Africa's Global Engagement: Perspectives from Emerging Countries

Series Editor
Ajay Dubey
African Studies Association of India (ASA India)
Centre for African Studies, Jawaharlal Nehru University
New Delhi, India

The 21st century has been characterized by a global rush to engage African countries. Unlike in the past, globalization has given African countries options to select and diversify their engagements. Though traditional powers are still trying to reinforce their links, African countries have generally found it more empowering to reduce their traditional dependence and develop more equitable relations with counties of the South, especially with emerging economies. Different regions and countries of the world find different opportunities and challenges in their attempts to engage the African region. Similarly, African countries, along with the African Union and other regional organizations, find different advantages in diversifying their traditional dependence. However, the new engagements have neither replaced the traditional engagement of Africa, nor are they wholly unproblematic from African perspectives. In this context, it is essential to understand and analyse emerging Africa's global engagements.

To that end, this series will cover important countries and regions, including traditional powers, that engage African countries, the African Union and African regional organisations. The book series will also address global and regional issues that exclusively affect African countries. Books in the series can be either monographs or edited works.

Expected Content:

The series will focus on the following aspects, among others:

- In its current global engagement, is Africa still a "helpless" player? Who dictates the terms of Africa's new engagement, and how it impacts various African countries?
- In the current competition between traditional powers and emerging economies to engage Africa, is Africa's global engagement merely undergoing a geographical shift, or is it moving toward increasingly equitable international relations? How traditional powers have re-strategised themselves to retain their influence on Africa and how Africa is responding to them?

How is Africa involved in the issues of global governance and how it negotiates and navigates its positions on issues of global concerns?

More information about this series at
http://www.palgrave.com/gp/series/15417

Yongkyu Chang
Editor

South Korea's Engagement with Africa

A History of the Relationship in Multiple Aspects

Editor
Yongkyu Chang
Division of African Studies
Hankuk University of Foreign Studies (HUFS)
Yongin-si, South Korea

Africa's Global Engagement: Perspectives from Emerging Countries
ISBN 978-981-32-9012-9   ISBN 978-981-32-9013-6 (eBook)
https://doi.org/10.1007/978-981-32-9013-6

© The Editor(s) (if applicable) and The Author(s), under exclusive licence to Springer Nature Singapore Pte Ltd. 2020
This work is subject to copyright. All rights are solely and exclusively licensed by the Publisher, whether the whole or part of the material is concerned, specifically the rights of translation, reprinting, reuse of illustrations, recitation, broadcasting, reproduction on microfilms or in any other physical way, and transmission or information storage and retrieval, electronic adaptation, computer software, or by similar or dissimilar methodology now known or hereafter developed.
The use of general descriptive names, registered names, trademarks, service marks, etc. in this publication does not imply, even in the absence of a specific statement, that such names are exempt from the relevant protective laws and regulations and therefore free for general use.
The publisher, the authors and the editors are safe to assume that the advice and information in this book are believed to be true and accurate at the date of publication. Neither the publisher nor the authors or the editors give a warranty, expressed or implied, with respect to the material contained herein or for any errors or omissions that may have been made. The publisher remains neutral with regard to jurisdictional claims in published maps and institutional affiliations.

Cover illustration: boommaval, shutterstock.com
Cover design: eStudio Calamar

This Palgrave Macmillan imprint is published by the registered company Springer Nature Singapore Pte Ltd.
The registered company address is: 152 Beach Road, #21-01/04 Gateway East, Singapore 189721, Singapore

Preface

My personal encounter with 'Africa' was through TV. A TV drama, Tarzan, an epic hero, was aired every Saturday when I was a little boy. Tarzan was a guardian and savior who protected the dark jungles of Africa from all villainous and carnivorous forces: his mighty capability to communicate with animals and his power to overpower enemy was phenomenal to my eyes. 'It' became my hero. The documentary of the animal kingdom cast me endless curiosity about Africa. Watching him struggle between predatory animals and their scapegoats was wondrous and the fixed image of Africa, nature, primitive, and carnivorous, was inscribed in my mind.

A more realistic experience came when I read Professor Kim Chan Sam's book series, *Kim, Chan Sam's World Tour*. In the late 1960s and early 1970s, he traveled wide and visited a number of African countries, and South Africa was one of them. His lively description of South Africa about Apartheid and the life of South Africans struck me hard and it was the first time to realize the political situation in South Africa. But that was all, and my interest in Africa had faded out soon.

But about ten years later, interestingly, I enrolled in the Department of KiSwahili (currently the Division of African Studies) at Hankuk University of Foreign Studies in 1983. The department was just established, and I was one of the first students of the department. My choice of African studies was obviously not due to the romantic memory of Tarzan or the animal kingdom, nor Professor Kim Chan Sam's Africa tour. It was rather mysterious because Africa was absolutely alien to me, and I was not serious about thinking Africa-related things as my profession. Anyhow, I decided to continue to study after my graduation and went overseas for further studies: first to India for master's degree and later to South Africa for a Ph.D.

Returning from South Africa after obtaining a Ph.D. in 2000, I started to teach at my old department of the university. I have actively involved in Korean-African studies since then and witnessed the development of African studies and social engagement with Africa in South Korea. In short, the progress of social discourses and various social and national engagements with Africa have been remarkable since 2000. In particular, the declaration of the African Initiative by the Korean government in 2006 was a turning point that has brought about a shift in the perception of Africa. As such, I have observed for decades the progressive relationship between South Korea and Africa. This is one reason I was able to edit this book.

Since the 2000s, the relationship between South Korea and Africa is in full blossom. In academia, African studies began to gain attention, and scholars and research institutes dedicating their researches on Africa have increased. Once the South Korean government joined the DAC, the volume of ODA to Africa has increased massively after the result of the government's joining to DAC, and ODA volunteers began to pour into all corners of the African continent. After the completion of service, some of these volunteers have started social enterprises related to Africa. The number of African migrants in South Korea and the presence of South Koreans in Africa have become remarkable since 2000.

It is not strange to meet Africans in the high streets of Seoul, and the number of Koreans to visit Africa has also increased. Now, over 20,000 Africans live in South Korea and 19 African embassies represent their countries. About the same number of Koreans reside in the African continent, and a similar number of South Korean embassies are present across the continent. As I summarized so far, the relationship between South Korea and Africa is active in many ways. As an Africanist, for some years, I wished to write a book that could shed light on the relationship between South Korea and Africa that has become so diversified and intensified.

For this reason, there is a thrill waiting for the book to be published. At the same time, as an editor of the book, I feel a vague sense of responsibility. I hope that the publication of the book will serve as an opportunity to explore the relationship between South Korea and Africa.

Yongin-si, South Korea   Yongkyu Chang

Acknowledgments

This book is the outcome of scholarly collaboration, and I owe many people in the process of publication. First of all, I express my deep appreciation to all contributors in this edition. The selection of contributors was based on the academic expertise and field experiences in relation to Africa. Obviously, there are other highly esteemed scholars and professionals who possess profound knowledge and expertise in Africa. The choice of contributors for the book is personal, and I like to make it clear that the abilities of other Korean Africanists are less than those of the contributors of this book. Therefore, I would like to extend my gratitude not only to this edition's contributors but also to the other Korean Africanists who have dedicated their efforts.

The idea of the book came from Professor Ajay Dubey who is a professor at the School of International Studies, Jawaharlal Nehru University (New Delhi), and the series editor of the book series *Africa's Global Engagement: Perspectives from Emerging Countries*. We have known each other since some years back when I, as the director of Institute of African Studies at Hankuk University of Foreign Studies (IAS-HUFS), organized an academic conference and invited him to the institute. I realized that he initiated the Asian Africanist Network that was what I dreamed on as a part of the institute's project. Academic exchanges have continued, and a couple of years ago, he suggested me to publish a book on Korea's engagement with Africa. I accepted the suggestion immediately because I thought it was timely to overview South Korea's relationship with Africa in both academic and practical perspectives.

The idea was shared with Eun Kyung Kim, an assistant professor in IAS-HUFS, who was instrumental in the composition of the book proposal. We discussed the outline of the edition and agreed on that the publication should contain both academic and practical perspectives of South Korea's engagement with Africa. We worked together to categorize the book into three sections: academic, political and economic, and sociocultural engagement. Based on the proposal, I contacted contributors. Fortunately, all contributors were willing to accept my suggestion, which made the publication possible. Contributors are all professionals as scholars and field activists; therefore, I think this edition faithfully reflects South Korea's engagement with Africa.

The edition's contributors come from various academic backgrounds and institutions; nevertheless, it is undeniably IAS-HUFS that has actually provided the venue for the process of publication. For instance, IAS-HUFS has organized a series of seminars and academic conferences at which the issues on Korea's engagement with Africa were widely discussed. Therefore, the edition is practically the collective work of Korean Africanists whose knowledge and experiences are shared and embedded in this edition. In particular, the idea of the publication was shaped as part of IAS-HUFS's long-term project, Humanities Korea-Overseas Research Grant (NRF-362-2010-1-B00003), sponsored by National Research Foundation of Korea (NRF).

My personal thanks go to Graduate School of Asian and African Area Studies (ASAFAS) and Professor Masayoshi Shigeta at Kyoto University. During the last winter break, ASAFAS invited me as a visiting professor and provided me with all facilities and support to write a manuscript and edit this volume. The completion of this edition would have been very difficult without the all favorable provision of ASAFAS.

Finally, I indebt much to the editorial team of *Africa's Global Engagement: Perspectives from Emerging Countries*, Palgrave Macmillan, for the reification of our publishing idea. Special thanks to Ms. Sandeep Kaur whose effective communication has been a boost to the smooth running of this publication.

CONTENTS

1 Introduction   1
Yongkyu Chang

2 Reflections on South Korean African Studies   7
Yongkyu Chang

3 South Korean Social Science Research on Africa   33
Dong Ju Choi, Soojin Han, and Sooho Lee

4 Issues Raised on Korea's Official Development Assistance to Africa: Future Perspective   71
Jin-sang Lee

5 Korea–Ethiopia Relations Since the Korean War   103
Eun Kyung Kim and Mark W. DeLancey

6 Dynamics of Korea-Africa Cultural Engagements   133
Suweon Kim

7 South Korea's Civil Engagement with Africa   159
Sookhee Yuk

Index   193

Notes on Contributors

Yongkyu Chang is a professor at the Division of African Studies, Hankuk University of Foreign Studies (HUFS), South Korea. He holds a PhD in anthropology from the University of KwaZulu-Natal, Durban, South Africa. He specializes in African belief systems and the creolization with other cultural and religious elements in the wave of globalization. He has conducted researches in South Africa and Ghana respectively on the topic.

Dong Ju Choi is a professor in the School of Global Service at Sookmyung Women's University and serves as Executive Director of Sookmyung Institute of Global Governance, South Korea. His field of interest includes international political economy, conflicts and economy, and state finance and development model in developing and underdeveloped countries. He holds a PhD in political economy from the University of London, UK, and an MA in international affairs from the American University, USA.

Mark W. DeLancey has served as a Fulbright Scholar at Universitas Riau, Indonesia; the University of Western Cape, South Africa; and the University of Yaoundé, Cameroon. He has been a visiting professor at the University of Nigeria, Somali National University, Rand Afrikaans University (South Africa), and Duke University (USA). He has published several books and numerous articles on African politics and international relations and, most recently, the politics of health and the HIV/AIDS problem. He was a professor at the University of South Carolina, Columbia, SC, USA and Sookmyung Women's University, Seoul, South Korea.

Soojin Han is a senior researcher in the Institute of Global Governance at Sookmyung Women's University, South Korea.

Eun Kyung Kim is an assistant professor in the Institute of African Studies at Hankuk University of Foreign Studies (HUFS). Her research interests include political and economic development in Africa and the relationship between the two. Her current works chiefly focus on elite alliances and economic policy choice in relation to African countries' democratization status. She has been writing articles for *Comparative Politics*, *International Area Studies Review*, *Politics & Policy*, and others.

Suweon Kim is extraordinary researcher in the Department of Political Studies at the University of the Western Cape in South Africa. Her research interests are soft power and development in the context of Afro-Asia Studies. Her works include 'The misadventure of Korea aid: Developmental soft power and the troubling motives of an emerging donor' (2019) and 'Who watches Korean TV dramas in Africa?' (2018).

Jin-sang Lee is a professor at SUNY Korea and has been working on African economic development since 1994. His works mainly focus on economic policies, industries, education sector, and science and technology promotion in Africa. He was awarded his PhD by the University of Strathclude, UK, Masters from Lancaster University and undergraduate degree from the University of Glasgow.

Sooho Lee is a researcher in the Institute of Global Governance at Sookmyung Women's University, South Korea.

Sookhee Yuk has been working at the diverse civil society organizations in Nepal, India, Uganda, and Ghana. Her research interests are women economic activities about the value chain and social and economic power of market women. She is currently in charge of the Shea nut value chain business projects in Uganda, Inclusive Business Solution project partnering with KOICA (Korea International Cooperation Agency), and two other civil organizations.

Abbreviations

CBO	Community Based Organization
CCEJ	Citizens' Coalition for Economic Justice
CPS	Country Partnership Strategy
FBO	Faith-Based Organization
GCAP Korea	Global Call to Action against poverty KOREA
INGO	International Non-Governmental Organization
JTS	Join Together Society
KCOC	Korea NGO Council for International Cooperation
KOICA	Korea International Cooperation Agency
KoFID	Korea Civil Society Forum on International Development Cooperation
NGDO	Non-Governmental Development Organization
NGO	Non-Governmental Organization
NPO	Non-Profit Organization
ODA	Official Development Aid
OECD	Organization for Economic Cooperation and Development
USAID	The United States Agency for International Development

List of Figures

Fig. 3.1	Diplomatic relations with African countries, 1958–1970 (Source: Ministry of Foreign Affairs of Republic of Korea; Wertz et al. (2016))	44
Fig. 3.2	Keywords cluster map, 1970s–1980s (Source: Author's own work)	45
Fig. 3.3	Diplomatic relations with African countries, 1971–1990 (Source: Ministry of Foreign Affairs of Republic of Korea; Wertz et al. (2016))	50
Fig. 3.4	GNI per capita of South Korea, Kenya, and Nigeria, 1970–1990 (current USD) (Source: World Bank)	51
Fig. 3.5	Keyword cluster map, 1990s–2010s (Source: Author's own work)	53
Fig. 3.6	South Korean total and proportional ODA to Africa 1987–2016 (current USD) (Source: Economic Development Cooperation Fund Korea)	55
Fig. 4.1	Korea's Development Cooperation Management Architecture (2017) (Source: ODA Korea 2017: 44)	77
Fig. 4.2	Korea's ODA Coordination and Process (Source: ODA Korea 2018: 55)	78
Fig. 4.3	ODA Selection Process (Source: ODA Korea 2018: 56)	79
Fig. 4.4	Trend of Korea's bilateral and multilateral ODA (Source: ODA Korea 2018: 111)	80
Fig. 4.5	Korea's ODA by region in 2015 (Source: ODA Korea 2018: 117)	85
Fig. 4.6	ODA model for holistic approach (Source: Modified from LEE, YH and LEE JS (2015))	96

Fig. 5.1	Personnel exchanges between Korea and Ethiopia (Source: Embassy of the Republic of Korea in the Federal Democratic Republic of Ethiopia; Embassy of Ethiopia in Seoul, the Republic of Korea; and Won (2012))	112
Fig. 5.2	Korea's ODA to Ethiopia since 1991 (Source: Korea International Cooperation Agency)	116
Fig. 5.3	Korea-to-Ethiopia ODA trend by sector (Source: Korea International Cooperation Agency)	118
Fig. 5.4	Korea's ODA to Ethiopia versus other African countries by sector (Source: Korea International Cooperation Agency. Note: African countries categorized as "Others" vary by year, but "Others" comprise of all the African states receiving ODA from Korea in each corresponding year)	119
Fig. 5.5	KOICA volunteers to Ethiopia (Source: Korea International Cooperation Agency)	122
Fig. 7.1	Status for foreign residents in Korea (2013–2017) (Source: Kosis.kr)	183

List of Tables

Table 3.1	Number of South Korean social science studies on Africa	38
Table 3.2	Research trends by discipline	39
Table 3.3	Distribution by study type (single/joint)	39
Table 3.4	Distribution by research method (empirical/interpretive)	40
Table 3.5	Research grant trends	40
Table 3.6	Keywords by period	40
Table 3.7	Frequently mentioned keywords in the 1950s and 1960s	41
Table 3.8	Discipline distribution in academic research, 1970s–1980s	49
Table 3.9	Distribution of disciplines in academic research, 1990s–2010s	55
Table 4.1	Trend of world development aid	74
Table 4.2	Priority sectors of CPS in Africa	82
Table 4.3	Scale of Korea's ODA between 2006 and 2015	83
Table 4.4	Share of grants and concessional loans	84
Table 4.5	Largest recipient countries of Korea's ODA between 2011 and 2015 (unit: USD million)	85
Table 4.6	Trend of Korean ODA to Africa 1991–2017 (Unit: US$ million)	87
Table 4.7	Sectors of grants to Africa in 2017 (unit: KRW million, %)	88
Table 4.8	Sectors of the EDCF loans to Africa in 2017 (unit: USD million, %)	88
Table 4.9	Korea's ODA by income groups	89
Table 4.10	SWOT of Korea's ODA to Africa	95
Table 5.1	African states in the list of top 20 recipient countries Korea provides most ODA (by within-Africa ranking; Unit: KRW)	117
Table 5.2	KOICA's humanitarian aid and small grants to Ethiopia	120
Table 5.3	KOICA's project type cooperation	121

Table 6.1	Number of embassy projects in public diplomacy by continent	142
Table 7.1	Aid for civil society organizations 2010–2016 in Korea (USD million, disbursements, Constant 2015 prices)	167
Table 7.2	Project Expenses by continent (Unit: 1 million KRW)	169
Table 7.3	African Countries where Korean CSOs operate	169
Table 7.4	List of Buddhist-based organizations in the development sector	175
Table 7.5	Priority partner countries in Africa continent	180
Table 7.6	Numbers of African students by nationality in Korea from 2012–2017	185

CHAPTER 1

Introduction

Yongkyu Chang

South Korea's Engagement with Africa is the first scholarly attempt to overview South Korea's relationship with Africa, since its first establishment of diplomatic tie with some African countries in the early 1960s. In describing this relationship, the book mainly focuses on Korea's attempt to cooperate with African countries in diverse perspectives: academic engagement, developmental cooperation, civic and cultural interactions. The volume does note that the quantity and quality of South Korea's relations with Africa differ not only from those of the major international stakeholders, such as the United States, the United Kingdom, France, and other European countries but also from those of the other Asian countries, such as China, India, and Japan.

This is because South Korea has a different historical and geopolitical connection to Africa, and until recently, South Korea had never considered Africa as a significant diplomatic and economic counterpart. For example, South Korea's share in the total volume of Africa's trade occupied only 1.8% in 2009 (Kang 2011), and the volume even decreased into 1.5% in 2017 (Kang 2017). In terms of diplomatic relations, Africa has hardly

Y. Chang (✉)
Division of African Studies, Hankuk University of Foreign Studies (HUFS), Yongin-si, South Korea
e-mail: ykchang@hufs.ac.kr

© The Author(s) 2020
Y. Chang (ed.), *South Korea's Engagement with Africa*, Africa's Global Engagement: Perspectives from Emerging Countries, https://doi.org/10.1007/978-981-32-9013-6_1

been a major partner to the South Korean government. Moreover, in terms of economic cooperation the African continent has been reserved as the 'last blue ocean'. In South Korean academia, African studies are always isolated from the mainstream. Overall, it would still be going too far to say that the relationship between South Korea and Africa has entered into a full-fledged stage. Nevertheless, no one can deny that recently there have been dramatic changes in this same relationship.

Since the de-escalation of tension and constraints on international affairs in the post-Cold War era, the international collaboration between South Korea and Africa has opened up unlimited possibilities. In particular, the South Korean government's entry to the Development Assistance Committee (DAC) in 2006 was a historical turning point in the relationship between South Korea and Africa. With this, South Korea has become a significant stakeholder in international development cooperation, and Africa becomes one of the major recipients. This book illuminates the whole arc of the historical development of South Korea's engagement with Africa. It also recognizes that South Korea–Africa relations, though relatively new, also break ground by acknowledging the importance of a constant endeavor to carry out international development and that they continue to grow as we find encouraging progress and fresh opportunities in the cooperation between these two partners.

This book is all inclusive, covering South Korea's academic, economic, diplomatic, and civil and cultural engagements with Africa. It is unique in that it investigates many hitherto untold aspects of South Korea–Africa relations. Part One introduces the trends in African studies that have been conducted in South Korea with two chapters. These chapters examine specific topics, approaches, and methodologies, as well as limitations found in the existing research, particularly in the fields of humanities and social sciences.

In Chap. 2, Chang describes the 40 year-history of the institutionalization of Korean African studies and evaluates the achievements and challenges therein. The first institutionalization of African studies began in 1977 at Hankuk University of Foreign Studies (HUFS) under the name of the Institute of African Affairs (now Institute of African Studies [IAA]). Chang contends that along with the Korean Association of African Studies (founded 1982) and the Department of KiSwahili (1983, now the Division of African Studies) at HUFS, IAA has led Korean African studies for the last four decades years.

Chang continues to argue that, 40 years from now, some major universities and para-governmental institutions will have partaken in African studies, thus expanding and diversifying the boundaries of this area of study. African studies has also been developed from without 'traditional' boundary of academia. Para-governmental and government-affiliated institutes, such as the Korea-Africa Center (2015), a consultative institute affiliated to the Ministry of Foreign Affairs, Korean Institute for International Economic Policy, have primarily focused on more practical and economic researches on African countries. All these recent academic developments are positive signals, as Chang points out, for the further development of South Korea and Africa's relationship.

The chapter then continues with a critical look at the challenges that Korean African studies faces. Chang diagnoses that the most severe challenges are academic sectionalism among researchers and the isolation of Korean African studies from international African studies. He suggests that Korean Africanists should open their doors and deliberately interact with other academic disciplines and institutes, and even civil societies related to Africa.

In Chap. 3, Choi, Han, and Lee analyze the development of social sciences in Korean African studies. They categorize the development of social sciences in African studies into three periods. Choi's team stress that, since its advent in the 1950s, Korean social science research on Africa has grown immensely in scope and scale. As both international and domestic political and economic environments have evolved, research too has adapted to meet the demands of the time. They point out that, during the 1950s and 1960s, research mainly focused on diplomacy and political factors within the context of the Cold War and diplomatic competition with North Korea. But researchers then began to shift their attention to economic and trading factors in Africa, as Korea's economy grew and Africa became an attractive choice for foreign market entry. Finally, they describe how, after Korea's admission to the OECD DAC in 2010, researchers have increasingly focused on official development assistance (ODA) and how aid can be effectively utilized in Africa.

Choi and his team use a bibliometric analysis method to analyze common keywords in research sources from the 1950s–1960s, 1970s–1980s, and 1990s–2010s. The results of this analysis led to the development of cluster maps, in which terms were grouped by frequency of occurrence and their relationship to one another. An examination of these clusters can readily depict the major research trends in South Korea according to era, thereby showing the evolution of research over time as well as providing a basis for the direction of future research on Africa.

In Part Two, the authors discuss the Korean government's practical engagements with Africa. Two chapters in this part also describe patterns of development cooperation in the form of trade, investment, development assistance, and military missions, and thereby consider how these aspects address mutual interests.

Lee, in Chap. 4, mainly focuses on Korea's ODA policies in Africa. For instance, in 2017 Korea's total ODA was USD 2.3 billion, which was 0.16% of its GNI (gross national income). African countries shared 23% of this total ODA, largely centered on rural development, education, health, social and economic infrastructure, and so on. The scale of Korea's ODA projects has been small in many cases; in such instances, it has been claimed that they are fragmented and less efficient. There were 47 African recipient countries, including seven priority countries, within the Country Partnership Strategy. The Country Partnership Strategy is the formulation that the Korean government has initiated for the better engagement with recipient countries in the international development cooperation. Seven African countries are selected as priority countries.

Lee argues that, in recent years, there has been a growing demand for Korean partnerships from African countries that wish to share Korea's development experiences. Prior to this, the partnership between Korea and Africa was rather inactive for many years due to political and economic factors and progress was slow until the 1990s. As many developing countries, especially in Africa, have been inspired by the Korean case of economic development, the Korean government has increased activities to foster partnerships with Africa. To strengthen these connections, from the early 2000s Korean presidents have visited Africa more often and organized regular forums and conferences among the public and private sectors in Korea and Africa. The Korea-Africa Foundation was established in 2018 as a government entity to enlighten partnerships with Africa. Korea's ODA to Africa has increased and could be consolidated by focusing on projects related to the development of specific countries. This could be made possible through a holistic approach by bringing together academia, private companies, and public institutions.

In Chap. 5, Kim and DeLancey present a case study of the Korea–Africa relationship by discussing Korea's engagement with Ethiopia. They argue that Ethiopian troops' participation in the Korean War in 1950 was a laborious and uncommon effort to be made by an African country. Despite their honorable service, the Ethiopian Korean War veterans were badly treated by the communist government under Mengistu Haile Mariam in the Cold

War era. That endeavor to fight for South Korea in the past, however, was brought to light after the Cold War and started to yield favorable diplomatic outcomes in the relationship with South Korea. In the chapter, Kim and DeLancey briefly review Ethiopia's participation in said war, its motives and actions, and then investigate the Korean government's efforts to (re)engage with an old ally in a new context. Examining the dialogues, attitudes, and actions Korea has taken to engage with Ethiopia, the authors find that the fact that Ethiopia dispatched its troops to combat in aid of South Korea within the United Nations mission has very heavily weighed on Korean government decisions to calibrate its foreign policy toward favoring Ethiopia.

Part Three concerns Korea's civil and cultural engagements with Africa. In the era of globalization, culture has become a central topic of international relations. Korea has undertaken cultural ODA in cooperation with UNESCO in order to promote the recipient countries' capabilities in the field of human resources. Kim, in Chap. 6, describes Korea's growing cultural engagement with Africa in this context. A distinctive feature of Korea's cultural engagement is that its cultural policies, in large part, are driven by the government and reflect the changing global dynamics of cultural soft power. Even though North Korea outpaced South Korea in its initial cultural engagement with Africa in the 1960s and 1970s, current transcontinental cultural exchange is predominantly led by the South.

The chapter discusses the patterns of growing cultural engagement between Korea and African states. Kim examines the reception of Korean pop culture in Africa and Korea's development projects in the cultural sector, and highlights the Korean government's understanding of cultural engagement as public diplomacy. Even though the volume of cultural engagement has been increasing, with other dynamics in trade and distribution of cultural products enduring, the question remains as to which side will benefit from this growth.

In Chap. 7, Yuk, a civil activist-com-scholar, argues that civic engagements with Africa began to appear late in the 2000s. Since Korea joined DAC, the Korean government has been asked to undertake humanitarian actions on global issues such as poverty and famine in Africa, so that South Korea has entered into new relations with Africa led by civil society organizations (CSOs). In the past, due to geographic and cultural similarities, most Korean CSOs preferred to work in Asian countries. However, as the Korean government's engagement with African countries evolves, CSOs have begun to collaborate more with African societies. The number of CSOs operating development projects and humanitarian campaigns in Africa significantly increased when South Korea promised to increase ODA.

Furthermore, religious groups that initially carried out mission work in Africa have tended to convert to development NGOs in the same period. According to a report issued by KCOC (Korea NGO Council for Overseas Development Cooperation) in 2015, 59 South Korean CSOs were working on 700 projects in 39 countries in Africa. Moreover, these were mostly targeted at education, health, social welfare, agricultural development, water, and hygiene at the grassroots level. Yuk, in this chapter, analyzes how Korea's CSOs have been working on the issues African countries face due to their particular geographical exigencies, as well as how those CSOs act on matters such as rights of Africans immigrants to South Korea and improving awareness of Africa in the home country.

The unique contribution of this book is that three different approaches—academic, economic-developmental, and civil and cultural—are combined in the process of offering an overview of the relationship between Korea and Africa. Korea's, or more precisely the Korean government's, prime focus with Africa is in economic interests and developmental cooperation, as is the case with other major stakeholders in the continent. The contributors to this book reflect this trend in some chapters, but also try to introduce broader academic and sociocultural engagements with Africa. We would be rewarded if readers find themselves better able to understand the contemporary relationship between South Korea and Africa through this book.

References

Kang, G. S. (2011). The Korea-Africa Partnership: Beyond Trade and Investment. AfDB. *Africa Economic Brief, 2*(9), 1–8.

Kang, K. H. (2017). Korea-Africa Business Forum Statement. Retrieved July 29, 2019, from http://www.mofa.go.kr/www/brd/m_20140/view.do?seq=302567&srchFr=&srchTo=&srchWord=&srchTp=&multi_itm_seq=0&itm_seq_1=0&itm_seq_2=0&company_cd=&company_nm=&page=2.

CHAPTER 2

Reflections on South Korean African Studies

Yongkyu Chang

INTRODUCTION

On May 22–24, 2018, South Korea hosted 51st annual African Development Bank (AfDB) meeting and 5th KOAFEC ministerial conference in Busan, a south-eastern harbor city in South Korea. The main event was the Korea–Africa Economic Cooperation (KOAFEC) ministerial conference, but various other social events were also held to celebrate the conference—among them a compelling exhibition: "2018 Busan Museum Special exhibition, AFRICA." This was organized by Busan Metropolitan Museum and I was invited to give a public lecture at the exhibition. On the day of the lecture, I happened to drop into the exhibition hall. Unfortunately, the exhibition disappointed me as it exhibited museum pieces such as age-old sculptures and grotesque masks as if they were a fair representation of Africa today. A section that riled me especially was 'Africa's daily life.' Therein, to my great surprise, bows and arrows, masks and swords were scandalously displayed as 'Africans' daily utensils.'

Y. Chang (✉)
Division of African Studies, Hankuk University of Foreign Studies (HUFS), Yongin-si, South Korea
e-mail: ykchang@hufs.ac.kr

© The Author(s) 2020
Y. Chang (ed.), *South Korea's Engagement with Africa*, Africa's Global Engagement: Perspectives from Emerging Countries, https://doi.org/10.1007/978-981-32-9013-6_2

Some consolation for my disappointment, though, could be found in one particular section of the exhibition. A beautiful copy of a world map was displayed in the middle of the exhibition hall. The caption to the map indicated that it was drawn by literati in the time of the Joseon dynasty.[1] A particularly striking feature was that the map depicted the shape of the African continent so accurately, albeit there was a clear exaggeration in its geographic features: the Victoria Lake occupied most of the continent. The narration attached to the map explained its meaning as such:

> On maps produced by the Islamic world and Europe, Africa is mostly distorted, with its southern end crooked to the east or connected to a vast fictitious continent. The actual shape of Africa, which a pointed southern tip, first appeared on *Honil yeokdae gukdo gangni jido* (混 ·歷代國都疆理地圖) which is a map produced by Joseon. Maps produced in sixteenth-century Europe were disseminated to Asia ... They were introduced to Joseon where most of the Joseon nobles became familiar with geography, including Africa. (2018 Busan Museum Special Exhibition, AFRICA)

The map had been meticulously redrawn by two Korean literates Keun Kwon (1352–1409) and Hoe Lee (late thirteenth–fourteenth century) who consulted two Chinese world maps and one from Japan, and so it was the result of intellectual exchanges between Joseon literates and scholars from these other lands.

Another intriguing display was a translated book about a journey by Scottish missionary David Livingstone, entitled *Explorations in Africa by Livingstone, Stanley, and Others*, which was believed to have been read by Joseon literates at the end of nineteenth century. The original book was translated by a Chinese scholar and contained the letters exchanged between David Livingstone and James Gordon Bennett about the slave trade in East Africa, which expressed criticism of the practice.

Yet, these pieces of historical evidence do not prove that our ancestors had built up a profound knowledge of Africa. The map was merely a compilation of two or more world maps that had been published abroad. The translation of *Explorations* was also not an original academic work from Korea. However, these publications impressed me because they show the extensive knowledge of the world among the Joseon dynasty's literate. The contemporary worldview of the Joseon dynasty is that its knowledge was strictly confined to the Korean Peninsula and its proximal regions, in particular China and Japan. Furthermore, the Joseon Dynasty had closed its boundaries to foreign countries since the seventeenth century. During this time, information acquisition on foreign countries was practically blocked. Therefore, it was surprising to discover that knowledge of Africa was being circulated among the Joseon dynasty's intellectuals, albeit the amount of this knowledge was limited. The limited access to Africa continued as Korea faced political and social turmoil in the following centuries.

In the aftermath of the Korean War of 1950–1953, the country was divided into two and South Korea's diplomatic relations in the twentieth century were confined to those of pro-capitalist countries in opposition to North Korea's pro-communist alliance. Most African countries adopted either socialist or non-alignment policies and had a more amicable relationship with North Korea. It was only in the 1980s that South Korea strategically approached Africa in order to gain international support to bid for a the seat on the United Nations. Since then, diplomatic relations between South Korea and Africa have continued to go through highs and lows depending on the changing international situation.

The full diplomatic relationship between South Korea and Africa began in 2016 after the South Korean government's "Korea Initiative for African Development." Through this scheme, relations with Africa have been initiated or renewed in many aspects, including in academia. Although the first institutionalization of South Korean African studies began in 1977, this area of enquiry had really remained dormant until the beginning of the 2000s. As an established area of study, South Korean African studies has been influenced by various initiatives and research institutes and the numbers of individual scholars on African studies have burgeoned since its first establishment.

Reflecting on the previous decades of African studies in Korea, my overall evaluation is positive and I feel that there has been gradual progress over time. I must admit that all the benefits we enjoy today are possible because of the dedication of the previous Korean Africanist generation. In fact, the previous generation started study from scratch, but they have achieved concrete advancements, in particular in an institutional way. The number of scholars and research institutes has been multiplying ever since, and the public engagement with Africa has also become much more prominent in recent years.

Korea is now in immediate proximity to Africa in many dimensions. The presence of the African population in Korea is no longer alien to its native citizens and travel to Africa is not exclusive to a particular group. Under these changing circumstances, we need to consider the position of Korean Africanists, who, I firmly believe, have a certain degree of duty to Korean society more broadly: the obligation of sharing our academic knowledge with the public for the better understanding of Africa.

This chapter is divided into two parts. The first is a quantitative illustration of the history of South Korean African studies, in particular the institutional development thereof. The second part is more of a qualitative interpretation of South Korean African studies. These two parts are independent but interdependent at the same time, in terms of their relevance to the advancement of African studies. I begin with a sketch of the history of African studies in Korea since the establishment of the Institute of African Affairs (IAA) in 1977. This institutional development of South Korean African studies is crucial, for it has provided shelter for Korean Africanists conducting their research.

A Chronology of African Studies in Korea

A History of South Korean African Studies: From the 1950s to the Early 2000s

The establishment of South Korean African studies saw a key moment in the late 1970s. It was in the late 1970s and early 1980s that three primary research and pedagogical institutes related to African studies were established. In the history of South Korean African studies, no research and educational institutes are more salient than these institutions, and they have led South Korean African studies ever since their first appearance.

The full history of African studies in Korea dates back as early as the 1950s, when academic and governmental publications on African issues appeared for the first time. Cho (2012: 141) states that the first Korean academic article on Africa appeared in 1955, concerning France's political engagement with Francophone Africa (Han 1955). The first governmental report on Africa followed a couple of years later (1959) from the Ministry of Foreign Affairs. However, it was a decade later (1972) when Dr. Ha published the first academic book on Africa, *African Politics*, as one of the series of introductory books on developing world politics. Nevertheless, before the end of 1970s, there was no single academic institute focusing on African studies in Korean academia.

A consequential setup of a research institute for African studies came in 1977. Hankuk University of Foreign Studies (HUFS) established the first research institute of African studies, the IAA. In the history of African studies, the central importance of HUFS is undeniable. HUFS is a private university. As its name shows, the primary goal of the university is to produce competent international professionals—that is, diplomats, journalists, and scholars—armed with proficient knowledge on foreign languages and cultures. As HUFS's academic orientation foregrounds research and education on foreign studies, area studies has become a professional research field of the university. The government and the public shown little attention on Africa, and it was HUFS that had foreseen the value of Africa and African studies in Korea. The establishment of that institute was succeeded by establishment of the Department of KiSwahili, and a graduate school for African studies.

HUFS has the only full-fledged educational institutions in Korea that provide B.A., Master's and Ph.D. degrees in area studies: African linguistics, literature, cultural studies, political science, and economics. The university's Center for International Area Studies, which was established in 1993, is one of the leading centers for international area studies in Korea. It has 12 affiliated area research institutes, and the IAA was one of them. The institute changed its name to the Institute of African Studies (IAS-HUFS) in 1999 and pioneered African studies.

However, the motivation of embarking African studies in Korean academia was not yet fully-grown; there was no single clear meaning of the term 'Africanist' in Korean academia; there were no full-scale diplomatic relationships between Korea and the independent African countries that had been established; public awareness on Africa was practically non-existent. Nevertheless, discussion of the possible establishment of the institute went on and a group of people, including scholars, diplomats, and government officers, took initiative from the discussion.

The group perhaps agreed that some realistic diplomatic measures should be taken to secure African countries as international partners. South Korea's diplomatic relations in those days were mainly confined to the United States and Japan, and some European countries. The Korean government was looking for the possibility of joining the United Nations in order to gain international support for resolving various diplomatic issues related to North Korea. Under these circumstances, diplomatic support from non-alignment countries, mainly in Africa and Latin America, was mandatory. Major newspapers backed this idea and published articles urging expansion of the government's diplomatic relations toward Africa and Latin America (Daily Economics, October 18, 1976). In my understanding, it was sought that a research institute for African studies should be established either at a national university or as a government-affiliated institute, if the intention was to provide consultation for the government's diplomatic policies on the African continent. The problem was that the government did not take any action to establish such a research institute, and national universities did not show any interest either.

The government's financial support for African studies was insignificant. It was predictable, considering the delicate diplomatic relationship and weak academic foundations of Africa in Korea, that the activity of the institute fell far short of expectations: IAA did little to contribute both to the government's decision-making process on African issues and the improvement of public awareness on Africa. Nevertheless, the institute's symbolic value as the first academic institute on African studies in Korea was immense, although it did not play a significant role as an academic or consultative body.

South Korean African studies in the 1970s was in an embryonic state. There were certain efforts by a group of professionals who, by no sense Africanists themselves, had laid the foundations for African studies in Korea. The initiation of IAA-HUFS was unique and symbolically significant as there were no institutional foundations before its establishment, although its contribution to academia was limited. It is nonetheless undeniable that the foundation of IAA was the keystone in the development of African studies in the 1980s and onwards.

The early 1980s were crucial for the advancement of South Korean African studies as two momentous institutes were founded: the Korean Association of African Studies (1982) and the Department of Swahili language (1983). The establishment of these two bodies was partly the effect of a political event: the first Korean presidential visit to Africa in 1982.

This was a monumental year for Korea–Africa relations. A month prior to the presidential visit to various African countries in June, the group that had mobilized the establishment of IAA organized a nationwide association of African studies, the Korean Association of African Studies (KAAS). At the first meeting, the association's agenda was set on building up "mutual understanding of African politics, societies, cultures, and economies" (Kyunghyang Daily, July 20, 1982). It manifested that the association's academic orientation was 'multidisciplinary' by encompassing humanities and social sciences. KAAS began with 20 members from universities, government research institutes, and diplomats. Since then, KAAS has remained the sole national-level academic association of African studies.

Since KAAS had undertaken academic and research functions, the establishment of the Department of KiSwahili at HUFS played a crucial role in the development of education on African studies. The department was significant as the first full-fledged educational department focusing on African studies in Korea. Initially, the department specialized in linguistics and literature, which had long been the academic strength of HUFS, expanding later into other academic disciplines. Some graduates of the department went overseas for further study and came back about a decade later, taking up key positions in the constellation of South Korean African studies.

There had been negotiations about setting up the department much earlier, in 1976, between the Ministry of Education and HUFS. As the Korean government became aware of the importance of the Third World—the likes of Africa, Latin America, and Eastern Europe—the Ministry of Education and other government departments took responsible actions. An executive director of the Ministry of Education, Dr. Taesoo Jung, consulted with HUFS about the foundation of departments on African and East European studies at HUFS. An Emeritus Professor, Hanjin Oh, of the Department of Russian Studies, recollected the moment when he and Dr. Jung wrote a proposal for the establishment of the Department of African Studies at HUFS (Oh 1991). An anecdote: HUFS is a university specialized in foreign language-based education combined with international area studies. In discussing the establishment of a new foreign language and area studies department at the university, however, the problem emerged that there was not a single Africanist not only at HUFS but also nationwide. University set up an executive board and examined foreign universities' curricula that taught African languages. The board finally chose one African language, Swahili, and suggested to the university to establish the Department of KiSwahili. Subsequently, two students were given National Scholarships on Swahili Literature and Language. Two students from the department of German language applied for this scholarship and went to England and Germany for further study, one for Swahili literature and the other for Swahili linguistics.

The Ministry of Education announced the inauguration of the Department of Swahili language at HUFS in 1981. HUFS announced the first recruitment of students at the end of 1982, and the first lectures began in 1983. The department has changed its name twice,[2] but it has remained as the sole educational department for African studies in Korea. The two students who were granted National Scholarships came back after finishing their studies and initiated their own lectures at the department. They are considered the first generation of African studies graduates and in turn have produced the next generation of Korean Africanists. This process took over a decade, from when the graduates from the department completed their study overseas and began to contribute to the development of South Korean African studies. This group of scholars became the core group of South Korean African studies and the triangular combination of IAA, KAAS and the department of Swahili language have indisputably led the development of African studies in Korea.

The development of African studies has entered another phase in that there has been a remarkable emergence of African studies outside this academic tradition, as some universities, such as the Institute of French Studies at Seoul National University and the Institute of African Studies at Kyunghee University, have embarked on their own African studies. Some other universities have initiated Africa-related courses. Scholars from diverse academic disciplines have started to take African studies more seriously. While scholars from HUFS and the Department of Swahili language have mainly focused on the study of African literature and languages, an emerging group has paid more attention to other academic dimensions.

A History of African Studies: From 2006 to Today

In a true sense, South Korean African studies began to burgeon in early 2000, both in terms of local and international perspectives. As we have seen, there has been an institutional development of African studies since 1970s; nevertheless, academic activity has been exclusively confined to the circle of the small number of Africanists. It is only after 2000 that the volume of research institutions and Africanists visibly increased and the academic boundaries of the discipline have expanded locally and internationally.

The year 2006 marked a turning point in the Korea–Africa relationship. In order to foster diplomatic relations between Korea and Africa, the president of Korea visited some African countries, and the Korean government started the first Korea-Africa Forum in the same year as a triennial initiative. At the same time, Korea finally joined in Development Assistance Committee (DAC) and began to offer official development aid and Economic Development Cooperation Fund (EDCF) to Less Developed Countries in South East Asia and Africa. The African continent has gained serious attention as many developmental projects have been proposed and delivered. Now some scholars, especially those who are work in economics and developmental studies, rushed into the field of African studies, and some Africanists enlarged their interests to developmental issues. Thus, a third group—developmental studies in Africa—has emerged since 2006.

A series of events followed the third Korean presidential visit to African countries in 2011: the first Korean Airline flight to Nairobi the subsequent year; the proclamation of 'Africa's New Era' by Korean National Assembly Forum; and the establishment of the Korea-Africa Center as an affiliate of the Ministry of Foreign Affairs and Trade in 2015. The activities of NGOs and civil society groups began to flourish and provided opportunities for the young generation to go over to various parts of the African continent. This young generation has become a valuable human resource for the advance of African studies as some of them moved into academia and tried to compound their personal experiences with academic knowledge. Others launched projects aimed at getting to 'know Africa better and correctly' and tried to enhance the public image of Africa. Some scholars have engaged themselves vividly with these movements. For instance, IAS-HUFS is keen to merge its academic knowledge with civil society and has launched various events, from public seminars to African festivals. All of a sudden, the physical and psychological distance between Korea and the African continent seems to have narrowed.

Another opportunity for the expansion of African studies arose from a crisis within academia. Since 2000, Korean academia, especially in the humanities, has faced a serious challenge as it has lost popularity among students and scholars. As globalization and neoliberalism have massively influenced Korean society, more practical and technical academic disciplines such as economics, financial management, and public policy have emerged as the most desirable areas of study. The humanities began to wane in popularity and university departments dedicated to humanities, such as philosophy, history, linguistics, and literature, began to close, rename, and merge with more practical academic disciplines. The Ministry of Education undertook various projects to aid the endangered humanities. One of them was 'Humanities Korea', which launched in 2007. The project was to provide academic and financial support for ten years to help humanities-related institutes lay the foundations for self-reliance.

This project included an Overseas Research Grant for which a special research budget was allocated. South Korea's regional studies were in no less trouble than the humanities, especially in some areas classified as 'isolated areas.' Therefore, particular 'academically neglected areas' were given major support for ten years. IAS-HUFS, which initiated South Korean African studies, has been selected as a beneficiary institute. Besides this project, the National Research Foundation of Korea (NRF) has launched short and mid-term projects for overseas area studies, which are good signals for the development of international area studies, including African studies.

In this changing environment, new academic and governmental institutes related to Africa have been established, and some pre-existing research institutes, which were not related to African research, began to move into the field of African studies either by changing their names or enlarging their research boundaries to include Africa. The most significant changes have taken place in some university French departments. In order to recover waning popularity, French departments have attempted to change their academic direction to cover Francophone African countries. Some French departments have even changed their name to the likes of 'Department of Francophone African studies.' For instance, the Institute of Francophone Studies, Seoul National University has extended its academic interest to 'Francophone African countries.' Previously, the institute had confined its field of study to France and some other Francophone areas but excluding Francophone African countries. Another institute for Francophone African studies, the Institute of Maghreb Studies (founded 2009) at Baejae University has become specialized in Maghreb studies. Kyunghee University opened the Institute of African Studies in 2013 and started research on Francophone Africa's folktales. Jeonbuk University set up the Institute of Francophone African Studies and the Graduate course on Francophone African studies in 2016. Korea National Open University opened a Department of Africa and Francophone studies as part of its graduate school in 2013. Also in 2013, the Institute of European and African Studies of Hanyang University has changed its name from the former Institute of European Studies, so as to deal with the political and economic situations of African countries too. The Institute of Africa and the Indian Ocean at Kwangwoon University was established in 2013. All these establishments and changes have happened since 2010, and it is interesting to see their development.

Although it is not an academic development per se, the establishment and the role of the Forum for Africa's New Era is also remarkable. The forum was founded in 2013 by the members of the National Assembly and some lawmakers in order to enhance the overall relationship between Korea and the African continent. I do not have detailed information about the establishment of the forum and also register some doubts about its contribution to African studies. Nevertheless, I agree that the forum has the power to influence the decision-making the process of national policies. This forum has no direct relation with Korean Africanists and instead focuses on friendly diplomatic cooperation with African diplomats, but the forum holds a bi-weekly morning seminar at which Korean Africanists are sometimes invited as speakers.

The Ministry of Foreign Affairs and Trade established its fourth affiliate of the Ministry, the Korea-Africa Center in 2015, and changed its name and structure in 2018 to the Korea-Africa Foundation. Although this foundation is independent of the Ministry now, its annual budget comes solely from the government. The foundation was established with the aim of cementing the "partnership with Africa"[3] and claims that research on various African issues is a part of its function.

In sum, South Korean African studies has become relatively opulent, at least in a quantitative dimension, since 2000. The year 2006 was crucial as it marked the Korean government's engagement with the African continent. In 2009, the Korean government became a full-fledged member of the DAC and began full-scale international development cooperation with partner nations, including many African countries. It cannot be denied that this government's interest in the issue of international cooperation has been a certain influence on African studies—in particular, African countries and development issues have become part of an attractive academic agenda and open the door to developmentalists to join take part in African studies.

According to Hong (2016), the number of Master's and doctoral theses on Africa has increased dramatically since 2000. She analyzes that since 1957 the overall number of Master's and doctoral theses has climbed to 686 and 48 respectively.[4] This is comparable with Park's findings (1996: 5) that before 1996 only 70 Master's theses and nine doctoral dissertations were registered to the Research Information Sharing Service (RISS). Hong's analysis shows that the number of Master's theses has sharply escalated since 2007 and that most of these came from the social sciences (75%), especially developmental studies. Academic humanities disciplines, such as linguistics, literature, history, religion, and so on, comprise only 10% of the total number of theses.[5]

The increasing number of academic articles in the field is also impressive, and these too have shown a sharp increase since 1996. The trend reveals that African issues have occupied academic attention on a bigger scale. Another critical but hidden figure is that of the group of Korean Africanists who have completed their academic degrees overseas. Toward the end of the 1980s and from the beginning of 1990s onwards, growing numbers of students who completed undergraduate courses either in African studies or in other disciplines began to go overseas for further study. Their destinations diversified too: Some African countries, mainly South Africa and Kenya, as well as the United States, Germany, France,

Belgium, Netherlands, England, and so on. The discipline also expanded from just literature and linguistics to economics and political science. These graduates began to return from the mid-1990s and became a driving force for the advancement of African studies in Korea. Hong's data proves that South Korean African studies has made rapid progress in a relatively short period, despite disadvantageous academic and social environments on the one hand and limited research resources on the other. It is undeniable that the growth of African studies since the late 1970s has been dramatic, in particular the advancement of African studies in a quantitative sense is truly impressive.

THE OVERSEAS EXPANSION OF SOUTH KOREAN AFRICAN STUDIES: 2012–2018

At the beginning of 2010, another notable development of African studies in Korea commenced: the internationalization of South Korean African studies. Certainly, there has been a steady stream of academic exchange between Korean and foreign Africanists. Most Korean Africanists received doctoral degrees overseas and so academic exchanges naturally occurred with the countries they studied. Therefore, there was only a limited number of countries, mostly Western countries and some of the African countries, where Korean Africanists had been engaged in academic exchanges. Even such academic exchange had been casual and sporadic, depending upon individual researcher or institute's capabilities.

The overseas network of South Korean African studies marked a turning point in 2012. In order to initiate one of the project goals, IAS-HUFS initiated an overseas academic network and the focus was to build up the network among Asian Africanists. The logic for having such a network was that, ideologically, Korean Africanists needed to be able to undertake a balanced academic engagement in international African studies. The international partnership of South Korean African studies had thitherto been skewed, as the main routes of academic exchange were centered on Western scholarship. IAS-HUFS attempted to find an alternative way of achieving international cooperation, and this is the second logic of networking among Asian countries. The institute turned its eyes on neighboring Asian countries. Japan has the longest history of African studies in Asia; India's geopolitical proximity to Africa has given the country a head start in African studies; China is an emerging power widely and profoundly engaged with Africa, and its academic engagements with Africa have been visible. Therefore, from a realistic perspective, IAS-HUFS tries to interact with Asian Africanists in Asian countries such as China, India, and Japan.

Coincidently, some other Asian Africanists had a similar idea as that of IAS-HUFS. The initiator was Prof. Ajay Dubey from the Centre for African Studies, Jawaharlal Nehru University (CAS-JNU), India. Along with a Japanese Africanist, Prof. Kitagawa, he had a meeting in New Delhi in 2011. Since then, CAS-JNU has played a central role in the network. The efforts of Prof. Takuo Iwata from Japan should also be highlighted, since he has traveled widely among some major institutes and centers for African studies in Asian countries and promoted the idea of having an Asian Africanist Network since 2011 (Iwata 2018: 224). He visited IAS-HUFS in 2011 and proposed the possibility of having an Asian conference on African studies, and IAS-HUFS willingly took up the responsibility for this. IAS-HUFS organized the 2nd international (Asian) conference 'Asia in Africa, Africa in Asia' in 2012, inviting Asian Africanists from China, India, Japan, Korea, and some African and European countries. The conference was significant in that it was the first conference where all four major Asian countries took part. It was a smooth start, and after the first conference in 2012, IAS-HUFS has hosted Asian Africanists for an annual conference. IAS-HUFS, the Center for African Area studies of Kyoto University (CAAS-KU), and the CAS-JNU hosted international conferences for Asian Africanists subsequently too. For instance, for the commemorative international symposium celebrating its 50th anniversary the Japanese Association of African Studies organized the 'second' Asian conference of African studies (Iwata 2018: 225).[6] IAS-HUFS and CAAS-KU had a memorandum in 2017 and agreed on cooperation in academic exchange.[7]

Due to their geographic connections, Korea and Japan have maintained a mutual academic relationship most easily. IAS-HUFS and the Research Institute of Social Sciences at Ryukoku University, Japan, had an agreement to have a seminar exchange twice a year which lasted for several years. After that, IAS-HUFS and CAAS-KU, a mecca for Japanese African studies, made a memorandum of understanding in 2017 to set up a scholarly exchange between them. The two institutes have mutually invited scholars and students and are looking forward to further academic collaboration.

The Asian Africanist Network is still in its infancy. It is obvious that the network has enough potential, but it has an explicit limitation at the same time. First of all, except India, its academic centers and institutes are exclusively centered in East Asian countries. There is a movement for African studies in South East Asia (Iwata 2018: 225); however, it may take some time before we see academic partners from Asian countries other than China, India, Japan, and Korea. Second, although the network has been up and running since 2011, it still needs a catalyst in order to attain some significant achievements. The best way so far for the network to function has been to host academic meetings themed around a specific research field and topic.

Now it is time to move forward from this initial stage. In the course of numerous academic exchanges, we have been able to distinguish the academic orientations of each country's African studies, and it is time to combine them in order to find out something deeper about the Asian approach African studies. Fortunately, there has been a number of publication projects in which Asian Africanists have collaborated and shared their academic knowledge. Sustainability is yet another challenge for Asian Africanists. We can try to form a joint project team and conduct work together, in that we can harmonize the different academic viewpoints from one country to another. This is one way of producing a specifically Asian academic perspective on African studies. The significance of an Asian Africanist Network is thus very clear to us. For Korean Africanists, since the domestic academic milieu is not favorable to Africanists and the resources for African studies are scare, we need to turn our eyes outside and expand our horizons beyond the immediate domain. However, any action plan must be sustainable. My suggestion is that via a national-level association of African Studies each country should take action collectively and create new environments for future academic collaboration.

In the first part of this chapter, I described the institutional development of South Korean African studies. Notwithstanding its fragile sustainability, South Korean African studies has laid its institutional foundations in Korean academy. We must agree that, despite its politico-economic and historical distance from the African continent, the institutional setup of African studies in Korea has been exceptionally successful. Furthermore, it is not only the institutional achievement but also the quantity of academic publishing that has improved enormously since the late 1970s.

Poverty in the Midst of Plenty: The Current Situation of African Studies

'Poverty in the midst of plenty' is probably the most suitable phrase for explaining the contemporary academic situation of African studies in Korea. In light of a brisk series of interactions between Korea and Africa in diverse areas—diplomatic, economic, cultural—South Korean African studies has undeniably made progress. However, the field faces some prolonged challenges. These challenges can be put into three points: the question of academic sustainability, academic sectionalism, and its poor intellectual contribution to Korean society.

A Definitional Problem for South Korean African Studies

Before we discuss the challenges faced by South Korean African studies in detail, I am going to elucidate the academic categorization of African studies as classified by the NRF. This is necessary because the categorization of African studies currently reflects the confused status of African studies in Korea. Above all, African studies in Korea is characterized as an 'isolated' branch of academia that requires academic protection and support.

The NRF asserts that the primary purpose of this categorization is to offer adequate support and management for academic research projects (www.nrf.re.kr). The NRF provides three general classifications of academia: (1) National Science and Technology Standard classification, (2) Academic and Research classification and (3) Program manager classification. Academic and Research classification is again subclassified into eight general classifications: humanities, social sciences, natural sciences, and so on. Diverse disciplines of African studies are thus subclassified into humanities and social sciences. The problem is that African humanities, that is, African linguistics, literature, history, and philosophy, are classified as 'unclassified other' disciplines. For instance, under general humanities, literature, philosophy, history, and language (linguistics) are subcategorized and there are no specific subcategories for African literature, history, and linguistics.[8] They are classified as 'unclassified others.'

It is only the social sciences that contains African studies under the subcategory of area studies. Nevertheless, this classification is still problematic. For the purpose of study, Africa is divided into five zones: East, West, South, Central, and North—but this is only covering 32 countries and these countries are arbitrarily classified. Therefore, I assume that this classification given by NRF reflects the ignorance and indifference of Korean academia on African studies.[9] In sum, the academic position of African studies in Korea is not clear, spread as it is over diverse academic disciplines, albeit it *is* an established academic discipline.

Challenges Faced by South Korean African Studies

Now I come back to discussion of the challenges South Korean African studies faces. There are number of analytical reviews on the topic (Park 1996; Cho 2012; Han 2013; Hong 2016). As mentioned beforehand, the advancement of South Korean African studies since the early 2000s has been very significant. It is in this period that researchers and research institutes of African studies have multiplied, and the issue of African development also caught government and the public attention. Nevertheless, these positive aspects cast gloomy shadows at the same time. For instance, Park (1996) listed the problems of African studies in Korea: lack of research funds, shortage of researchers, and social sciences-dominated research environments. About 16 years later, Cho (2012) pointed out again the lack of research funds and the factional tendencies of individual and group researchers. Han (2013) and Hong (2016) diagnose that the factionalism among South Korean African studies is a critical issue. To generalize these criticisms, I can categorize the problem thus:

1. shortage of research institutes and researchers;
2. shortage of research funds;
3. failure of communication among different disciplines.

Such criticisms are correct on some points, and these problems are not solely our problems. Other countries where African studies are marginalized suffer similar issues. Even countries that have a long and well-established academic history of African studies may face similar trials. Fortunately, the situation in Korea is getting better year on year. The shortage of research institutes and researchers does not matter, as there is an increasing tendency for new researchers to enter into African studies of late. For this reason, one cannot argue that the lack of researchers and research institutes act as barriers to the development of South Korean African studies. Rather, as mentioned above, I consider three other barriers as substantial hindrances to development of the discipline: lack of sustainability, sectionalism, and poor academic contribution to the public realm.

The question of academic sustainability is an essential condition for the development of South Korean African studies but, unfortunately, the field suffers from structural weakness. Most research institutes, if not all, are in fragile situations in terms of their management, as they exclusively rely on external sources for carrying out research. An individual researcher and institute cannot afford the massive amounts required for research funds from their own pockets. So, they seek research sponsors outside of academia, mainly from government affiliates such as the NRF, Korea International Cooperation Agency (KOICA), Korea Foundation, or Korean Institute for International Economic Policy (KIEP). Except for some fortunate researchers and institutes able to gain specific support for a certain period, the rest will face languishment. This structural weakness could cause certain dependencies in academia and put researchers at risk of conducting research tailored to suit the tastes of sponsor agencies rather than following their own ideas.

There is another kind of structural fragility at work. Korean researchers, including Africanists, become self-censoring when they apply for research funds from sponsor bodies, such as the NRF and others, and tend to cut back the duration and amount of research funds required; this causes researchers to adjust their original projects according to the funding streams, compromising their work and reducing the duration allocated for field research. Moreover, the lion's share of annual national research funds always goes to some significant research institutes or universities that have comparatively (politically) advantageous positions. For example, when a certain research project for humanities was initiated in 2007, overseas studies (area studies) was included as a part of the project brief. The goal was to support financially 'isolated' overseas studies, and the NRF picked up African studies as a typically isolated overseas study. But in reality, above all, the lion's share of overseas studies fund went to well-established academic institutes. The research fund was allocated by who had academic powers and full-fledged research systems. This kind of structural fragility may partly cause the withering of African studies in Korea.

Since the 2000s, an intriguing academic phenomenon in South Korean African studies has been that diverse academic projects have been attempted by non-Africanist researchers. The entry of humanities and developmental studies is particularly curious. Studies on African masquerade, African costume and textiles (Choi 2007, 2015), African music (Lee 2000, 2011), and African religion (An 2008) have emerged as new topics. Nevertheless, these projects have not been prolonged and the main reason for this was that they were presumably not designed to be long-term projects, mainly due to the lack of sufficient research funds.

Academic sectionalism is a further deterrent to the advance of South Korean African studies, and I count this as the most difficult problem Korean Africanists face. As Han (2013) aptly points out, the confrontation or contestation of two rival groups within the circle of African studies is an endemic problem. He classifies these rival groups of South Korean African studies into two: a group of scholars from African studies backgrounds and a group of those who hail from other academic disciplines. In the first group are the scholars who have been trained in African language and literature at HUFS and dedicated their academic lives to African studies. The second group come from diverse disciplines, particularly the social sciences, and have designated African studies as the second field for their research objectives. The former group is suspicious of the second group, denigrating them as not 'serious' and 'unorthodox' in the discipline of African studies, casting them as opportunist academic fence-sitters looking for ways to take advantage. The second group argues that the first group lacks scientific theories and methodologies as scholars, for they are mere 'area specialists.' The question is about who takes authority and has authenticity in their studies. I believe this is a silly question since no one can claim academic authority and authenticity for South Korean African studies.

I see the situation more complicated than the conclusions reached in Han's analysis, because there are confrontations among at least four different academic groups concerned with African studies. First, there is a scholarly confrontation between humanities and international area studies, which has deepened at HUFS. Arguments are ongoing between a group of scholars who major in languages and literature, and who conceive that the true academic research of international studies should be based around this work. Furthermore, there are counterarguments from scholars of area studies, especially majors in social sciences who insist that international studies should focus on area studies. Therefore, it must be more practical and directly applicable to the regions in question. I argue that this rivalry is derived from a structural problem in the tradition of HUFS—a long-standing confrontation between pure and ideal academic disciplines and practical and applicable area disciplines.

There is another form of rivalry that has developed between a group of scholars who think they are 'orthodox' Africanists and the new entries from other disciplines and area studies. This has been a phenomenon since the early 2000s, in that various other academic disciplines, especially political science and economics, and area studies, such as Middle Eastern studies and Francophone studies, have found their attention drawn to African studies. The Africanists are suspicious of such new researchers who take African studies as secondary or supplementary topic, while the second group contends that the supposed 'orthodox' Africanists are mere 'area specialists' and generally lack the theories and methodologies of an established academic discipline. Of course, this does not mean that the antagonism is readily visible among these groups, but there are tensions. It is unfortunate to see this kind of argument going around as it would only produce adverse effects for the development of African studies, and without these academics resolving the rivalry among themselves, the future of South Korean African studies is not terribly bright.

Another challenge is the poor intellectual contribution that discipline has thus far made to Korean society. Academia has a certain degree of obligation to somehow take academic achievements back into society at large; the popularization of academic knowledge is one way of communicating with the broader public. The NRF has incorporated 'outreaching' academic achievements to wider society as a part of project guidelines. This is in order to boost the sharing of academic knowledge. Some critical reviews (Hong 2016; Kim et al. 2015, 2016) indicate that the Korean public has created a distorted image of Africa. These reviews diagnose the reasons of this distorted image of Africa as being the misreporting of the media (Kim et al. 2015), factual errors in school textbooks (Kim et al. 2016), and scholarly indifference to correcting this state of affairs. For instance, Kim et al. (2016) and Hong (2016) argue that addressing the lack of proper information related to Africa is the top requirement for formulating the appropriate image of the continent.

My main question lies in this point: how should we understand the gap between the quantitative increase of academic publication (both in terms of journals and books), while on the other hand there is outcry about the lack of information related to Africa? Does this mean that the quality of scholarly publication does not meet the public demands for necessary knowledge? My personal experience says 'yes.' I often get complaints from audiences when I deliver public lectures that there are 'no' reference works available on Africa. Of course, this is not true. There is a full list of publications on Africa to be found in libraries and book shops. Hong (2016) has already shown us that publication on African studies has been skyrocketing in recent years. Then, why do my audiences complain about the lack of information? Quantitatively, there is indeed an abundance of academic publication but, qualitatively, the number of references out there for public use is dramatically shrinking. The public needs 'useful' knowledge which is readable and usable for them. I term this academic sectionalism and the academia–society divide as epitomized by the idea 'poverty in the midst of plenty.'

Conclusion: What Is the Place of South Korean African Studies?

African studies is an inclusive academic discipline that has its genetic roots in the studies of African linguistics and anthropology during the period of European colonial dominion. As an academic discipline, the essential and underlying purpose of the study is the accumulation and generalization of comprehensive knowledge of humankind, but it also entails the practical aim of obtaining necessary information and knowledge of colonized peoples and societies. Over time, the study has expanded to other academic disciplines, and when the United States initiated area studies after the Second World War, African studies, as a part of area studies, became globalized. For the United States, the initiation of area studies had a strategic reason: to gather information on different parts of the world and expand American influence over them. Therefore, historically, for practical reasons African studies is closely related to the European colonialism and the United States' global paradigm plan.

Naturally, Western scholarship has dominated the field of study by attempting to analyze and generalize the nature of African societies and cultures. For instance, as the forerunner of Western African studies, anthropology, in the late nineteenth and early twentieth centuries, pioneered the attempt to classify African societies into a number of 'structural forms' (Radcliffe-Brown 1952). Armed with the spirit of enlightenment and social evolutionism, anthropologists objectified African societies as 'primitive' and 'savage' people who lived in a social unit called a 'tribe.' To the West, exotic African societies and people have been considered 'tribal.' The influence of such thinking was wide and deep.

Korea has an ambiguous position in this regard. South Korea's political engagement with Africa was not direct. 'Traditionally,' South Korea's economic interests in Africa have remained in low and cultural interactions were rare. South Korea's developmental cooperation with Africa is a recent phenomenon. Under these conditions, South Korean African studies has been isolated from wider international academic discourses.

So, what is the place of South Korean African studies in this discourse? With these minimal prior engagements, what is the point of South Korean African studies?

I consider that South Korean Africanists have dual goals: academic and practical achievements. Academically, we attempt to construct systems of knowledge useful for ourselves. Practically, we try to contribute to wider Korean society by providing something useful for societal engagements with Africa. So, how much have we done to achieve both aims?

As I have mentioned, knowledge construction is possibly the ultimate interest and goal of any scholarly work. In this vein, the knowledge production of African studies in Korea has dramatically increased from its academic establishment and particularly since the 2000s. I also pointed out that there is a considerable gap between the construction of academic knowledge and the demand for that knowledge beyond academia. Thus, the question remains: If one of the roles of academia is to contribute the fruits of its academic activities to society, and African studies are no exception, then how do we construct knowledge and for what?

As Hong (2016: 388) aptly mentioned, the problem of South Korean African studies, in terms of knowledge construction, is that diverse disciplines of African studies have not produced synergy effects at all, mainly due to the lack of interactions among academic institutes and individual researchers. Boundaries between social sciences and humanities on the one hand, and among individual Africanists on the other, are so robust that the breaking down of these boundaries does not seem to be a realistic aim, reflecting the past trajectory of African studies. The problem is that there is no catalyst to merge different academic disciplines and individual researchers. The KAAS, which is a single national-level academic association, should take on this catalytic role. The association has gone some way to doing this, but only an insignificant distance in terms of the expectations.

We need to shake off the idea that scholars should stay away from the 'secular' world and nest in 'ivory towers' for the yielding of in-depth knowledge exclusively for ourselves. This scholarly exclusiveness only isolates academia from society. Now the times insist that scholarly knowledge should meet the demands of societies. I doubt that most of Korean Africanists take this seriously, since we tend to think that our scholarly devotion and academic neutralism are the primary conditions for scholarship. The crisis of academia and, in particular, the crisis of African studies comes from this solitude. To resolve the problem, we should open the gates of the ivory tower and try to make active exchange with the outside world.

I suggest two approaches here. Domestically, we need to interact with areas outside of academia. There are demands for knowledge from the government, civil societies, and the public. Knowledge desired and required by the government and civil societies are the knowledge that can be practically applied by them. Korean Africanists cannot monopolize the process of knowledge production, since the emergence of Africa-related civil society organizations has led to the accumulation of their own knowledge based on direct experiences in Africa. I urge that this 'alternative' knowledge should be merged with academic knowledge in order to produce 'appropriate' knowledge which might be useful for both academia and the public.

In this sense, it might be worthwhile to consider a unique cultural event recently introduced in the Korean capital: Seoul Africa Festival. The festival was initiated by IAS-HUFS and one of its stated aims was to share Africa-related academic knowledge with the public. The institute suggested the idea with a civil enterprise, Africa Insight, to co-organize the festival. The research institute and civil enterprise formulated the idea and hold the first such festival in 2016 at which participated seven African embassies and 18 Africa-related organizations, along with a number of academic institutes. The following year, in 2017, the festival extended its boundary even wider and 40 Africa-related civil organizations took part. In 2018, the number increased again as 50 Africa-related civil and public organizations were in attendance. The festival was divided into five zones: knowledge, culture, community, market, and friends. At each festival, IAS-HUFS has designed the knowledge zone so as to popularize academic knowledge that has been produced by institute researchers through intensive field research. For instance, in 2017 the knowledge zone presented Africa's coffee cultures by introducing rare knowledge such as different regional coffee brewing and consuming cultures. The theme of African coffee cultures attracted the public as interest in coffee culture is high in South Korea, and the festival has proven that the popularization of academic knowledge is acceptable by the public if that knowledge meets the public demand.

Producing this kind of popular knowledge is, as a matter of fact, one of the conditions that the NRF always asks of research projects. It is not an easy task since there is a huge gap between academic and applied (practical) knowledge, and scholars are in general reluctant to try and bridge it. However, there have been attempts to popularize academic knowledge by publishing readable books for the public. In the field of African studies, compared to the publication of academic books, the volume of trade book publication is insignificant. This is comparable to the situation of humanities, which, facing crisis, declares the 'popularization of the humanities' and actively tries to broaden the reach of its publications.

The second way of expanding South Korean African studies is to internationalize domestic African studies. Considering the size of South Korean African studies and the issues faced in terms of the sustainability of study, international collaboration is indispensable. Academic networking in African studies seems to be an international trend. For example, the Africa-Europe Group for Interdisciplinary Studies (AEGIS), which is the biggest and the most influential academic organization in international African studies, is now connected to Asian Africanist groups. The African Studies Association of India and the Japanese Association of African Studies have become Asian members of AEGIS (Iwata 2018: 226). KAAS should itself consider membership seriously for, in this era of globalization, internationalization is a necessary condition for enriching academic study.

There have been good signs for the last few years as African studies in Korea has actively engaged with international collaborations, in particular with other Asian countries. The problem is that this activity has been led by a particular institute, IAS-HUFS, which cannot represent South Korean African studies as a whole. I assert that KAAS, as a national representative body of African studies, should take the appropriate role for international networking. KAAS is a national-level research institute, which has many academic potentialities to lead South Korean African studies, both domestically and internationally.

Notes

1. The Joseon dynasty (1392–1910) was the last empire before the establishment of the Republic of Korea.
2. The Department of Swahili language changed its name to the Department of African Studies in the late 1990s, and then again expanded its structure into the Division of African Studies in 2008.
3. http://www.k-af.or.kr/load.asp?subPage=120, accessed July 30, 2019
4. This year was selected because it was the year that first master thesis on African studies was registered at the RISS.
5. Master's theses on religion have a share of 7%, and most of these theses are on African theology, composed by missionaries and mission school students.
6. The Japanese Association of African Studies' Asian international symposium might be the third after India (2011) and South Korea (2012).

7. Scholarly and student exchanges have been initiated since the memorandum between CAAS-KU and IAS-HUFS.
8. This is comparable to the situation with other area humanities, such as Middle Eastern literature, history, linguistics, and philosophy, which are subclassified as semi-independent categories. The same goes for South East Asian humanities, European humanities, Latin American humanities; it is only Africa that does not have such fuller classification.
9. The current categorization of academic disciplines was done in 1999, and no significant change has occurred since then.

REFERENCES

An, S. (2008). Recent Trends and Prospect in the Study of African Religions: Limitations in Western Understanding of African Religions and Alternative Approach of Phenomenology. *Korean Journal of African Studies, 27*(1), 131–160. (in Korean).

Cho, W. B. (2012). Korean Research Trends in African Studies. *Asian Review, 2*(2), 129–148. (In Korean).

Choi, H. J. (2007). The African Style in Fashion Designs in 2000's. *Journal of Korean Clothes and Foods, 57*(3), 150–164. (in Korean).

Choi, J. Y. (2015). Consideration of Textiles of African Tribes. *The Association of Korean Design and Culture, 21*(3), 685–697. (in Korean).

Daily Economics. (1976, October 18). Institute of African Studies and Latin America, Urgently Need To Be Set Up… Construction and Export Potential Are Great, p. 7. Retrieved July 30, 2019, from www.newslibrary.naver.com, in Korean.

Daily Economics. (1982, August 27). Korea-Senegal, Agreed on a Free Trade Zone in Dakar, p. 1. Retrieved July 30, 2019, from www.newslibrary.naver.com, in Korean.

DongA Daily. (1982, June 18). President Chun, National Visit to Four African Countries and Canada, p. 1. Retrieved July 30, 2019, from www.newslibrary.naver.com, in Korean.

Ha, G. G. (1972). *African Politics*. Seoul: Bupmunsa. (in Korean).

Han, G. R. (1955). The Concern of France Over Violence in Africa. *Regional Administration, 4*(10), 18–22.

Han, G. S. (2013). A Methodological Reflection on African Studies in Korea and a Review for Research Topics. *Asian Review, 3*(5), 159–193. (In Korean).

Hong, M. H. (2016). The Current State and Task of African Studies in Korea. *Cross-Cultural Studies, 44*, 373–391.

Iwata, T. (2018). 14. Africa-Asia Relations in Academic Network Formation. In P. M. A. R. de Medeiros Carvalho, D. Arase, & S. Cornelissen (Eds.), *Routledge Handbook of Africa-Asia Relations* (pp. 216–232). London; New York: Routledge.

Kim, C. S., Chae, Y. I., & Jung, N. W. (2015). Exploring Media Portrayals and Public Image About Africa. *International Area Studies, 18*(5), 219–252.

Kim, J. M., Park, J. Y., Kim, Y. A., & Kim, J. Y. (2016). *The Study on the Improvement of Understanding Africa*. Seoul: Korea-Africa Center.

Kyunghyang Daily. (1982, July 20). The Establishment of the Association of African Studies, Dr. Park, Sang-shik was Elected as the First President, p. 11. Retrieved July 30, 2019, from www.newslibrary.naver.com, in Korean.

Lee, S. W. (2000). The Influence of African Music on Ligeti's Work. *Institute Journal of Western Music, 5*, 225–246. (in Korean).

Lee, J. B. (2011). The Sources of African Musics and Its Hybridities. *Music and Culture, 25*(25), 177–202.

National Research Foundation of Korea. www.nrf.re.kr.

Oh, H. J. (1991). Recruitment of the Department of Eastern European Studies and KiSwahili. In C. Taesoo & C. Kyuhyang (Eds.), *The Developmental History of Korean Educational and Policy* (pp. 765–767). Seoul: Yejugak. (In Korean).

Park, W. T. (1996). Current Situations and Questions of African Areas Studies. *African Studies, 12*, 1–15. (In Korean).

Radcliffe-Brown, A. R. (1952). *Structure and Function in Primitive Society: Essays and Address*. Glencoe, IL: The Free Press.

CHAPTER 3

South Korean Social Science Research on Africa

Dong Ju Choi, Soojin Han, and Sooho Lee

Introduction

South Korean social science research on Africa began in the mid-1950s, following the establishment of diplomatic ties between the South Korean government and African countries, with Han Ki-ryun's essay in Korean, titled 'The Troubles of France and the Riots of Africa', published in the fourth volume of the *Local Administration Review* in 1955 (Cho 2012). Seventy years later, South Korean social science research on Africa has achieved remarkable growth, both quantitatively and qualitatively, especially at the university and research institute levels. Taking the time to look back at the path of South Korean social science research on Africa can be

D. J. Choi (✉)
School of Global Service, Sookmyung Women's University, Seoul, South Korea
e-mail: djchoi@sookmyung.ac.kr

S. Han • S. Lee
Institute of Global Governance, Sookmyung Women's University, Seoul, South Korea

© The Author(s) 2020
Y. Chang (ed.), *South Korea's Engagement with Africa*, Africa's Global Engagement: Perspectives from Emerging Countries, https://doi.org/10.1007/978-981-32-9013-6_3

a valuable tool for researchers both to appreciate its growth and to find meaningful future directions for research.

There have been few trend analyses conducted on African studies that focus solely on the social sciences. Most of the existing studies were included in a comprehensive analysis of the origins and history of research on Africa (Abbink 2001; Kirk-Greene 2002). In addition, from a geographical perspective, with the exception of research from China and Japan (Li 2005; Ichikawa 2005), these studies were mainly conducted by researchers hailing from former African colonizers.[1] The majority of this research exhibits a strong common link with Africa's colonial past; the origins, development, and themes of research cannot help but to be influenced by the legacy of colonialism. Therefore, it is of special significance that a study aims to analyze the trends of social science research focused on Africa in a country that bears no colonial ties to Africa, such as South Korea.

Several attempts have been made to conduct trend analyses of South Korean research on Africa. The first attempt, made by Park (1996), examined quantitative changes in the volume of research on Africa published between 1959 and 1995 both by period and by academic discipline. Several years later, Cho (2012) further examined quantitative trends specific to the field of social sciences, distinguishing sources ranging from 1955 to 2012 by publication type (professional journals, degree theses, and books) and discipline. In the following year, Han (2013) analyzed characteristics in terms of research areas and themes by period from the viewpoint of regional studies.

These analyses have made a great contribution to South Korean research on Africa, in that they attempted to determine the origins and record the growth of research despite its emergence in an environment not conducive to such research. Building on their achievements, this study is an attempt to more systematically analyze South Korean social science research on Africa through the use of scientific methods not yet attempted in existing research.

Through the analysis of journal articles, degree theses, government-funded research reports, and books published in the field of social sciences between 1955 and September 2018, this study reviewed topics of academic interest over time. Additionally, although statistical methods have been employed in research trend analysis when it comes to Africa in general or specifically for the social sciences, no trend analysis has been conducted using scientific analytical methods. This study used cluster map analysis, a useful method to analyze bibliographic information. This aids researchers in understanding which topics are most frequently addressed in a set of sources, and terms are mapped in clusters based on frequency of appearance and their relationships with one another. The result is a single, visualized map which allows viewers to easily grasp a vast amount of bibliographic information. It is also a useful tool for identifying research trends and researcher interests, especially when cluster maps from different periods are compared, allowing for the determination of trends over time.

This study is organized into four sections. The following section introduces the research methods employed. Section "Basic Statistical Information" provides basic statistical information about the data collected, including quantitative data about increases and decreases in the volume of research, and the distribution and changing trends of research by field, types of research, research methods, and grant sources. Section "South Korean Social Science Research on Africa" presents the results of the bibliometric analysis of term occurrences as well as the relationships among keywords and is followed by the conclusion.

Research Methods

Analysis Methods

The bibliometric mapping technique visualizes bibliographic results and can display large amounts of data at a glance (Small and Greenlee 1980). The Visualization of Similarities (VOS) Viewer, developed by Waltman et al. (2010), was the software of choice for this study. The VOS Viewer uses similarity measures to map the clusters, which are determined by calculating co-occurrence among keywords based on strength of association (van Eck and Waltman 2007).

The similarity between items i and j is stated as $S_{ij} \cdot C_{ij}$ and indicates the number of co-occurrences of items i and j, where $W_i \cdot W_j$ denotes the total number of occurrences of items i and j as follows:

$$s_{ij} = \frac{c_{ij}}{w_i w_j}.$$

With the establishment of the similarity matrix, the distance between items can be measured as follows:

$$V(x_1,\ldots,x_n) = s_{ij}x_i - x_j^2,$$

V denotes the distance between items i and j, whereas denotes the Euclidean norm of items i and j.

$$D_p(X) = \sum_{i=1}^{n} I_p(i) w_i K\left(\frac{X-X_i}{(\bar{d}h)}\right).$$

The VOS Viewer can visualize data in various ways. This study opts to use the cluster density map for data display. This is a particularly efficient tool for identifying which words are included in each cluster and how the words are related. On a cluster density map, each cluster has its own item density at a specific point. The item density for a point x in a cluster p is denoted as $D_p(X)$, and w_i is the weight of the item i. $I_p(i)$ denotes an indicator function that equals 1 if item i belongs to cluster p and that otherwise equals 0. The kernel function K is given, and $\bar{d}$ denotes the average distance between items. h denotes a parameter called kernel width (van Eck and Waltman 2009).

The cluster density maps display several unique features. Differently colored clusters represent stronger associations between keywords. In other words, words that fall within a cluster of the same color are more closely related to one another than to those words in other clusters. Furthermore, keywords that occur more frequently are larger and bold, whereas less frequently occurring terms are smaller and non-bold. The VOS Viewer also corresponds to a distance-based map, developed through another bibliometric research method (van Eck and Waltman 2009; Han 2015). Therefore, the distance between keywords is also indicative of their association; a shorter distance between words indicates a closer relationship in terms of co-occurrence. The ability of the VOS Viewer to display not only the frequency of words but also the relationship among words made it a powerful tool for this study.

Data Collection and Preparation

This study utilizes keywords in African studies, specifically targeting social science fields in South Korea as the main data source. Keywords drawn from selected sources were used to develop term cluster maps by period in order to identify overall research trends. When possible, keywords provided by the source authors were included in the analysis. If no keywords were provided, five to ten keywords were arbitrarily selected from the source, excluding general terms (e.g., method, survey) or obvious terms (e.g., Africa, Korea). The Korean keywords were translated into English by the researcher for the purposes of this study. Of the total sources, 915 were in Korean and 190 were originally in English.

Following data analysis, cluster maps were developed for three periods: 1950s–1960s, 1970s–1980s, and 1990s–2010s. In the second and third maps, two and three keyword clusters, respectively, were created, especially due to much higher number of studies on Africa conducted compared to the 1950s–1960s, for which it was impossible to make such a map. Words displayed in the cluster maps are those that appeared frequently in sources, as well as surrounding and highly related terms based on the research environments of each time period, and the distance between terms is representative of their degree of relatedness.

Period classification was determined based on significant changes in South Korea's international status or policy changes toward Africa. The 1950s–1960s marked the beginning of diplomatic relations with African countries, as well as the beginning of South Korean scholarship on Africa. The 1970s–1980s was a period of rapid economic growth for South Korea, and domestic companies became interested in the African market, while the strategic diplomatic approach of the Cold War toward African countries continued until the late 1970s. Finally, the end of the Cold War and South Korean admission to the United Nations (UN) in 1991 signaled a policy change for the 1990s–2010s. Since then, South Korea's diplomatic status in the international community has risen, and development assistance to developing countries has come to play an increasingly important role in foreign policy toward the Third World, including toward African countries.

Basic Statistical Information

For this study, researchers surveyed journal articles, degree theses, government-funded research reports, and books, using a different database for each source type. Under the search term 'Africa', results were limited to social science disciplines as defined by the classification table of academic research from the National Research Foundation of Korea (NRF). A total of 785 journal articles and degree theses were drawn from the Korea Education and Research Information Service (KERIS) website, excluding overlapping results. Of these, 444 articles were from Korea Citation Index (KCI) certified journals, while 73 were from noncertified journals. An additional 245 government-funded research reports were obtained from the National Knowledge Information System (NKIS) and National Research Foundation (NRF) of Korea websites, the primary source for national policy reports in South Korea. Furthermore, a total of 75 books were retrieved from the National Assembly Library. It was observed that, over time, the number of results increased almost 40-fold, from 14 results in the 1950s and 1960s to 540 results in the 2010s (See Table 3.1).

When it comes to specific disciplines addressed in the sources, business and economics were the most common areas of interest, followed by sociology. The remaining fields, in order, were political science, international development, anthropology, public administration, law, education, geology, and military science (See Table 3.2).

Journal articles and government-funded research reports were categorized as single-research or joint-research projects. A total of 94 journal articles (18%) were classified as joint-research, whereas 160 government-funded research reports (65%) were classified as joint-research (See Table 3:3).

Table 3.1 Number of South Korean social science studies on Africa

	Journal articles	*Degree theses*	*Research reports*	*Books*	*Total*
1950s	2	0	0	0	2
1960s	11	1	0	0	12
1970s	17	11	39	1	68
1980s	61	58	53	4	176
1990s	58	20	6	12	96
2000s	141	25	33	12	211
2010s	227	153	114	46	540
Total	517	268	245	75	1105

Source: Author's own work

Table 3.2 Research trends by discipline

	B	P1	S	P2	I	L	A	E	G	M
1950s	0	1	0	1	0	0	0	0	0	0
1960s	0	2	3	2	0	5	0	0	0	0
1970s	39	13	3	0	7	5	1	0	0	0
1980s	107	41	7	2	15	1	2	1	0	0
1990s	32	20	22	3	7	0	5	7	0	0
2000s	42	54	65	6	26	5	10	3	0	0
2010s	131	114	97	16	131	11	20	16	1	3
Total	351	245	197	30	186	27	38	27	1	3

B Business & Economics, *P1* Political Science, *S* Sociology, *P2* Public Administration, *I* International Development, *L* Law, *A* Anthropology, *E* Education, *G* Geology, *M* Military Science

Source: Author's own work

Table 3.3 Distribution by study type (single/joint)

	Journal articles	Research reports	Total
Single-research	423	85	508
Joint-research	94	160	254

Source: Author's own work

Additionally, journal articles and degree theses were classified based on the type of research employed—empirical or interpretive. Of these, 459 journal articles employed interpretive research, a rate approximately 8 times higher than empirical research, while 219 degree theses employed interpretive research, a rate over 4 times higher than empirical research (See Table 3.4).

Furthermore, research grant organizations were categorized as governmental institutions, universities, or private institutions, with research that received no grant funding included in the 'None' category. Almost half of the research examined was conducted without grant funding. The government has provided research grants since the 1970s, and although the grant rate declined sharply in the 1990s, it has again risen steadily since the 2000s. Data on research conducted by government-affiliated institutions were included in the 'Government Institution' category (See Table 3.5).

The keywords analyzed were classified into three categories—'most frequently mentioned', 'new keywords', and 'most frequently mentioned countries'. The top five words based on frequency of occurrence are listed by category and period, with those in the category 'new keywords' listed in order of frequency. Through a review of these three categories, one can get a rough idea of research trends over time (See Table 3.6).

Table 3.4 Distribution by research method (empirical/interpretive)

	Journal articles	Degree theses	Total
Empirical research	58	49	107
Interpretive research	459	219	678

Source: Author's own work

Table 3.5 Research grant trends

	Government institutions	Universities	Private institutions	None
1950s	0	0	0	2
1960s	0	0	0	11
1970s	39	0	0	17
1980s	53	0	0	61
1990s	9	1	1	53
2000s	70	27	0	77
2010s	177	39	3	122
Total	348	67	4	343

Source: Author's own work

Table 3.6 Keywords by period

	1950s–1960s	1970s–1980s	1990s–2010s
Most frequently mentioned keywords	Democracy Colony Nationalism	Economy Trade Market entry Country overview Export	ODA China South Africa Sub-Saharan Africa Development
New keywords		Economy Trade Market entry Country overview Export	ODA Soft Power MDGs Refugee HIV/AIDS
Most frequently mentioned countries		Nigeria Kenya Soviet Union Senegal China	China South= Africa Ethiopia Kenya Nigeria

Source: Author's own work

South Korean Social Science Research on Africa

1950s–1960s: Strategic Approach for Inter-Korean Issues

In the 1950s and 1960s, very little social science research was conducted on Africa by South Korean researchers. The first academic study was published in 1955, and a total of 13 additional studies were conducted throughout the 1950s and 1960s. From 1955–1970, the most frequently appearing keywords were *colony, democracy,* and *nationalism,* appearing three times each, followed by *Cold War, decentralization, foreign policy, local administration, neutral nation,* and *politics* (See Table 3.7).

Most articles published at the time focused on the newly established African countries and concentrated on issues such as constitutional systems (Han 1965), political ideas of the ruling elite (Kim 1965), and the status of women (Byun 1970). These articles seem to be, for the most part, based on the personal interests and specialties of the researchers. At the same time, however, the appearance of the terms *Cold War* and *neutral nation* among the keywords for this period reflect the international system dominated by the American-Soviet antagonism of the time, with many researchers choosing to focus on African ideologies and activities in the international community. This is also particularly indicative of South Korea's diplomatic competition with North Korea. South Korean scholars conducted case studies of Non-Aligned Movement countries, comparing African countries with Asian countries (Shin 1963), as well as studies on African nationalism (Han 1964).

Prior to the 1950s, South Korea had little to no relationship with any African country. There was very little public knowledge of Africa itself due to extremely limited sources of information. Korean public interest in

Table 3.7 Frequently mentioned keywords in the 1950s and 1960s

Rank	Keyword	Instances
1	Democracy	3
2	Colony	3
3	Nationalism	3
4	Cold War	2
5	Decentralization	2
6	foreign policy	2
7	local administration	2
8	neutral nation	2
9	Politics	2

Source: Author's own work

Africa seems to have begun in the early twentieth century when Koreans began taking a greater interest in international affairs, and Korean news agencies began obtaining information from foreign agencies. Thus, articles on Africa occasionally appeared in the international sections of domestic newspapers (Kim and Yang 2012).[2]

The absence of an African department in the first ministry of foreign affairs of the Republic of Korea, established in 1948, indicates South Korea's lack of immediate interest in pursuing a relationship with Africa. Rather, considering its independence from Japanese colonial rule and US control of the southern half of the Korean peninsula following the end of the Korean War in 1953, the South Korean government focused its attention on gaining recognition as the sole legitimate government within the international community (Lee 2012). South Korea's desperate need for aid to rebuild the war-torn peninsula, as well as military support through a US-ROK alliance, led the government to focus all its efforts on the relationship with the USA rather than other so-called 'Third World countries' (Park 2007). As a result, there was very little research on Africa conducted in the 1950s. It was not until the United Nations took control of inter-Korean issues following the Armistice Agreement in 1953 that the South Korean government realized the importance of establishing relations with African countries.

In 1954, 15 members of the United Nations, which participated in the Korean War as UN troops, as well as the Soviet Union and China, met with representatives from both North and South Korea in Geneva to discuss peaceful reunification of the two Koreas. However, due to differing allegiances, with Communist countries such as the Soviet Union supporting North Korea on the one hand and countries that had participated in the Korean War as UN troops (including the USA) on the other, the talks were suspended after 50 days with no resolution, and inter-Korean issues subsequently became the responsibility of the General Assembly, with an annual report published by the UN Commission for the Unification and Rehabilitation of Korea (UNCURK). Although neither was a UN member at the time, both North and South Korea employed aggressive diplomatic measures aimed at other UN members to gain support for their own initiatives for relief, reconstruction, government recognition, and unification. Inter-Korean issues were therefore transformed from a matter of force to a matter of diplomacy.[3]

The increasing membership of African nations in the UN made them naturally subject to competition between the diplomacy of North and

South Korea. In 1957, South Korea made its first goodwill mission to African countries as part of the first official South Korean visit to the Middle East and Africa. The delegation visited a total of 11 countries with the expressed intention of showing gratitude for support and participation in the Korean War, especially to Ethiopia, Sudan, Libya, and Tunisia. The delegates also worked to obtain commitment from these countries for support at the General Assembly, and it was reported to the president after returning home that this was a major achievement of the tour (Ministry of Foreign Affairs 2010). The mission's delegation subsequently wrote the first government report on Africa, titled 'Report on the goodwill mission to Africa and the Middle East', which was published by the Ministry of Foreign Affairs in 1959 (Park 1996).

In the 1960s, diplomatic rivalry between South and North Korea intensified, as South Korea expanded its program of diplomatic relations in 1961 through official visits and the extension of diplomatic invitations to African countries, and worked to establish official relationships with newly independent Africa countries, beginning with Côte d'Ivoire, Niger, and Chad (See Appendix 1). In 1965, ambassadors were dispatched to nine countries in East and West Africa, and South Korea committed to attending the second Asia-Africa Conference in April 1965, although it was eventually canceled. Further large-scale ambassadorial missions were conducted from August to October 1967 to secure support in the United Nations ahead of the 22nd General Assembly (Kim and Yang 2012).

Various internal and external factors contributed to the growth of South Korea's active diplomatic engagement with Africa. Specifically, the South Korean government was keenly aware that North Korea could easily gain an advantage at the diplomatic level. Park Chung-hee, who seized power in South Korea through a 1961 military coup, was critical of the former Rhee government on the grounds that it was excessively anti-communist to the point that South Korea's diplomatic options were actually limited and diplomatically isolated the country in the international community, leading to a diplomatic disadvantage compared to North Korea. Specifically, the Rhee government adhered to the Hallstein Doctrine,[4] adopted in the 1950s to keep North Korea in check.

The year 1960, dubbed 'The Year of Africa', was a promising year for South Korean diplomacy as several African countries declared independence from the colonial powers. Prior to 1960, there were only ten independent countries in Africa, including Ethiopia and Liberia. Although these nations were already United Nations participants and therefore

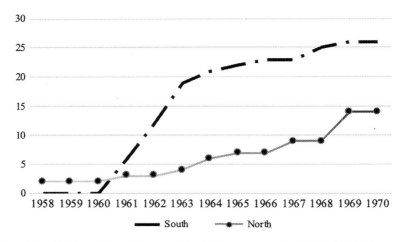

Fig. 3.1 Diplomatic relations with African countries, 1958–1970 (Source: Ministry of Foreign Affairs of Republic of Korea; Wertz et al. (2016))

attractive targets for Korean diplomacy, they alone did not wield enough power to influence the passage of resolutions in the General Assembly, which was dominated by Western nations (Yoo and Seol 2015). However, the wave of independence in the 1960s reinforced Africa's presence in the international community. Not only did these new nations actively support the principles of sovereignty and neutrality but also refused to belong to the majority camps led by the USA and the Soviet Union. The rise of such states caused a shift in the power structure of the United Nations, and the traditional stronghold of the USA began to falter. The South Korean government, taking advantage of this shift, continuously strived to expand its engagement with African countries, establishing official diplomatic relations with 26 countries in 1970, while North Korea achieved official relations with only 14 (See Fig. 3.1).

1970s–1980s: Seeking Cooperation Amid a Changing World Order

From 1971 to 1990, a greater diversity of keywords began to appear in research publications, following an increase in the number of studies conducted in general—from 14 in the 1950s and 1960s to 244 in the 1970s and 1980s. During this period, the most frequently appearing keyword was *economy*, which appeared 66 times, followed by *trade* and *market entry* 58 times

3 SOUTH KOREAN SOCIAL SCIENCE RESEARCH ON AFRICA

and 44 times, respectively (See Appendix 2). This is in clear contrast to keywords that appeared more than twice in the previous period, which were mostly political. This difference becomes especially evident when viewing the cluster map, which visualizes the links between keywords. Based on keywords from the 1970s and 1980s, two clusters were made.

As shown in Fig. 3.2, the keywords in Cluster 1 are mostly associated with the economy and business. Terms such as *export*, *trade*, *market entry*, and *FDI* are shown in close proximity above economy, which has the highest frequency. In addition, *import*, *natural resources*, *mineral resources*, and *resource* appeared together, showing close connectivity right next to words representing trade and markets. Accordingly, it can be understood that extensive research was conducted during this time on the economic situation in and business activities with Africa, and researchers became increasingly interested in Africa's natural resources. The close proximity of keywords such as *plant construction*, *company*, and *FDI* are also indicators of South Korean corporate intentions to penetrate the African market.

Additionally, the close proximity of *Nigeria* and *Kenya* in the middle of the cluster indicates that there was a strong interest in these two countries.

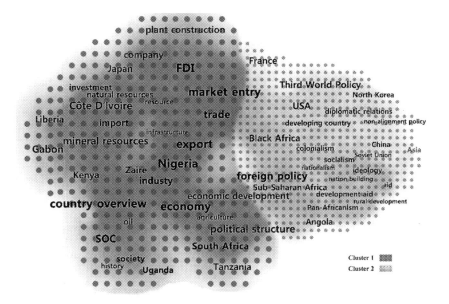

Fig. 3.2 Keywords cluster map, 1970s–1980s (Source: Author's own work)

It was in the late 1970s that specific countries began to appear as keywords. *Nigeria* and *Kenya* appeared 27 and 18 times, respectively, in the 1970s–1980s, and ranked first and second in the list of most-mentioned countries during the same period (See Appendix 2). As both country names are surrounded by words such as *export* and *industry*, most of the research on these countries covered topics such as trade environment, foreign investment climate, and distribution of natural resources, including oil and development potential (Pyo 1985; Kim 1978; Park 1985; KIET 1977). Terms such as *history*, *society*, and *SOC* are also closely related, indicating that scholars were beginning to drift toward accumulating basic knowledge on Africa and investigating the status of African infrastructure for market entry and investment.

On the other hand, Cluster 2, on the right side of Fig. 3.2, is composed of keywords related to social and political aspects of Africa. In particular, the terms *economic cooperation* and *development aid* appeared for the first time and are connected to *foreign policy*, which appeared 35 times, marking the advent of studies on cooperation with and development in Africa in terms of foreign policy. However, the presence of terms such as *ideology*, *socialism*, and *nationalism*, closely linked in this cluster and appearing more than ten times each, demonstrates a continued interest in political factors, carrying on from the 1950s and 1960s. Most of these keywords appeared in data sources normally focused on the characteristics of African socialism and nationalism, the background of and factors behind the adoption of ideologies by socialist African countries, and Soviet and Chinese policies on Africa (Yoon 1978; Na 1986). Within a Cold War context, political factors continued to play an important role in the social, political, and economic development of Third World countries, a classification that included most of the African countries.

Development aid, *rural development*, and *nation-building* are shown together in the bottom right of the cluster, demonstrating that development assistance to African countries was one of the popular topics of this period alongside *Pan-Africanism*, representing regional cooperative efforts of Africa itself. Another notable group in this cluster contains terms such as *Third World policy*, *North Korea*, *diplomatic relations*, and *non-alignment policy*, which are placed at the top of the cluster. Considering that diplomatic competition continued between South Korea and North Korea until the 1970s, these topics remained relevant during this period.

Based on the clusters, two main trends in Korean social science research on Africa during the 1970s and 1980s can be established. The first is the emergence of practical research for African market entry and investment. Table 3.1 shows that government-funded research on Africa was not published in the 1960s, but 39 studies were published in the 1970s and 53 in the 1980s. In the 1970s, government-funded research reports accounted for a little more than half of all the social science research on Africa conducted in South Korea, reflecting the government's growing interest in industrial policy.

Since the 1970s, as South Korea sought economic growth and to earn foreign exchange, companies were encouraged to enter foreign markets at the national level. To aid these efforts, government-affiliated institutions actively researched the industrial environment and economic structures in African countries, in order to provide overseas market information to South Korean firms and build up data for the national industrial development policy. In particular, the late 1970s to the early 1980s marked a period of increased research, supporting South Korean entry into the African construction market. The 'Middle East Construction Boom' had proven to be a blessing for South Korean companies, providing copious amounts of foreign currency and spurring South Korean economic growth (Disney 1977). This experience piqued South Korean interest in the African market, leading to active research, especially focused on advancement strategies into Africa for the construction firms. At the same time, in 1975, following a European Economic Community (EEC) tariff-free agreement with African countries, Africa became attractive as a potential stepping stone into the European import market, considering the lower trade costs and entry barriers.

Many government agencies made great efforts when it came to industrial research on Africa and the promotion of Korean industry in Africa. The Korea Institute of Industrial Economics and Trade (KIET), established in 1976, conducted a number of studies on the overall economy and business environment in Africa and strategies for market entry. In 1977, KIET began the publication of research papers on Africa, releasing 18 reports in the first year. These reports included such titles as *Import structure of Nigeria*, *National Development Plan of Botswana*, *Oil industry in Africa*, *Economic overview and outlook on Africa*, and *Agricultural resources in Africa*. KIET also published at least 90 research reports during 1970s–1980s, and in particular it published county handbooks for business and investment since 1983. Among the countries that were objects of focus for KIET, Kenya, Nigeria, Gabon, Libya, and Cameroon were frequently mentioned. Kenya was considered a suitable base for entering the

African market, while Nigeria and Gabon were identified as countries rich in natural resources, being oil-producing countries, which were also experiencing economic growth. Meanwhile, the Korea Trade-Investment Promotion Agency (KOTRA) held seminars for South Korean companies seeking industrial advancement toward the African market, beginning in the early 1980s. Additionally, in June 1979, the Export-Import Bank of Korea opened a branch office in Abidjan, the capital of Côte d'Ivoire, in order to provide services to Korean companies.

Another significant trend in the evolution of research during this period was the emergence of purely academic research on African society and politics. Especially in the 1980s, the volume of academic journal articles and degree theses increased by more than five times compared to the 1970s and far exceeded the number of government-funded research reports published. Additionally, the formal establishment of academic institutes and research journals on Africa played a significant role in the increase of research, including the establishment of the Institute of African Studies at Hankuk University of Foreign Studies in 1977.

In addition to the establishment of the Institute, a graduate course in African Area Studies was established two years later in 1979. This was the first formal research institute at the university level in South Korea solely devoted to African studies, and later, in 1983, a Department of Swahili Studies was established at the same university, leading to a class of researchers who specialized in African studies at the undergraduate level (Hwang 2016). Additionally, academic journals—*African Affairs* from the Institute of African Studies in Hankuk University of Foreign Studies, and the *Journal of the Korean Association of African Studies*, from an association of that name—were first published in 1979 and 1986, respectively. These two journals collectively dealt with linguistics, literature, and the social sciences and are still published regularly. Although many journal articles and theses still concentrated on economics, business, and diplomacy, this period signaled the beginning of discipline diversification within South Korean social science research on Africa, as research began to cover new topics such as sociology, public administration, international development, law, anthropology, and education (See Table 3.8).

The growth of African research in South Korea in this period can be attributed to several external and internal factors. Following the ascension of more non-aligned countries[5] to United Nations membership, the power structure of international politics shifted from a bipolar system, dominated by the USA and the Soviet Union, to a more multipolar system, concurrent

Table 3.8 Discipline distribution in academic research, 1970s–1980s

	B	P1	S	P2	I	L	A	E	G	M
1970s	39	13	3	0	7	5	1	0	0	0
1980s	107	41	7	2	15	1	2	1	0	0

B Business & Economics, *P1* Political Science, *S* Sociology, *P2* Public Administration, *I* International Development, *L* Law, *A* Anthropology, *E* Education, *G* Geology, *M* Military Science

Source: Author's own work

with an easing of tensions in the Cold War. Additionally, following US shifts in foreign policy to increase contact with communist countries, as well as summits between East and West Germany, the new atmosphere of détente in international politics led South Korea to revise its staunchly anti-communist foreign policy. Likewise, North Korea attempted to strengthen its position for legitimacy by expanding its diplomatic relationships with non-aligned nations. As a result, South Korea's hopes for unifications were dashed as a 'Two Koreas Policy' seemed to be the viable future of the peninsula (Do 2017).

Under such a series of changes, the Park Chung-hee government's declaration of Foreign Policy for Peace and Unification (1973) provided momentum for the expansion of South Korea's diplomacy toward Africa. The South Korean government began to establish diplomatic relations with non-aligned African nations and also worked to establish relations with countries that had already established diplomatic ties with North Korea (Do 2017). Later, in 1975, the South Korean government designated some non-aligned countries in Sub-Saharan Africa, including Uganda, Cameroon, and Côte d'Ivoire, as 'strategic posts' in Africa and subsequently dispatched high-level diplomats to the region (Kim and Yang 2012). South Korea also signed formal declarations of diplomatic relations with other non-aligned nations, including Ghana and Sudan in 1977, and Equatorial Guinea in 1979. As a result, South Korea emerged as a competitor of North Korea for participation in the Non-Aligned Movement. While participating in the Non-Aligned Foreign Ministerial Conference in Peru in August 1975, ahead of the 5th Non-Aligned Conference, the South Korean delegation proposed a simultaneous enrollment or observer qualification scheme to prevent North Korea from being the sole Korean member in the organization. However, only North Korea's membership was accepted. According to a contemporaneous press release, some African and Arab nations, including Zambia, Sierra Leone, Gabon, Saudi Arabia, and Oman insisted on the simultaneous admission of both Koreas, while

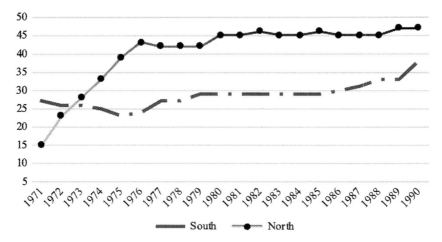

Fig. 3.3 Diplomatic relations with African countries, 1971–1990 (Source: Ministry of Foreign Affairs of Republic of Korea; Wertz et al. (2016))

Asian and Latin American countries were against such a move (Hong 1975). Despite the South's efforts, in the early 1970s, North Korea began to outpace South Korea (See Fig. 3.3), although South Korean diplomatic relations with African nations had outpaced North Korea's in the 1960s. North Korea worked to expand its influence in Africa by maintaining close political and military ties with many African countries, as well as guerilla groups that advocated socialism (Connell and Smyth 1998; Chitiyo and Rupiya 2005).[6]

The diplomatic rivalry between South and North Korea began to wane, following the South Korean decision to expand its cooperative relations, seeking relationships not only with non-aligned countries but also communist countries, as economic growth led to increased diplomatic confidence. South Korea's rapid economic growth bolstered its status in the international community, and it also led to changing expectations on the part of African countries when it came to their relationships with South Korea. Until the mid-1970s, South Korea had maintained an economic status similar to that of Nigeria and Kenya. However, following rapid economic development (a growth rate of ten times the GNI per capita in ten years (See Fig. 3.4)), African countries' perspectives of South Korea as a distant, new, and weak country shifted to that of a cooperative partner that could also assist them in their own development. As a growing influence,

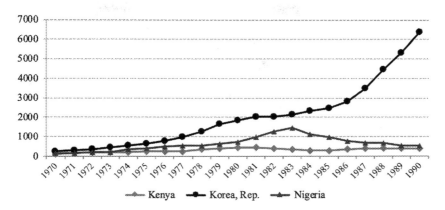

Fig. 3.4 GNI per capita of South Korea, Kenya, and Nigeria, 1970–1990 (current USD) (Source: World Bank)

South Korea also needed to adapt its foreign policy to focus on practical mutual benefits, especially in the economic sector, away from short-term, one-sided policies.

Against this background, it's easy to understand why economic cooperation began to appear as the most frequent keyword in research during the 1980s. Bolstered by South Korea's newfound economic strength and international reputation, Chun Doo-hwan's visit to Africa in 1982 marked the first visit of a South Korean president, during which he visited four countries, thereby increasing the African region's status in South Korean diplomatic policy. Since then, as the Korean economy achieved rapid growth, outpacing the competition with North Korea, the country has also worked to expand its foreign relations. As a result, South Korea has become more actively engaged in South-South cooperation with Africa, while also expanding its diplomatic relations with African countries as part of efforts to improve relations with communist countries.

Further, in 1987, South Korea established the Economic Development Cooperative Fund (EDCF) and its first official foreign aid program. EDCF's first project was the modernization of Nigerian railway vehicles. The establishment of the EDCF was concurrent with an increase in the amount of research related to economic cooperation strategies with African countries, particularly in academic research. Interestingly, while research conducted on socialist countries in Africa in the 1970s was conducted mostly through a critical lens or based on ideological and strategic connections with countries such as North Korea, China, and the Soviet Union, there was a shift toward a focus on cooperation between socialist African countries and South Korea, highlighting economic cooperation as a priority over ideological issues. In addition, President Roh Tae-woo, who took power in 1988, utilized Nordpolitik as his foreign economic policy with the aim of improving relations with communist countries. It widened the horizons of diplomacy and international economic cooperation of South Korea by dramatically shifting policy in a less hostile direction toward communist countries (Park 1990; Rozman 2007). As a result, South Korea, following the establishment of a formal diplomatic relationship with Algeria, which had close ties with North Korea in 1990, was able to pursue cooperative relationships with other countries in Africa.

1990s–2010s: Toward Partnership

Between 1991 and 2018, the most frequently used keyword was *Official Development Assistance (ODA)*, which appeared 103 times in total. Following this are *development, poverty, trade, economy, foreign policy, civil war*, and *education*. (See Appendix 3) Among countries, *China* appeared the most (70 times), followed by *South Africa, Ethiopia, Kenya, Nigeria, Tanzania, Rwanda,* and *Ghana*. Unlike previous periods, specific names of countries and regions topped the list. In general, the main feature of research from the 1990s onward is that research on ODA and development cooperation emerged as a new trend, along with interest in specific countries and regions.

In particular, the frequent mention of China demonstrates that there is continued interest in China's expansion and strategies in Africa, as evidenced by the increase in the volume of research conducted on such topics since the 1990s. In addition to China, South Africa was also mentioned 69 times—evidence that it was a country in the research spotlight. Research on South Africa rapidly increased after the abolition of Apartheid policy, with increased focus on democratization, economic reform, human rights, national construction, and other similar topics in South Africa and the surrounding region (Hwang 2007; Seo 2006; Kim 2001).

Additionally, mention of Kenya and Nigeria remained frequent, demonstrating South Korea's continued interest in both nations. However, contrary to previous periods, the topics of research regarding the two countries diversified from industrial status and market penetration to studies on ODA, political situation, the constitutional system, and poverty, in the case of Kenya. In the case of Nigeria, the topics of research have widened to include development cooperation, political situations, conflict, education, and marketing strategy. On the other hand, Ethiopia, Rwanda, and Ghana, countries which appeared frequently for the first time, were all designated as Priority Partner Countries[7] in the field of international development cooperation by the South Korean government in 2015.

An analysis of the keywords from the 1990s to the 2010s led to the development of three clusters. Cluster 1 consists of keywords such as *conflict, civil war, democracy, security,* and *economy,* showing an increase in the number of studies on regional security in Africa (See Fig. 3.5). This is noteworthy as a new field of research. In the upper part of the cluster, *politics, democratization,* and *economic integration* are closely linked to *ethnic conflict,* indicating that studies dealing with regional security issues can also be considered in terms of ethnic and racial conflict. As previously mentioned, the close relationship between the South African Apartheid

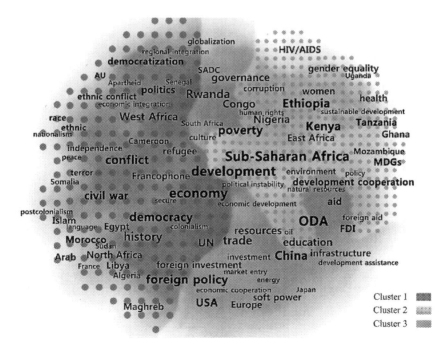

Fig. 3.5 Keyword cluster map, 1990s–2010s (Source: Author's own work)

system and democratization suggests that South Korean researchers' interest in Africa has expanded beyond political and economic ones to human rights and democratic values.

In the middle of the cluster, keywords such as *refugee, peace, Islam*, and *society* appear around *civil war* and *conflict* and are closely related to *West Africa* and *Somalia*, areas that have recently experienced extreme civil wars. This indicates a growing interest among researchers in civil war and its solutions. *Democracy, Libya, UN*, and the *Maghreb* are closely connected at the bottom of the cluster—words associated with the Arab Spring of 2011. Following the Arab Spring, research on civil war, civil revolution, and democratization movements has primarily focused on Libya out of the North African countries. South Korea's foreign policy and advancement strategies toward North African countries have also been studied in response to the changing circumstances of North African countries affected by the Arab Spring (Choi and Choi 2012).

In Cluster 2, the most frequently occurring term is *ODA*, and the entire cluster consists of countries and terms related to *ODA*. It is, therefore, possible to recognize specifically what South Korean research has recently focused on through a close examination of terms in this cluster. In order of frequency, the most common terms are *poverty, education, governance, human rights, women, agriculture, health, corruption, culture, HIV/AIDS*, and *environment*. Moreover, the frequent appearance of the terms economic development and economic growth in the clusters, appearing 36 and 25 times, respectively, indicates a close relationship between economic development and ODA. These topics are also representative of South Korea's dedication to contributing to the achievement of the United Nations Millennium Development Goals (MDGs).

Quantitatively, the number of studies conducted on international development cooperation with African states has increased significantly since the 2010s, growing from 26 in the 2000s to 131 in the 2010s, accounting for almost 25% of the total social science research on Africa (See Table 3.9). This sharp increase can be attributed in part to the fact that South Korea became a member of the Organisation for Economic Co-operation and Development (OECD) Development Assistance Committee (DAC) in 2010 and subsequently expanded its ODA support for Africa. This increase also brought about major changes in South Korean social science research on Africa. Prior to 2010, there were only nine papers published related to ODA—and only four prior to 2009—indicative of the relationship between DAC membership and South Korean scholars' interest in ODA as a research topic.

Table 3.9 Distribution of disciplines in academic research, 1990s–2010s

	B	P1	S	P2	I	L	A	E	G	M
1990s	32	20	22	3	7	0	5	7	0	0
2000s	42	54	65	6	26	5	10	3	0	0
2010s	131	114	97	16	131	11	20	16	1	3

B Business & Economics, *P1* Political Science, *S* Sociology, *P2* Public Administration, *I* International Development, *L* Law, *A* Anthropology, *E* Education, *G* Geology, *M* Military Science

Source: Author's own work

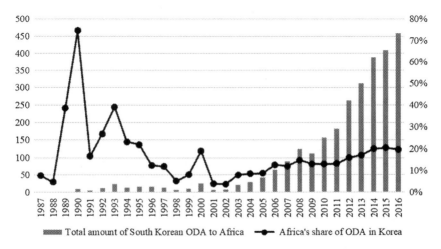

Fig. 3.6 South Korean total and proportional ODA to Africa 1987–2016 (current USD) (Source: Economic Development Cooperation Fund Korea)

South Korea's ODA to Africa has grown steadily, increasing almost 500 times over the past 30 years. Since 2010, when South Korea joined the DAC, the amount of ODA to Africa has increased by about 100 million USD annually (See Fig. 3.6). This growth led to an overall rise in cooperation and communication between South Korea and Africa, although the proportion of South Korea's total ODA expenditure provided to Africa has not increased that much, reaching 17% in the 2010s compared to 10–20% in the 1990s. Additionally, the private sector has also been active in providing aid to African countries, and naturally, attention to the African continent, which includes some of the poorest countries in the world, has increased. Following this, the amount of research conducted about ODA in Africa has also seen significant increase, while the specific topics related to ODA have varied based on changing government policies.

Since 2006, each South Korean government has pursued an active ODA policy toward African states. Following the first announcement of a plan for African ODA in 2006, the Roh Moo-hyun administration announced the 'Korean Initiative for Africa's Development', pledging to triple ODA to Africa. The plan also included policy recommendations for trade, IT, agriculture, health, and education. Compared to previous African policies, it was a distinctive strategy, which encouraged cooperation on the basis of aid provision, as well as the promotion of economic and social development in Africa. Following that, the Myung-bak Lee government pledged to achieve an ODA rate of 0.25% of the GNI in order to gain admission to the DAC, consequently resulting in an increase in ODA to Africa (although lacking specific African policies).

More recently, the ODA policy of the Park Geun-hye administration, while still focused on Asia, featured a slight increase in the proportion of ODA provided to Africa, including an increase in the number of recipient countries in Africa. Additionally, although President Park's 2016 visit to major African countries, despite drawing significant criticism for several reasons, marked a turning point in South Korea's humanitarian interest in Africa. The current South Korean government continues to maintain a basic policy of increasing aid to Africa and diversifying the target countries.

Considering the diversification of research topics related to ODA, topics have shifted from strategic approaches to the use of ODA (the early 2000s) to policy topics on areas such as the allocation of ODA resources. Since 2010, following the significant increase in the amount of ODA provided to Africa, many discussions have also emerged about the effectiveness of ODA and the evaluation of projects conducted in Africa.

Finally, Cluster 3 consists of keywords primarily related to business and industry, such as *trade, resource, investment, FDI,* and *infrastructure*. This indicates that researchers still have a marked interest in trade and market entry in Africa. On the left side of the cluster, *market entry, investment, trade,* and *oil* are closely connected to the main keyword, *resource*, indicating a high number of studies on securing natural resources in Africa, especially when it comes to oil. Additionally, *foreign policy* and *soft power* are closely linked in the same cluster, indicating that researchers draw a strong link between access to natural resources and foreign policy. On the right side of the cluster, *South-South cooperation* and *infrastructure* appear around the terms *FDI* and *aid*—further indications of research on economic cooperation.

Comparing this economic cluster to similar clusters developed based on the research of the 1970s and 1980s, the frequency of the term aid has increased, demonstrating its increased importance in the context of trade and industry in African countries. Additionally, some terms have increased or decreased in frequency compared to previous periods. While there are fewer mentions of *market entry* and *export*, the terms *resource*, *oil*, and *investment* were mentioned with increasing frequency.

This change can be attributed to a decline in interest in trade with Africa, considering that the share of trade with Africa in South Korea's total trade volume has remained around 1.5% since the 1970s, although access to energy and mineral resources has become a priority issue since the 2000s, due to the steady rise of international oil prices since 2004. Accordingly, the South Korean government has strengthened its efforts to obtain overseas resources, leading to diversification in oil import countries and the targeting of Africa as a new resource development area. Since the mid-2000s, South Korea has embarked on natural resource development projects in Nigeria, Africa's largest oil producer, as well as Algeria and Madagascar (Yoo and Seol 2015), and was also able to secure a stake in national gas development projects in Mozambique (Ministry of Trade, Industry and Energy 2014). Nigeria and Mozambique have been both designated as key partner countries under the South Korean government's 5th Overseas Resource Development Basic Plan, which runs from 2013 to 2022.

Important to note is the active role that the South Korean government is taking in overseas resource development, contrary to the USA and the UK, where the government does not directly engage in business activities related to resource development. South Korea's high dependency on energy resources (96%) necessitates a secure and stable supply, and energy security is thus an important policy issue and closely tied to South Korean national security and thus also prioritized in foreign policy (Chae 2014).

South Korea has worked to secure stakes in resource development projects through negotiations and dialogues at summits and high-level talks with resource-rich nations, parallel to other diplomatic exchanges (Chae 2014). These exchanges have thus taken the form of 'resource diplomacy', conducted together with discussions on ODA and economic cooperation. Therefore, returning to Cluster 3, it is evident why, in a policy context, research on natural resources is closely linked to economic cooperation.

In general, since the 2000s, the number of journal articles and degree theses related to social science research on Africa has skyrocketed compared to the number of government-funded research reports, which has yet to recover to the 1960s numbers. Additionally, as mentioned earlier, in academic research of the 2010s, the number of papers in the international development field increased explosively, while the number of studies in the fields of economic management, political science, and sociology has also steadily increased. In short, South Korean social science research on Africa has experienced significant quantitative growth since the 2000s, as well as greater topic diversification (See Table 3.9).

Topic diversification can be understood as a natural phenomenon, resulting from changes in domestic and international attitudes since the end of the Cold War, as well as South Korea's admission to the United Nations as a member state. Following the deviation from adherence to policies of diplomatic competition or market entry in Africa, South Korea has shown increased interest in UN agenda topics such as human rights, poverty reduction, peacebuilding, gender equality, and security. Furthermore, increased interest in stability and democratization in Africa can also be linked to ODA and economic cooperation, due to the institutional basis of democracy and social stability as essential conditions for sustainable social and economic development. In addition, the increase in research on risk factors in Africa, such as civil war, conflict, and security, also reflects interest in risk identification and response when it comes to increased ODA, market expansion, and FDI toward Africa, within the context of feasibility research.

Conclusion

South Korea and Africa have a relationship of fewer than 70 years, yet throughout this time, the purposes and characteristics of South Korean social science research on Africa have varied greatly and were highly dependent on both domestic and international circumstances. A relationship that initially focused on diplomatic competition with North Korea evolved into one focused on market entry and economic development and further expanded to also focus on mutual cooperation and the realization of humanitarian goals. Accordingly, the volume and diversity of South Korean research on Africa have grown remarkably, especially since the 2000s, due to increased efforts by researchers to establish an academic foundation for African studies in South Korea (e.g., establishing a university research institute) and also to receive increased government support for research. Although not addressed in this study, there has also been significant growth in South Korean tourism to and NGO activity in Africa, as well as private sector growth, forming another basis for recent research (Hwang 2016).

This study sought to analyze the path of topic changes in South Korean social science research on Africa from 1955 to 2018. From the keywords selected from 1105 source documents, three cluster maps were developed, one for each period of focus (1950s–1960s, 1970s–1980s, and 1990s–2010s). While the first period (1950s–1960s) yielded only one cluster due to the limited amount of research, the 1970s–1980s and 1990s–2010s yielded two and three keyword clusters, respectively. It was therefore possible to draw specific conclusions about researchers' interests based on these clusters, by analyzing both the frequency of keywords and their proximity (and thus relationship) to one another in the cluster.

In the 1950s and 1960s, South Korean researchers first began to focus on Africa as an area of interest. In general, this interest stemmed from the academic curiosity of individual researchers and seems to have been conducted, on the whole, in a rather fragmentary manner. Following the independence of several African countries from 1960 onward, the South Korean government's diplomatic rivalry with North Korea to gain support in the UN led to a period of research representative of the Cold War environment, covering topics such as African socialism and relations between Africa and the Soviet Union.

In the 1970s and 1980s, the scope of research expanded significantly to focus on economic issues, including African economy and industry, industrial structure, investment environments, and trade. This trend reflects the increased interest in South Korean overseas market entry at the national level, as well as the fact that South Korean government became more actively engaged in cooperation with African countries as it achieved rapid economic growth. These changes also contributed to the pursuit of in-depth research on social, political, and economic aspects of Africa, as well as focus on individual countries such as Kenya and Nigeria.

The third period (1990s–2010s) also reflects major domestic and foreign changes, following the end of the Cold War and South Korea's admission to the United Nations, as well as its 2001 admission to the OECD with significant outcomes for South Korean research on Africa. Compared to previous periods, the most striking feature of this third period was the overwhelming progress of ODA research. Research on various topics related to development cooperation, including poverty, education, governance, women, agriculture, and health, was conducted alongside studies on conflict and resolutions, all of which together accounted for a significant part of the research during this period. It is of note that although a significant amount of research on trade and market entry and natural resources has continued, research moved beyond political and economic intentions to address humanitarian issues. The shift to focusing on cooperation and humanitarian issues is representative of South Korea's 'resource diplomacy' strategy—that is, using humanitarian and economic cooperation as a point of leverage for natural resource access, as a matter of national security—an active government policy since 2004.

Aside from showing the general trends of research on Africa over the past 70 years, this study is significant for its research method as well—specifically its use of cluster map analysis of bibliographic information. The creation of cluster maps aided in the visualization of research themes, providing a fresh perspective on data rather than the standard (and somewhat limited) numerical comparisons and interpretive narratives.

Nevertheless, there are some weaknesses of the study that need to be addressed. First, because data collection was conducted only through online database searches, there may be more related sources that have not been digitized and thus were not available for inclusion in this study. This is particularly true for studies published before the 2000s when digitization was not the norm. In the future, the inclusion of additional data from offline sources would contribute to a more comprehensive analysis of research topic trends.

Second, keyword analysis was based on the frequency of occurrence of each keyword. Accordingly, it is difficult to evaluate the qualitative value of each source. For example, a source that may have significantly affected the relationship between South Korea and Africa may have had a low frequency of certain keywords, or vice versa. As this study focused only on topic coverage, further research could also attempt to include qualitative factors such as research value in terms of influence.

Furthermore, research trends carried out within a certain country are strongly shaped by government policy and social perception. It is impossible to separate research from these factors, but to improve the quality of South Korean research on Africa in general, it would be useful to compare the results of this study with similar studies in other countries to get an understanding of global trends and develop a sense of some kind of international standard. If such a study was conducted, the results would be of immense value when it comes to policy recommendations for the South Korean government, as well as research and academic institutions.

Appendix 1: Timeline of Diplomatic Relationships with African Countries

South Korea		North Korea
	1958	People's Democratic Republic of Algeria
		Republic of Guinea
Republic of Benin	1961	Republic of Mali
Republic of Cameroon		
Republic of Chad		
Republic of Côte d'Ivoire		
Republic of Niger		
Republic of the Congo		
Burkina Faso	1962	
Gabonese Republic		
Kingdom of Morocco		
Republic of Madagascar		
Republic of Senegal		
Republic of Sierra Leone		
Republic of Mauritania	1963	Arab Republic of Egypt
Central African Republic		
Democratic Republic of the Congo		
Federal Democratic Republic of Ethiopia		
Republic of Rwanda		
Republic of Togo		
Republic of Uganda		
Republic of Kenya	1964	Republic of Mauritania
Republic of Liberia		Republic of Ghana
		Republic of the Congo
Republic of Malawi	1965	United Republic of Tanzania
Republic of the Gambia		
Kingdom of Lesotho	1966	
	1967	Federal Republic of Somalia
Republic of Botswana	1968	
The Kingdom of Eswatini		
Tunisian Republic	1969	Central African Republic
		Republic of Chad
		Republic of Equatorial Guinea
		Republic of the Sudan
		Republic of Zambia
Republic of Mauritius	1971	Republic of Sierra Leone

(continued)

(continued)

South Korea		North Korea
	1972	Burkina Faso
		Democratic Republic of the Congo
		Republic of Cameroon
		Republic of Madagascar
		Republic of Rwanda
		Republic of Senegal
		Republic of Uganda
	1973	Republic of Benin
		Republic of Liberia
		Republic of Mauritius
		Republic of the Gambia
		Republic of Togo
	1974	Libya
		Gabonese Republic
		Republic of Botswana
		Republic of Guinea Bissau
		Republic of Niger
	1975	Democratic Republic of Sâo Tomé and Príncipe
		Republic of Angola
		Republic of Cabo Verde
		Republic of Mozambique
		Tunisian Republic
		Union of the Comoros
Republic of Seychelles	1976	Federal Democratic Republic of Ethiopia
		Federal Republic of Nigeria
		Republic of Namibia
		Republic of Seychelles
Republic of Djibouti	1977	
Republic of Ghana		
Republic of the Sudan		
Republic of Equatorial Guinea	1979	
Union of the Comoros		
Libya	1980	Kingdom of Lesotho
Federal Republic of Nigeria		Republic of Zimbabwe
	1982	Republic of Malawi
Republic of Guinea Bissau	1983	
	1985	Republic of Côte d'Ivoire
Federal Republic of Somalia	1987	
Democratic Republic of Sâo Tomé and Príncipe	1988	
Republic of Cabo Verde		
	1989	Kingdom of Morocco

(*continued*)

(continued)

South Korea		North Korea
People's Democratic Republic of Algeria	1990	
Republic of Mali		
Republic of Namibia		
Republic of Zambia		
Republic of Burundi	1991	
Republic of Angola	1992	
Republic of South Africa		
United Republic of Tanzania		
Republic of Mozambique	1993	Republic of Djibouti
State of Eritrea		State of Eritrea
Republic of Zimbabwe	1994	
Arab Republic of Egypt	1995	
	1998	Republic of South Africa
Republic of Guinea	2006	
	2008	Republic of Kenya
Republic of South Sudan	2011	Republic of South Sudan

Source: Ministry of Foreign Affairs of Republic of Korea; Wertz et al. (2016)

APPENDIX 2: FREQUENT KEYWORDS, 1970s–1980s

Rank	Cluster 1		Cluster 2	
	Keyword	Instances	Keyword	Instances
1	Economy	66	Foreign policy	35
2	Trade	58	Economic cooperation	28
3	Market entry	44	Nationalism	15
4	Country overview	37	Socialism	15
5	Export	37	Soviet Union	15
6	Political structure	31	Ideology	13
7	Industry	27	Development aid	12
8	Nigeria	27	Sub-Saharan Africa	11
9	FDI	26	China	10
10	Agriculture	22	Colonialism	10
11	SOC (Social Overhead Capital)	22	Third World Policy	10
12	Infrastructure	19	Aid	9
13	Kenya	18	North Korea	8
14	Economic development	16	Developing country	7
15	Construction	15	Diplomatic relations	7
16	Import	13	Marxism	7
17	Mineral resource	13	Non-alignment policy	7
18	Company	12	Pan-Africanism	7

(continued)

(continued)

Rank	Cluster 1		Cluster 2	
	Keyword	Instances	Keyword	Instances
19	Oil	11	Rural development	7
20	Senegal	11	Black Africa	6
21	Côte d'Ivoire	10	France	6
22	History	10	USA	6
23	Gabon	9	Angola	5
24	Japan	9	Nation building	5
25	South Africa	9	Asia	5
26	Resource	8		
27	Tanzania	8		
28	Zaire	8		
29	Uganda	7		
30	Investment	6		
31	Liberia	6		
32	Natural resources	6		
33	Society	6		
34	Plant	5		

Source: Author's own work

APPENDIX 3: FREQUENT KEYWORDS, 1990s–2010s

Rank	Cluster 1		Cluster 2		Cluster 3	
	Keyword	Instances	Keyword	Instances	Keyword	Instances
1	Economy	52	ODA (Official Development Assistance)	103	China	70
2	Civil war	37	Sub-Saharan Africa	68	South Africa	69
3	Conflict	35	Development	57	Trade	54
4	North Africa	35	Poverty	54	Foreign policy	50
5	Democracy	34	Ethiopia	40	Resources	34
6	Democratization	29	Kenya	38	Economic cooperation	29
7	Colonialism	28	Education	37	Oil	28
8	History	27	Economic development	36	FDI (foreign direct investment)	28
9	Security	25	Nigeria	32	Aid	25

(continued)

(continued)

Rank	Cluster 1 Keyword	Instances	Cluster 2 Keyword	Instances	Cluster 3 Keyword	Instances
10	France	25	Tanzania	32	Developing countries	24
11	Politics	23	Rwanda	28	Infrastructure	18
12	West Africa	21	Governance	26	Soft power	18
13	UN (United Nations)	18	Economic growth	25	Investment	17
14	Independence	16	Human rights	23	Southern Africa	17
15	Peace	16	Women	23	Export	17
16	Francophone	16	Ghana	22	Energy	15
17	Algeria	15	Cooperation	21	Market entry	14
18	Egypt	15	Development cooperation	21	South-South Cooperation	14
19	Refugee	15	Sustainable development	21	EU	14
20	Ethnic conflict	15	Agriculture	18	US	14
21	Apartheid	14	East Africa	18	Mozambique	13
22	Cameroon	14	Health	18	Angola	12
23	Libya	14	MDGs	18	Development assistance	12
24	Morocco	13	Congo	17	Natural resources	12
25	Senegal	13	Corruption	16	Japan	11
26	AU	12	Uganda	16	Political instability	11
27	Regional integration	12	Culture	15	SADC (Southern African Development Community)	11
28	Terror	12	Globalization	15	Migration	11
29	Arab	12	Gender equality	14	Europe	10
30	Language	12	Policy	13		
31	Economic Integration	11	HIV/AIDS	12		
32	Islam	11	Environment	11		
33	Middle East	11				
34	Sudan	11				
35	Society	11				
36	Ethnic	10				
37	Maghreb	10				
38	Nationalism	10				

(continued)

Rank	Cluster 1		Cluster 2		Cluster 3	
	Keyword	Instances	Keyword	Instances	Keyword	Instances
39	Somalia	10				
40	Election	10				
41	Post-colonialism	10				
42	Race	10				

Source: Author's own work

Notes

1. In the Netherlands, Abbink (2001) analyzed academic research processes for research on Africa, examining the period from the beginning of the colonial expansion in the sixteenth century to the twentieth century. In the UK, Kirk-Greene (2002) examined changes in research topics from 1926, the year of the establishment of the International African Institute, to 2002. Similar studies dealing with the origins, development, and status of research on Africa were conducted in Portugal (Nobrega 2002), France (Coquery 2002), the USA (Page 2002), and Belgium (Deslaurier 2003).
2. According to Kim and Yang (2012), four articles about Africa were printed by the Dong-A Ilbo newspaper between 1920 and 1930. In one article dated 8 December 1924, a country in Africa was reported to be 'dominated by women with a lot of gold, fighting against each other'. On 25 October 1925, it was reported that some explorers in Africa discovered a 'land of small people'. Further, African articles were published following the Italian invasion of Ethiopia in 1935, as the relationship between Europe and Africa became an international issue.
3. The South Korean government focused its diplomatic efforts on gaining support for UN recognition as the sole legitimate government on the Korean peninsula, while North Korea endeavored to move inter-Korean issues out of the General Assembly, deeming the Assembly unfair and unacceptable due to the leadership of the USA. In 1957, the 11th General Assembly passed a resolution to hold a nationwide Korean election under the UN auspices. However, North Korea refused to acknowledge the resolution, asserting that Korean elections should be held only by the Korean people rather than being managed by the UN (Korean Institute for National Unification 2011).
4. The Hallstein Doctrine formed the bases of West Germany's foreign policy from 1955 to the mid-1960s. According to this doctrine, the West German government refused to engage in diplomatic relations with any government that recognized East Germany as a legitimate nation, since West Germany

claimed that title for itself. For more information on the Hallstein Doctrine, see Brzezinski, Z., & Griffith, W. E. (1961: 642–654). The Rhee government not only adopted this doctrine to a tee, but took the policy further, in that neutral states, which acknowledged both North and South Korea, were automatically classified as communist and therefore ineligible to conduct trade or communicate with the South Korean government.

5. The Non-Aligned Movement is rooted in a 1955 meeting, held in Bandung of Indonesia, by 29 Asian and African states, the two continents joined together for the first time to represent themselves as the 'Third World' (Gupta 1992). Since the first meeting in Bandung, Indonesia, Third World nations have moved to actively participate in international society, while refusing to ally with either the USA or the Soviet Union, based on shared colonial experience and 'weak country' identity. Following the official launch of the Non-Aligned Meeting in Belgrade, Yugoslavia, in 1961, the number of participating countries rose to 74 in the mid-1970s, constituting half of the United Nations, and making the organization an influential target for South Korean diplomacy.

6. As an Example, North Korea established diplomatic ties with the socialist government of Somalia in 1970 for ideological reasons, providing military training to the Somali army. This support was intended to assist Somalia in its conflict with Ethiopia—a further reason for North Korean support, considering that Ethiopia participated with UN troops against North Korea in the Korean War. However, after the collapse of the pro-American regime in Ethiopia and the establishment of a socialist regime, North Korea also provided support to Ethiopia (Ododa 1985). North Korea's military support continued into the 1980s, and in the early 1980s, Zimbabwe was also provided with military support totaling approximately 16.3 million USD and included weapons, equipment, and military training (Chitiyo and Rupiya 2005).

7. Under to the 2015 Framework Act, Article 8.2.3, the South Korean government outlined specific strategies for each priority partner country for ODA maximization. Out of 24 countries, 7 countries in Africa were selected as priority partner countries: Ethiopia, Ghana, Mozambique, Rwanda, Senegal, Uganda, and Tanzania.

References

Abbink, G. J. (2001). African Studies in the Netherlands: A Brief Survey. *African Research & Documentation, 8.*
Brzezinski, Z., & Griffith, W. E. (1961). Peaceful Engagement in Eastern Europe. *Foreign Affairs, 39*(4), 642–654.
Byun, M. (1970). Female Status and Role: Six Cases of East Africa. *Journal of Law and Political Science, 13*(70.2), 194–201. (In Korean).

Chae, J. (2014). A Study on the New Direction of Korea's Energy Diplomacy. *The Journal of Political Science and Communication, 17*(1), 77–98. (In Korean).

Chitiyo, K., & Rupiya, M. (2005). Tracking Zimbabwe's Political History: The Zimbabwe Defence Force from 1980–2005. In *Evolutions and Revolutions: A Contemporary History of Militaries in Southern Africa* (pp. 331–363). Pretoria: Institute of Security Studies.

Cho, W. (2012). Korean Research Trends in African Studies. *Asia Review, 2*(2), 129–148. (In Korean).

Choi, H., & Choi, C. (2012). A Study on the Resource Development and Entry Strategies in North-Africa Maghreb Area. *Journal of International Trade & Commerce, 8*(1), 95–118. (In Korean).

Connell, D., & Smyth, F. (1998). Africa's New Bloc. *Foreign Affairs, 77*, 80–94.

Coquery, C. (2002). *De l'"africanisme" vu de France : Le point de vue d'une historienne*. Paris: Gallimard.

Deslaurier, C. (2003). Afrique & histoire: revue internationale, *1*, 223–234.

Disney, N. (1977). South Korean Workers in the Middle East. *MERIP Reports, 61*, 22–26.

Do, J. (2017). South Korean Debates on Policy Alterations towards Neutral and Communist Countries in the 1960s. *Korean and World Politics, 33*(4), 59–90. (In Korean).

van Eck, N. J., & Waltman, L. (2007). VOS: A New Method for Visualizing Similarities Between Objects. In *Advances in Data Analysis* (pp. 299–306). Berlin, Heidelberg: Springer.

van Eck, N., & Waltman, L. (2009). Software Survey: VOS viewer, a Computer Program for Bibliometric Mapping. *Scientometrics, 84*(2), 523–538.

Gupta, A. (1992). The Song of the Nonaligned World: Transnational Identities and the Reinscription of Space in Late Capitalism. *Cultural Anthropology, 7*(1), 63–79.

Han, S. (1964). Nationalism in Africa. *Social Science Research Collection, 4*, 203–228. Sookmyung Women's University (In Korean).

Han, C. (1965). Constitutions of Burundi and Mali. *Social Science Review, 2*(1), 133–149. (In Korean).

Han, G. (2013). A Methodological Reflection on African Studies in Korea and a Review for Research Topics. *Asia Review, 3*(1), 159–193. (In Korean).

Han, Y. J. (2015). Analysis of Essential Patent Portfolios via Bibliometric Mapping: An Illustration of Leading Firms in the 4G Era. *Technology Analysis & Strategic Management, 27*(7), 809–839.

Hong, J. (1975). Non-aligned Countries and Korean Diplomacy. The Dongguk Post. In Korean.

Hwang, K. (2007). Presidency in South Africa: Focusing on the Political Structure and the Power Mechanisms. *Journal of the Korean Association of African Studies, 26*, 205–227. (In Korean).

Hwang, K. (2016). African Studies in Korea: Current Status and Future Task. *Journal of the Korean Association of African Studies, 47*, 157–181. (In Korean).
Ichikawa, M. (2005). The History and Current Situation of Anthropological Studies on Africa in Japan. *African Anthropologist, 12*, 2.
Kim, S. (1965). Non-Western Perception of Social Scientists Toward Newly Founded Countries. *Journal of Law and political science, 1*, 141–150. (In Korean).
Kim, H. (1978). *Market and Economic Condition of Six Black Horn African Countries: A Search for the Way of Korean Export.* M.A. thesis, Hankuk University of Foreign Studies. (In Korean).
Kim, K. (2001). The Cultural Identity of South Africa. *Asian Journal of African Studies, 13*, 81–144.
Kim, M., & Yang, J. (2012). The Place of Africa and the Middle East in the Diplomatic History of the Republic of Korea: Perceptions behind Diplomatic Organizational Changes. *Korean Political Science Review, 46*(5), 267–295. (In Korean).
Kirk-Greene, A. (2002). The Changing Face of African Studies in Britain, 1962–2002. *African Research and Documentation, 90*, 17–27.
Korea Institute for Industrial Economics & Trade. (1977). *Research on Kenyan Economy and Business Environment.*
Lee, C. (2012). Syngman Rhee's 'Survival Diplomacy Against the US. *Journal of Korean Politics, 21*(3), 179–206. (In Korean).
Li, A. (2005). African Studies in China in the Twentieth Century: A Historiographical Survey. *African Studies Review, 48*(1), 59–87.
Ministry of Foreign Affairs, Republic of Korea. (2010). *Goodwill Mission to the Middle East and Africa.*
Ministry of Trade, Industry and Energy, Republic of Korea. (2014). *The Fifth Overseas Resource Development Plan.*
Na, Y. (1986). Nation Building and Development of African Socialist Countries (in Korean). *Journal of the Korean Association of African Studies, 1*, 1–38.
Nobrega, A. (2002). African Research and Documentation: The Journal of the African Studies Association of the UK and the Standing Commission [Conference] on Library Materials on Africa, *90*, 71–89.
Ododa, H. (1985). Somalia's Domestic Politics and Foreign Relations Since the Ogaden War of 1977–78. *Middle Eastern Studies, 21*(3), 285–297.
Page, L. (2002). African Research and Documentation: The Journal of the African Studies Association of the UK and the Standing Commission [Conference] on Library Materials on Africa, *90*, 53–57.
Park, D. (1985). Distribution and Development of Underground Resources of the African Countries (in Korean). *Social Science and Policy Research, 7*(1), 59–89.
Park, J. (1990). Political Change in South Korea: The Challenge of the Conservative Alliance. *Asian Survey, 30*(12), 1154–1168.

Park, W. (1996). Research on Current Status and Tasks of African Area Studies. *Asian Journal of African Studies, 8*(9), 1–15. (In Korean).

Park, T. (2007). The Economic Development Plans of the Rhee Government After the Korean War. *Journal of World Politics, 8*(0), 203–242. (In Korean).

Pyo, H. (1985). Research on Characteristics and Progress of Economic Development Strategy of African Countries. *Social Science and Policy Research, 7*(1), 35–58. (In Korean).

Rozman, G. (2007). South Korea and Sino-Japanese Rivalry: A Middle Power's Options Within the East Asian Core Triangle. *The Pacific Review, 20*(2), 197–220.

Seo, S. (2006). A Theoretical Approach to Democratization in South Africa. *Journal of the Korean Association of African Studies, 23,* 37–77. (In Korean).

Shin, B. (1963). Research on Neutral States During the Cold War. *The Law & Public Administration Review, 16,* 147–154. (In Korean).

Small, H., & Greenlee, E. (1980). Citation Context Analysis of a Co-citation Cluster: Recombinant-DNA. *Scientometrics, 2*(4), 277–301.

Waltman, L., Van Eck, N. J., & Noyons, E. C. (2010). A Unified Approach to Mapping and Clustering of Bibliometric Networks. *Journal of Informetrics, 4*(4), 629–635.

Wertz, D., Oh, J. J., & Insung, K. (2016). DPRK Diplomatic Relations. *The National Committee on North Korea. Dostupné na internete.* Retrieved February 8, 2019, from http://www.ncnk.org/resources/briefing-papers/all-briefing-papers/dprk-diplomatic-relations.

Yoo, H., & Seol, G. (2015). Paradigm Change of Korea's Foreign Policy towards Africa. *OUGHTOPIA, 30*(2), 217–245. (In Korean).

Yoon, G. (1978). Special Characteristics of African Ideology. *Journal of Law and Political Science, 13*(1), 7–13. (In Korean).

CHAPTER 4

Issues Raised on Korea's Official Development Assistance to Africa: Future Perspective

Jin-sang Lee

INTRODUCTION

The Republic of Korea (herein after 'Korea') became a donor country when the Korea International Cooperation Agency (KOICA) was established under the Ministry of Foreign Affairs (MOFA) in 1991. Korea transformed from an aid-recipient country to a donor country in 30 years. The transformation was possible with an achievement of economic development, which started in the early 1960s.[1] The country was completely destroyed during the Korean War between 1950 and 1953. Korea rose to become the 12th largest economy in the world with the GDP of USD 1530 billion and the sixth largest trading country with the trade volume of USD 1135 billion in 2018 (IMF 2019). The Korean economy is heavily dependent upon international trade as it shared 74% of its GDP last year. The partnership was very different from other Asian countries such

J. Lee (✉)
Department of Technology and Society, SUNY Korea, The State University of New York, Incheon, South Korea
e-mail: jinsang.lee@sunykorea.ac.kr

© The Author(s) 2020
Y. Chang (ed.), *South Korea's Engagement with Africa*, Africa's Global Engagement: Perspectives from Emerging Countries, https://doi.org/10.1007/978-981-32-9013-6_4

as China and India. The trade volume between Africa and Asia grew more than ten times between 1990 and 2005, which marked a 13–18% growth rate per annum (Broadman 2007: 69–70). Korea's trade with Africa was recorded at USD 7.5 billion, which was only 1.5% of total Korea's trade in 2017.

There are two institutions engaged in bilateral aid in Korea. The KOICA is the grant aid agency under the Ministry of Foreign Affairs (MOFA) and the Economic Development and Cooperation Fund (EDCF) in the Korea Export Import Bank (KOEXIM), under the Ministry of Strategy and Finance (MOSF), and facilitates concessional loans to developing countries. Apart from these two aid institutions, more than 30 government institutions are engaged in ODA activities which include central government ministries, regional governments, government-sponsored research institutions and state-owned enterprises.

In 2017, the total amount of Korea's ODA reached USD 2.3 billion and 0.16% of gross national income (GNI), which was lower than many OECD Development Assistance Committee members.[2] The Korean government committed to increase its ODA to 0.2% of GNI by 2020 and 0.3% by 2030.[3] In a recent peer-review report by OECD DAC, Korea should set a time frame and targets for allocating 0.3% of GNI by 2030, untie its aid, and focus resources on countries most in need (OECD DAC 2018). Korea's ODA to Africa was not expanded as much as in other regions for many years until the end of the 1990s.[4] Geographically, Africa is far from Korea and that induces a lot of expenses to process ODA projects. Many African countries were struggling with political instability, which caused inefficiency and low level of absorptive capacity of ODA projects.

Korea's ODA to Africa increased rapidly since the year 2000. It was associated with the decrease in the share of its ODA to Asia.[5] Korea's ODA to Asian countries was maintained at over 50% from the early stage of foreign aid, and gradually reduced as some Asian countries managed to develop to middle-income countries.

There are a growing number of Korean companies to promote businesses in African countries. The Korean government has been supporting to foster the partnership between Korea and African countries. It is worth discussing how Korea could bring ODA policies to foster the partnership.

Understanding Korea's Official Development Assistance

Official Development Assistance Debates

Since the early 1960s, large sums of money have been spent in many developing countries. Some countries made good use of aid money and effectively managed to develop, while majority of African countries hardly succeeded to promote their economies. Korea's development was not comparable to any other developing countries after World War II. The Korean economy was as bad as many African countries in the early 1960s, but remarkably succeeded to industrialize the country and transformed from an aid-recipient to a donor country by 1991. Hence, questions arise as to how ODA should be managed for better results for the development of African economies.

There were active debates on the effectiveness of ODA to Africa in the early 2000s. Moyo (2007) wrote that Africa received more than USD 1 trillion of ODA from donor countries since the 1960s (Moyo 2007). Despite the large scale of foreign aid to Africa, its impact on African countries was not significant. Easterly (2007) insisted that foreign aid had not been properly managed in many developing countries, and there should be some ways of monitoring aid activities so that aid could bring better results in recipient countries. He wrote that it could be necessary to have incentive systems in ODA. Collier (2005) and Sachs (2005) wrote that the amount of foreign aid was not sufficient enough to impact the developing world. The scale of aid money should be increased dramatically so that ODA could bring fruitful outcomes. Sachs (2005) argued that Goal 1 in the Millennium Development Goals (MDGs), which was the reduction of the poverty ratio by 50% between 2000 and 2015, would be achieved if ODA volume increased from USD 65 billion as of 2002 between USD 135 billion and USD 195 billion a year by 2015 (Sachs 2005). Nevertheless, most of the developing countries achieved the first goal of the MDGs by 2015. Somehow, the amount of ODA was raised from just over USD 65 billion in 2000 to USD 145 billion in 2017 (Table 4.1).

Despite the twofold increase in the total international ODA between 2000 and 2017, a large number of African countries are still underdeveloped and based on the primary sector, which are mainly the agricultural

Table 4.1 Trend of world development aid

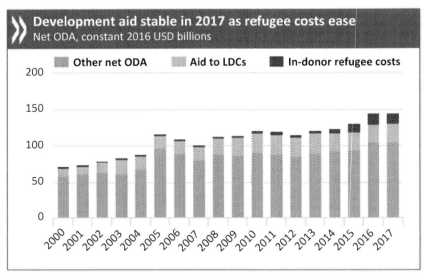

Source: OECD DAC Statistics 2018

sector and mining industries. It is estimated that more than 400 million Africans live in absolute poverty with USD 1.25 per day in 2018 (Golubski 2017).[6]

Korea's Development and Official Development Assistance

Korea has little quantity or almost none of the natural resources and relies on imported industrial raw materials and energy. Korea has a small size of land, and it is surrounded by big powers such as China, Russia and Japan. The country was separated in 1945 in the South and North and had the Korean War between 1950 and 1953, which completely destroyed its economy. Korea did not have favorable political and economic environments in the 1950s with political upheaval. From the early 1960s, the country began to work toward development. The government adopted economic policies focusing on export-oriented industrialization and managed to promote industrialization. The industrialization began with light industries, notably cotton textile and garment industries in the 1960s. The economy was showing positive growth by focusing on more capital-intensive heavy and chemical industries in the 1970s and more knowledge-intensive industries in the

1980s. By the middle of the 1990s, several industries such as petrochemical, steel, automobile, shipbuilding and Information and Communications Technology (ICT) sectors became internationally competitive. The volume of export reached USD 605.2 billion and the country became the sixth largest exporter in the world in 2018. The import volume was USD 535 billion and the ninth largest in the world.[7] Total volume of trade was USD 1135 billion in 2018 (IMF 2019). Korea's GDP was USD 1530 billion, which was the 12th largest in the world in 2018. The agricultural sector shared only 2.6% of GDP and the industrial sector 39.2% in the same year. The Korean economy is deeply integrated to the world economy, which means that the country needs to maintain stable relationships with many countries. Korea's unique development experiences can be utilized to enhance international efforts to promote developing countries to eradicate poverty (Marx and Soares 2013). One of the factors to Korea's development was ODA received between 1945 and 1990, which was accounted at USD 12 billion (Yoon and Moon 2014).[8] The country became one of the leading industrial economies and transformed from a recipient to a donor country in 1991.

Korea joined the OECD in 1996 and the OECD DAC (Development Assistance Committee) in 2010. Within two years of the membership of the OECD DAC, there was a peer review by the OECD DAC in 2012. There were some issues raised in the peer-review report. There was an issue on fragmented aid activities, which was a result of too many institutions committed in the process of ODA that could inhibit their aid effectiveness. DAC also recommended that there could be a single entity for grants and concessional loans that required coordination processes between the KOICA and the EDCF. The report also suggested that Korea needed to scale up ODA budget as its ratio to GNI was far lower than 0.7% of GNI recommended by OECD DAC (OECD 2018).[9]

At the dawn of the new millennium in 2000, the United Nations (UN) set the Millennium Development Goals (MDGs) as a road map to develop less developed countries. In 2005, OECD DAC endorsed the Paris Declaration (PD) to improve aid effectiveness. Korea began to actively participate in OECD DAC policies. As a part of its efforts on the OECD DAC, Korea hosted the High-Level Forum 4 (HLF 4) for aid effectiveness in Busan, Korea, in 2011. The HLF4 brought a resolution to enhance private sector participation and increase activities by NGOs and civil society organizations (CSOs). There were discussions on South-South partnership in the HLF4 (ODA Korea 2018).

The Korean government prepared for the Mid-term Strategy for Development Cooperation every five years. It clarified ODA policy directions and determined the priority countries where it would need to prepare for Country Partnership Strategy (CPS). The First Mid-term Strategy for Development Cooperation covered between 2011 and 2015 included the direction of ODA activities, areas, sectors, and types. That strategy emphasized active commitments on OECD DAC guidelines, scaling up the size, sharing Korea's development experiences, and inclusive partnership. The second Mid-term Strategy for Development Cooperation (2016–2020) included the private sector partnership, inclusive business model with public-private partnership (PPP), and corporative social responsibility (CSR). The second Mid-term Strategy pursued the implementation of Sustainable Development Goals (SDGs) as one of its principles.

Official Development Assistance Governance in Korea

The Office of International Development and Cooperation in the Prime Minister's Office operates the Committee for International Development and Cooperation (CIDC), which is chaired by the Prime Minister.[10] The CIDC is composed of 18 cabinet ministers and 6 experts from academia and the private sector. The CIDC is the final decision-making body for ODA policies, budget, projects, grants, concessional loans, bilateral and multilateral aids. As presented in Fig. 4.1, the KOICA and the EDCF are under the CIDC. The KOICA and the EDCF have working relationships as they coordinate and consult their ODA activities. All government institutions are subjected to report their ODA activities to the Prime Minister's Office (ODA Korea 2018).

The KOICA was inaugurated by the Korea International Cooperation Agency Act in 1991. The 'Foreign Migration and Development Agency (FMDA)', a government institution under the Ministry of Health and Social Welfare was established in 1965 and organized short-term training programs for Koreans who tended to immigrate, work, and travel to foreign countries. Korean workers employed at construction sites in the Middle East and South Asian countries had to take short-term training courses in the FMDA. The FMDA was newly established by the KOICA under the Ministry of Foreign Affairs in 1991.

Korea's ODA works on the 'Framework Act on International Development and Cooperation and the Presidential Decree' that was

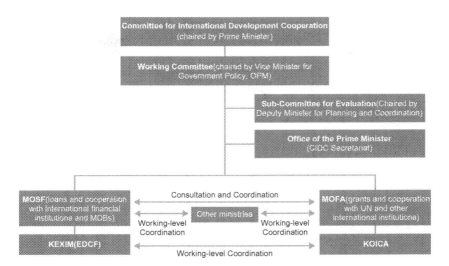

Fig. 4.1 Korea's Development Cooperation Management Architecture (2017) (Source: ODA Korea 2017: 44)

enacted in July 2010 (ODA Korea 2018). The Framework Act has set guidelines on poverty, human rights, gender equality, sustainable development, economic cooperation, and peace and prosperity in developing countries (ODA Korea 2018). In 1987, the Economic Development Cooperation Fund Act was a legal foundation for the EDCF to facilitate concessional loans. The final policy-making authority of the EDCF is the Fund Management Council, which is composed of 13 members from different ministries and experts chosen from outside the government.

Some ODA-related Acts were enacted for special purposes. For example, the Overseas Emergency Relief Act was enacted for emergency aid, covering relief teams and emergency relief supplies to disaster areas (ODA Korea 2018).

Official Development Assistance Coordination Process

ODA proposals are required to get through many steps in the Korean government. The final approval of ODA proposals is decided by the CIDC. Grant proposals should be submitted to the KOICA and passed to the MOFA. ODA proposals for concessional loans should be submitted to the EDCF and passed to the MOSF. Some proposals could be submitted directly to the relevant ministries. For instance, an ODA proposal on education should be submitted to the Ministry of Education (MOE).[11] In March every year, each ministry submits a ministerial budget with ODA projects to the MOSF. The MOSF is the supervising ministry for the government budget and compiles all ministerial budgets. By the end of May, the CIDC should receive ODA budgets from different government ministries and institutions through the MOSF. The approved ODA budget from the CIDC is passed to the National Assembly and included in the government budget before June. The budget is then endorsed in the plenary session of the National Assembly in December, and it is passed to the President's office.[12] The coordination of ODA project proposals is presented in Fig. 4.2.

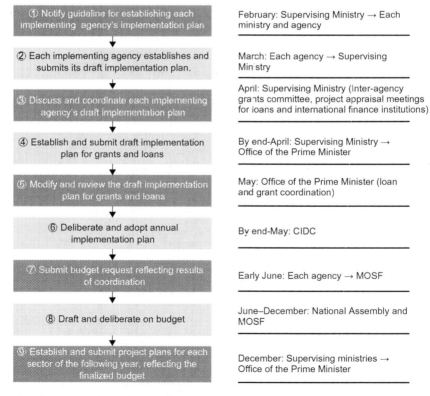

Fig. 4.2 Korea's ODA Coordination and Process (Source: ODA Korea 2018: 55)

Fig. 4.3 ODA Selection Process (Source: ODA Korea 2018: 56)

ODA projects are finalized after the formal agreement signed by the Korean and recipient governments. Each ODA proposal requires feasibility study by the implementation agency. Projects include monitoring and evaluation processes, and some projects require mid-term evaluations in case of multi-year projects. A project will be evaluated when it is completed. The process of ODA project is presented in Fig. 4.3.

Partnerships Between Korea and Africa

The partnership between Korea and African countries began to strengthen when former President Chun Doo-hwan visited four African countries, namely Gabon, Kenya, Nigeria, and Senegal, for the first time in 1982 (Yoon and Moon 2014). The visit was mainly for economic and political purposes. During the 1970s and 1980s, North Korea had more diplomatic missions than Korea in the African continent (Veras 2018).[13] When most African countries were liberalized from their colonies in the 1960s, many of them became close allies to the former Soviet Union. North Korea took advantage of the strengthening relationship with African countries with the same political system until the Soviet Union disintegrated in 1989. After African countries changed their political systems to democracy and open economies, Korea began to enhance partnerships with African countries.[14] The Korean government increased diplomatic missions to Africa over the past 20 years. There were 14 Korean Embassies in Africa in 2000, and this increased to 21 missions by 2018.

In 2006, former President Roh Moo-hyun visited three African countries, notably Algeria, Egypt and Nigeria, and declared the Korea's Initiative for Africa's Development. Korea's ODA to Africa was still small in

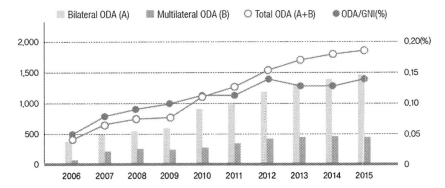

Fig. 4.4 Trend of Korea's bilateral and multilateral ODA (Source: ODA Korea 2018: 111)

proportion in comparison to other regions though the total amount of ODA budget increased (Yoon and Moon 2014).[15] Figure 4.4 presents the figures showing a big increase in ODA to Africa in 2006, which was associated with changes in government policies with the presidential visit. After the presidential visit to Africa, the Korean government began forums, workshops, and conferences with the African counterparts. The first Korea-Africa Forum (KOAF) began in Korea in 2008, which continues to this day, and it is held every three years. The MOFA organizes the KOAF with the African Union as its counterpart. KOAF agendum include how to stimulate Korea-Africa partnerships. In 2008, the Korea-Africa Economic Cooperation (KOAFEC) began as a biennial meeting between the MOSF and African Development Bank (AfDB), and it determines Korea's commitments toward African development. It includes financial support for the 'Korea Trust Fund' in AfDB. The Fund has been specially created to support projects to encourage Korea-Africa partnerships. At the KOAFEC meeting in October 2016 in Seoul, the Korean government and AfDB signed a memorandum of understanding (MOU) to facilitate a financial package of USD 10 billion toward cooperation.[16] Numerous projects were financed by the Korea Trust Fund, including the increase in the productivity in the agricultural sector, fisheries, and industrial policies. KOAFIC was started in 2008, and is now organized by the Ministry of Industry and Natural Resources (MINR) of Korea and the ministries connected to the industry from African countries. The KOAFIC meets annually and discusses industrial cooperation between Korean and African industries.

Korea's presidential visit to Africa became more frequent after 2010, with the previous two presidents visiting Africa (Mabaya 2018). Former President Myung-bak Lee visited three countries, namely South Africa, the Democratic Republic of the Congo (DR Congo), and Ethiopia, in July 2011. President Lee's visit was focused on sharing Korea's development experiences with African countries. The visit had some other objectives as the government was pursuing to secure energy and raw materials for Korean industries.

The President Lee's government was encouraging foreign direct investment in developing countries that were abundant in natural resources. Korea's ODA projects were also linked with the possible exploration of energy and minerals in Latin America and Africa. Several ODA projects were designed by the government in resource-rich countries. Many Knowledge-Sharing Programs (KSPs) were introduced in countries with abundant natural resources. In 2015, former President Park Geun-hye visited three African countries, namely Ethiopia, Kenya, and Uganda. During her visit, the 'Korea Aid' was initiated to focus on education, health, culture, and the Saemaul Undong.[17] Under the Korea Aid, several ODA projects were carried out in East Africa. Mobile clinics and libraries were included in remote areas in East Africa. Saemaul Undong projects were expanded in several countries in Africa that included South Africa, Uganda, Ethiopia, and DR Congo. Some projects were carried out through joint programs with the UN Village Program conducted by the United Nations Development Programme (UNDP).

The KOICA launched the 'Creative Technology Solution Program' by providing seed money for social entrepreneurs in 2015. They provided leverage fund of USD 4.3 million for the private sector to support small and medium-sized enterprises (SMEs) in recipient countries, which was implemented as the Inclusive Business Opportunity Creation Program (OECD 2017: 222). The 'Hope with Africa' was introduced as a regional partnership strategy. The strategy included four pillars, namely 'wealthy Africa, initiative Africa, thriving Africa and harmonious Africa' (KOICA 2016).

Country Partnership Strategy[18]

The Korean government formulated the Country Partnership Strategy (CPS) based on political, social, and economic environment of the recipient country. CPS includes mid-term strategy, priority sectors, and the scale of

Table 4.2 Priority sectors of CPS in Africa

Country	Priority sectors
Ethiopia	Health and Sanitation, Rural Development, Transport and Energy, and Education
Uganda	Rural Development, Education, and Health
Rwanda	Education, Rural Development, and ICT
Tanzania	Water Management and Health, Transport, Education, and Energy
Mozambique	Transportation, Energy, Water Management, and Health
Ghana	Agriculture and Rural Development, Public Health, Education, and Energy
Senegal	Rural Development, Agriculture and Fisheries, Education, Water Management and Health, and Transport

Source: KOICA 2018

ODA to recipient countries. The CIDC endorses priority countries every three years. The last selection of priority countries was in 2016. There are seven African countries, namely Ethiopia, Ghana, Mozambique, Uganda, Rwanda, Senegal, and Tanzania, at the moment.[19] CPS for priority sectors in African countries is presented in Table 4.2. Ethiopia has four key sectors, namely health and sanitation, rural development, transportation, and energy and education. Priority sectors are enacted to both grants and loans.

Korea supported 47 African countries, which means that Korea's ODA has diversified and is widely spread in the African continent. Priority countries have main sectors to support through ODA projects. Nevertheless, there are many other sectors not included in the CPS but included in ODA projects. Priority sectors in the CPS are aligned with the long-term development plan and determined by political and economic environment and the absorptive capacity of the recipient country.

Scale of Korea's Official Development Assistance

As presented in Table 4.3, the scale of Korea's ODA increased rapidly after the year 2000 and grew faster between 2005 and 2010. Korea's bilateral aid share was 83% in 2006 and reduced gradually to 77% in 2015, while the multilateral aid increased from 17% to 23% during the same period (OECD 2018). Figure 4.4 shows the trend of Korea's ODA and the changes in the share of bilateral and multilateral aids.

Table 4.3 Scale of Korea's ODA between 2006 and 2015

	2006	2007	2008	2009	2010	2011	2012	2013	2014	2015
Total ODA (A+B)	455.25	696.11	802.34	816.04	1173.79	1324.59	1597.45	1755.38	1856.73	1915.39
Bilateral ODA (A)	376.06	490.52	539.22	581.1	900.63	989.57	1183.17	1309.58	1395.77	1468.79
Multilateral ODA (B)	79.19	205.59	263.12	234.94	273.15	335.02	414.28	445.8	460.96	446.6
ODA/GNI (%)	0.05	0.07	0.09	0.1	0.12	0.12	0.14	0.13	0.13	0.14

Source: ODA Korea 2018: 111

Table 4.4 Share of grants and concessional loans

Year	Bilateral ODA	Loans		Grants	
		Amount	Share (%)	Amount	Share (%)
2009	581.1	214.13	36.85	366.97	63.15
2010	900.63	326.74	36.28	573.89	63.72
2011	989.57	414.55	41.89	575.02	58.11
2012	1183.17	468.29	39.58	714.88	60.42
2013	1309.58	500.58	38.22	809	61.78
2014	1395.77	512.12	36.69	883.65	63.31
2015	1468.79	562.37	38.29	906.42	61.71

Source: ODA Korea 2018: 113

Bilateral aid is composed of grants and concessional loans (Table 4.4). The grants share was 61.7% and concessional loans 38.3% in 2015 (Chun et.al. 2010). Concessional loans are classified as ODA if a grant element is at least 25% on the basis of interest rate between 1% and 4%.[20] At times, concessional loans and grants could be complementary (Iimi and Ojima 2005; Hulya Ulku and Tito Cordella 2004). Iimi and Ojima (2005) performed an empirical study among 61 developing countries and found that concessional loans affected economic growth, but grants was less effective, and the optimal condition could be a combination of the two.[21] The OECD DAC suggested to the Korean government to reduce the share of loans, as Korea maintains higher proportion of loans than many other DAC members (Table 4.4).

There is a belief that concessional loans would increase the ownership of ODA projects by stake holders as it would bring more accountability to beneficiaries. There are market failures to justify ODA, and loans could provide offer a better solution for development.[22]

More than half of Korea's ODA went to Asia with 52.7% and Africa 23.1%, in 2015. The large proportion of ODA to Asian countries was due to the geographical location that made the handling of projects easy with good accessibility. Korea has similar historical and cultural backgrounds with that of Asian countries, operational expenses for ODA projects are less in Asian countries than other regions (Fig. 4.5).

In 2015, the top ten recipient countries consisted of seven Asian countries, three African countries, and none from the Middle East, Central Asia, and Latin America. Vietnam received more than USD 200 million, which was a lot more than the total of the next three highest recipients together (see Table 4.5).

4 ISSUES RAISED ON KOREA'S OFFICIAL DEVELOPMENT ASSISTANCE... 85

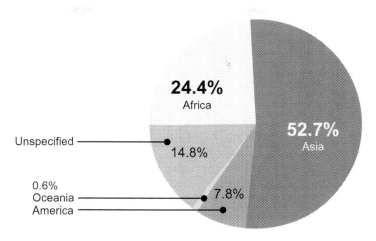

Fig. 4.5 Korea's ODA by region in 2015 (Source: ODA Korea 2018: 117)

Table 4.5 Largest recipient countries of Korea's ODA between 2011 and 2015 (unit: USD million)

Countries	2011	2012	2013	2014	2015
Vietnam	139.49	200.32	234.56	178.84	217.16
Laos	33.48	23.52	27.07	28.98	87.63
Cambodia	62.23	56.15	60.54	68.62	65.85
Bangladesh	80.02	46.76	44.71	68.06	52.16
Ethiopia	11.61	20.44	27.34	42.91	46.02
The Philippines	35.69	31.33	42.74	60.93	44.04
Mozambique	6.48	25.13	57.08	56.51	42.29
Ghana	5.06	23.44	9.85	15.82	39.84
Indonesia	24.29	37.23	31.5	21.49	39.55
Sri Lanka	43.36	51.49	44.93	44.78	27.46

Source: ODA Korea 2018: 185

Vietnam received more than USD 200 million, which was the largest recipient of Korea's ODA (see Table 4.8). Vietnam was one of the most successful cases of Korea's ODA and Korean direct investment. Vietnam was isolated from the West after the Vietnam War in 1976. The country took the Doi Moi policy in 1986, which encouraged foreign direct investment among the top multinational enterprises (MNEs) around the world. The USA,

Japan, and European countries as well as Korea have been supporting the country in the field of education, Technical Vocational Education and Training (TVET), health, economic infrastructure, and many others. With growing interest shown by businesses with Vietnam, Korean private companies increased direct investment and trading. Many Korean companies invested in textile, garment, and light engineering from the 1990s. It was well matched with Korea's ODA on skills and economic infrastructure. Vietnam had a large population of young employable age group earning low wages.

Korea became the largest foreign investor in Vietnam in 2017. Samsung established the largest factory for mobile phones in Vietnam near Hanoi employing more than 110,000 workers. The company exported over USD 60 billion, which was equivalent to 25% of the total export and 15% of Vietnam's GDP in 2017. Korea's ODA on training of skilled workers in Vietnam was well matched with the demand for skilled labor in the rapidly growing industrial sector. ODA projects, such as building roads, bridges, power supply, IT infrastructure, water supply, and so on, helped in Vietnam's industrial promotion.

Korea's Official Development Assistance to Africa

The total amount of Korean ODA to Africa was USD 35.6 million in 1991, which increased to USD 556.1 million in 2017. Its share was maintained between 20% and 26% in1991 and 2017, respectively. Korea's ODA share to other regions was fluctuating over the years due to changes in political and social environment in the Middle East. After the wars in Iraq and Afghanistan, Western donor countries increased ODA to these two countries for them to recover from the wars and to stabilize the region. Korea also took part by increasing ODA to these two countries and a lot of ODA resources were diverted. As a result, Korea's ODA to other regions, such as Asia and Africa, had to be reduced in the 1990s and the early 2000s. Grants to Africa were delivered to 47 African countries out of the total of 54 countries, which shows that Korea's ODA to Africa was widely dispersed in the African continent. Concessional loans were delivered to 20 African countries, which is fewer than that of grants.[23] The trend of Korea's ODA to Africa is presented in Table 4.6.

Table 4.6 Trend of Korean ODA to Africa 1991–2017 (Unit: US$ million)

Year	1991	1995	2000	2005	2010	2015	2017
Amount	35.6	8.9	59.2	74.7	523.1	517.6	556.1
% to total	26.3	3.8	16.7	10.4	26.7	23.1	23.9

Source: OECD Stat. 2018

Among African countries, Ethiopia is the largest recipient country for grants with 16.4% (approximately USD 150 million) of the total ODA to Africa, and Tanzania is the largest recipient of concessional loans which accounted for USD 371 million and 23% of the total concessional loans to Africa (KOICA 2018; KOEXIM 2018). Korea's ODA to Africa focuses on three sectors—education, health, and public administration which shared 68% of the total ODA to Africa in 2017 (KOICA 2018). In 2017, the education sector shared the largest proportion in Africa at 25.6% of the total, followed by health and public administration with 22.4% (USD 20 million) and 20.6% (USD 19 million), respectively. The high proportion of education ODA was induced by high illiteracy ratio and shortage of skilled labor in African countries.

The transport sector shared 31.3% of total loans to Africa, followed by the energy sector at 14.4% (USD 527 million) and health at 13.6% (USD 489 million) in 2017 (KOICA 2018; KOEXIM 2018). ODA projects in the transport sector include building roads, establishing urban transport systems, airports, and so on. Korea's ODA by sectors are presented in Table 4.7 for grants and Table 4.8 for loans.

Korea spent more than 40% of bilateral aid to the least developed countries (LDCs), followed by low middle-income countries with 36%. Aye and Lee (2018) find that the impact of foreign aid to middle-income countries tended to experience greater benefits on their economic growth than low-income countries in Africa (Aye and Lee 2018). This is because aid projects to least developed countries are more focused on basic needs, which would have a lower impact on economic progress. However, the middle-income countries already solved problems of basic needs, and aid projects could be directed to economic infrastructure. As presented in Table 4.9, the share of ODA to LDCs was 24% in 2006 and increased to 35% in 2015, while ODA to upper middle-income countries reduced from 31% in 2006 to 7.4% during the same period.

Table 4.7 Sectors of grants to Africa in 2017 (unit: KRW million, %)

Rank	Sector	Aid Amount	Disbursement (%)
1	Education	26,092	25.6
2	Health	22,839	22.4
3	Public administration	21,017	20.6
4	Agriculture, forestry and fishery	15,627	15.3
5	Technology, environment and energy	11,938	11.7

Source: KOICA 2018

Table 4.8 Sectors of the EDCF loans to Africa in 2017 (unit: USD million, %)

Rank	Sector	Amount	Proportion (%)
1	Transport	1119	31.3
2	Energy	527	14.4
3	Health	489	13.6
4	Public Administration	473	12.8
5	Education	394	10.8
6	Water sanitation	312	8.7
7	Agriculture	249	7.2
8	Communications	8	0.2
9	Others	38	1.0
	Total	3608	100

Source: KOEXIM (2018)

Official Development Assistance Sectoral Specifications to Africa

Education

Korea has heavily invested in the education sector for many years. The participation ratio in tertiary education is the highest in the world. Korea's ODA could include formulating education sector development plans, policies and reform education systems in African countries.

Projects can be classified into general education, TVET, and tertiary education. General education projects include establishing schools, improving school facilities such as expansion of classrooms, improving curricula setting, training of teachers, introducing pedagogy, and supplying education materials. Korean teachers can be dispatched to teach specific subjects such as mathematics, computers, IT, and physics. There were projects in Ethiopia, Kenya, Algeria, Zimbabwe, and Côte d'Ivoire.

Table 4.9 Korea's ODA by income groups

	2006	2007	2008	2009	2010	2011	2012	2013	2014	2015
Total bilateral ODA	376.08	490.54	539.21	584.96	900.61	989.52	1183.17	1309.58	1395.77	1468.79
Least developed countries (LDCs)	91.95	120.66	143.47	161.02	333.26	346.73	417	515.31	542	580.13
Other low-income countries (OLICs)	15.7	3.23	4.1	5.82	7.25	10.82	10.91	8.72	8.61	9.27
Lower middle-income countries (LMICs)	102.86	185.05	194.34	222.3	354.81	366.58	472.51	502.4	485.79	529.95
Upper middle income countries (UMICs)	120.57	121.56	107.73	93.41	111.17	120.93	107.56	101.76	140.09	109.74
Unallocated by income	44.74	59.5	90.49	100.48	96.22	144.46	175.08	181.28	219.28	239.71
More advanced developing countries	0.26	0.54	−0.92	1.93	−2.1	–	0.11	0.1	–	–

Source: ODA Korea 2018: 116

Technical Vocational Education and Training

TVET is one of the top-priority areas for Korea's ODA to Korea. TVET projects include the establishment of TVET institutes; curricula modification; supply of equipment; training of trainers; preparation of textbooks; and setting up for national skills competition, skill standardization, and certificate system. The MOE of Korea initiated Better Education for Africa's Rise (BEAR) project in 2011. The BEAR project was designed with UNESCO as a new strategy to enhance the capacity of TVET institutions in African countries. BEAR I project began in 2011 and was completed in 2016 in five countries, namely Malawi, DR Congo, Botswana, Namibia, and Mozambique. The project focused on the capacity building of TVET in recipient countries. Korea Research Institute of Vocational Education and Training (KRIVET) carried out the BEAR I project. In the designated country, UNESCO's local office acts as a coordinating agency between KRIVET and stake holders in the country. The outcome of BEAR I was very successful, and the Korean government decided to support the first five countries with the Vocational Development Cooperation ('V-Code'). It covers another three years of assistance on the project. BEAR II was initiated for other African countries in the East Africa region such as Ethiopia, Kenya, Uganda, Tanzania, and Madagascar.

Tertiary Education

Korean universities and colleges were able to collaborate with African universities and colleges. Activities included exchange programs for professors, researchers, and students. Many Korean universities had excessive capacities of laboratories, which could be utilized by inviting African professors and students for training. Higher education institutions in Africa have been decoupled from their societies and have limited capacity for research and development. Research capacity in African universities could be improved through university-industry cooperation with Korean universities.

Health Services

Korea's ODA share in the health sector stood at 22.4% of the total ODA to Africa in 2017. Korea's health services have improved remarkably well and it has become one of the top medical service countries in the world. Many health tourists are visiting Korea for medical services from developing countries. ODA of health services could include health policies, public health, maternal, reproductive health, malaria, and TB. In Ethiopia, a few projects were carried out to improve health network, train midwives, and monitor public health in rural areas. In Tanzania, the EDCF has financed the construction of Muhimbili Hospital near Dar es Salaam, which was the largest in sub-Saharan Africa. The project included the setting up of the management system and training medical staff. The KOICA joined the Tanzanian Health Basket Fund Program between 2016 and 2018. The Fund was used for medicine and health services. There was a project on m-Health System for integrated disease management of communicable and noncommunicable diseases. m-Health is a mobile application used to track the medication of the beneficiaries of diseases.[24]

Public Administration and Governance
The improvement of public administration is one of the top agendas in African countries. The capacity of planning and implementation of policies could determine the stability of the government. Korea's ODA could include capacity-building programs through restructuring government institutions and training of public officials. The e-government system can include wide range of public services, including population census, human resources, economic and social data, and agriculture and industrial outputs. The data and information will facilitate government policies.

Korea carried out several ODA projects on governance such as operation and management of government institutions, and modification of public administration system. E-government projects included the supply of equipment and software to run the e-government system. In Tanzania, Korea delivered the national identification system as a part of e-government project, including the registration of citizens, immigration control system, and public services. There was a project in Tunisia which included democratic governance and public accountability. It was carried out by the collaboration between Korea and the UNDP.

Economic and Industrial Development
Many African countries are demanding Korea's ODA, as Korea's development experiences would support their economic promotion. Some African countries have abundant natural resources, but some have very little. Industrial promotion strategies should be designed according to the factor endowment of each country. Many African countries have similar factor endowments and have similar industrial policies. Ethiopia, Kenya, Uganda, and Tanzania have policies to develop the cotton and textile industries.

Ethiopia and Kenya were promoting the horticulture industry with exports to the European and the Middle Eastern markets. Many horticulture farmers went bankrupt as there were too many producers in that region. Of late, several African countries are pursuing the development of the pharmaceutical industry. This calls for a policy coordination for industrial development at the regional level.

A Knowledge-Sharing Program (KSP) has been initiated by the Korean government to activate Korea's development experiences with recipient countries. The formation of KSP projects will be similar to ordinary ODA project proposals. KSP proposals will be managed by the MOSF, and Korea Development Institute (KDI) is the executing agency following government policies.[25] Equatorial Guinea had two KSP projects in a row—first one was on the modification of the mid-term economic development plan, and the second KSP project was on the determination of priority sectors and the promotion of the agricultural and fisheries sectors. KDI dispatched Korean experts to the country, and several civil servants visited Korea for site visits and seminars. The project included meetings between policymakers in Equatorial Guinea and Korean experts. Ethiopia had a KSP project on industrial development and transport system in Addis Ababa in 2011. The project analyzed economic and social environment and medium- and long-term development plans. Korea's development experiences were introduced in target industrial sectors, and included industrial zones, parks and export processing zones. Another KSP project in Morocco was focused on trade promotion and recommended priority industries for the export sector. Morocco has many automobile industries that supply car components to European car makers. The KSP project suggested that Morocco should build up technological capacity to achieve sustainable development.

PPP has been encouraged as it could develop business partnerships between Korean and African private sectors. The partnership could include the formation of business entities, operation, organizational structure, accounting, marketing, human resource management, and logistics.

Agricultural and Rural Development
Agricultural and rural development was included in the CPS of Ethiopia, Uganda, Rwanda, and Senegal.[26] Agricultural and rural development projects were implemented in Uganda, Ethiopia, Tanzania, Rwanda, DR Congo, Ghana, and South Africa. The KOICA, the Ministry of Public Administration and Safety (MPAS), and the Gyeongbuk Provincial

Government have been involved in the Saemaul Undong and rural development projects. The productivity of agricultural sector can be improved by adopting modern technology and mechanization. That will be related to the level of technology in machine tools and mechanical engineering in the recipient country. It is also necessary to improve storage system and post-harvest logistics for agricultural crops. The market for agricultural crops can be developed with agricultural cooperatives. Since 2017, there has been an ongoing ODA project for the capacity building of agricultural cooperatives in Northern Ghana. The project includes training and education of cooperative members, and built-up systems improve the productivity in agricultural crops and post-harvest managements. The project includes encouraging communal meeting to disseminate agricultural knowledge and technologies.

Information and Communications Technology Sector
The implication of ICT would improve the efficiency of the public and private sectors. ICT projects include hardware and software. One of the best examples of ICT projects in Africa was in Rwanda. The Rwandan government took initiative to promote the ICT sector as a strategic industry from the early 1990s. The country's land mass is small with ten million people. Korea helped in Rwanda's fiber-optic cable projects, and the country could boast of the most up-to-date ICT infrastructure. The country has one of the best ICT infrastructures in the African continent. Korea's ODA projects on ICT in Rwanda were carried out by a Korean telecommunication company.

There were several ICT projects on the establishment of ICT laboratories in higher education institutions in Africa. An ICT Center was established at the University of Dar es Salaam, Tanzania. The ICT center was equipped with computers and software technology labs. ICT could be applied in education, health, the financial sector, the agriculture sector, and so on, which can be accessed through mobile phone applications.

Science and Technology Innovation
Korea ODA on Science, Technology, and Innovation (STI) includes policy advocacy, the establishment of science parks and research institutions, enhancing academia-industry cooperation, and capacity building of research activities through education and training. Korea's ODA could involve in long-term science and technology development plans in African countries. Those projects could include science and technology education and increasing research capacity.

It is necessary to increase public awareness about science and technology with active student participation in science and technology studies. Korea has promoted public awareness of science and technology and managed to attract talented students in.

A science and technology project in Algeria included the establishment of science parks and providing a long-term development plan for science and technology. There is an ongoing project to establish science and technology parks and provide a long-term science and technology development plan for Tanzania. Science and Technology Policy Institute (STEPI) has been implementing the project since 2016.

FUTURE PERSPECTIVE OF KOREA'S OFFICIAL DEVELOPMENT ASSISTANCE TO AFRICA

Needs for Korea-Africa Cooperation

Darracq and Neville (2014) insisted that there are three factors that explain why Korea renewed engagement in sub-Saharan Africa: 'the pursuit of food and energy security, the establishment of new markets for its manufactured goods; and the enhancement of its credentials as a prominent global power, particularly in order to counter the diplomacy of North Korea' (Darracq and Neville 2014: 2). Kim (2014) states that Korea has been acting as a medium power in Africa.

Many African countries have abundant industrial raw materials and energy, but lack of technology and capital investment. Korea has many scientists and technical personnel with skills that could be shared with Africans. African countries need to develop education, health, gender, social infrastructure, and so on. One of the key success factors of Korea's development was human resource development and TVET. It is possible to organize ODA projects on pre-school education for early childhood education would bring positive impact to learning capacity later.[27] Korea could share the experience of health-care systems with African countries.

Korea's ODA to Africa could bring limited opportunity to harmonize their own activities with other institutions. There are a growing number of NGOs and CSOs joining ODA projects and even private companies for CSR. These movements would make Korean ODA more efficient as the chance for PPP could increase. PPP will stimulate the development of African private businesses. Table 4.10 presents Korea's ODA to Africa in the form of a SWOT analysis.

Table 4.10 SWOT of Korea's ODA to Africa

Strength	Weakness
• Korean development experience • High level of industrial technology and adoption • Good governance in Korea • Strong government policies • A lot of specialists who are capable of working in Africa	• Lack of experts and knowledge on Africa • Geographical location (long distance from Korea) • Limited work experience in Africa • Limited budget • Fragmented ODA agencies and activities
Opportunities	Threat
• Learning from early donors • Good public perception by Africans about Korea on development • Demand for Korean partnership in many African countries • Increase in demand for business partnership by Korean private sector	• Competition from big donors • Relatively small-scale projects that could be overshadowed by big projects from others • Security problems in the recipient countries • Political uncertainty in some countries • Low level of governance

Source: Author's own work

Future Perspectives of Korea's Official Development Assistance to Africa

Korea's ODA to Africa would be consolidated if ODA stakeholders work together. It is necessary to bring priority sectors for individual recipient country by considering factor endowment and absorptive capacity. Projects could focus on a few key sectors such as education, including TVET, health, industrial promotion, and technology promotion.

It is necessary for Korea to cooperate with international institutions, notably UN organizations, the World Bank, AfDB, African Union (AU), EU, and bilateral donors. Korea could harness partnerships, since the AU improved good governance and brought about far-reaching changes in policies while considering political, social, and economic aspects. For instance, Korea could collaborate on New Partnership for Africa's Development (NEPAD) programs in the AU as a multilateral ODA platform. The NEPAD projects are initiated by African countries with their ownership.[28] The AfDB launched the Partnership for Skill in Applied Science, Engineering, and Technology (PASET) in 2013.[29] Korea's ODA projects could be implemented by the cooperation with the PASET. Korea and UNESCO have been working on an education ODA project on TVET in ten African countries since 2011. There have been projects executed with AfDB and World Bank.

African countries require industrial promotion and need to promote science and technology. There could be capacity building of higher education institutions and research institutions. Korea's experience on human resources, science, and technology can be combined in the development and cooperation with African countries. This can be seen in a holistic approach to Korea's ODA to Africa. It is necessary to bring academia, the private sector, governments, NGOs, CSOs, and international institutions together. It will be a good opportunity to share Korea's development experiences with African countries.[30]

International organizations could play a pivotal role in aid activities as shown in Fig. 4.6. International organizations could bring academia, private companies, NGOs and CSIs, and governments together and provide an aid platform for cooperation among different stakeholders. Korean academic institutions need to develop partnerships with African institutions. Korean private companies need to have industry-academia linkages to build up capacity for technology development. Korean companies are increasing aid activities as a part of CSR (Corporative Social Responsibility). CSR

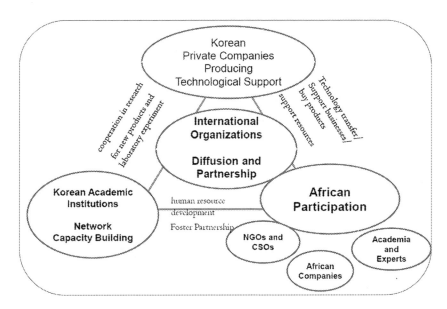

Fig. 4.6 ODA model for holistic approach (Source: Modified from LEE, YH and LEE JS (2015))

could bring positive effect to transfer technologies to Africa as it covers the global society. The development of science and technology is a key element to promote industries and sustain economic development in Africa. As Amoako (2000) insisted, Africa needs to build science and technology capacities to meet the development challenges of Africa (Amoako 2000). African institutions should strengthen partnerships with Korean institutions from academia, private companies, and public institutions. Areas of ODA projects could be aligned with the development plans of the recipient country and priority sectors included in CPS report provided by the Korean government. In the areas of economic development, projects could include technical assistance and technology transfer as shown in Fig. 4.6. There could be ODA projects on policymaking, implementation, monitoring, and evaluation.[31]

Concluding Remarks

Korea's ODA could facilitate the partnership between Korea and African countries. Korea has unique development experiences that could be shared with African countries where ODA can play a pivotal role. Many African countries are inspired by Korea's development experiences, and this has induced the need for the partnership between Korea and African countries. Korea's ODA was highly valued by the OECD DAC Peer Review Report (OECD 2018). As it wrote,

> As a former recipient country and now as a significant provider of ODA internationally its own right, Korea leads by example, bringing its direct knowledge and expertise to bear on how aid can drive economic and human development. (OECD 2018: 16)

Korea-Africa business partnerships were not significant to the Korean economy, as the share of total Korean trade with and foreign direct investment (FDI) to African countries remained a very small proportion. Korean government institutions, NGO institutions, academic institutions, and research organizations are trying to take part in the partnership projects with African partners, and these partners have made progress during the last few decades. The Korean government has made efforts to enhance the partnership through the diversification of diplomacy which lies in 3Ps—people, peace, and prosperity. The Korean government established the Korea-Africa Foundation under the MOFA. The Korea-Africa Foundation will be working on various issues to strengthen partnership with African countries including ODA, business linkages, educational, social, and economic relations with Africans. In May 2018, the Korean government hosted the 53rd Annual Meetings of AfDB in Busan. It was estimated that about 3000 people attended the meeting. There were ministerial meetings, business roundtable talks, and discussions by government officials as well as business leaders in Korea and Africa.

Socio-economic partnership includes any cooperation activities in the education, health, gender, governance, and economic sectors. The government could be in the driving seat to bring package deals with the private sector. Economic partnership starts with how African countries can benefit from their cooperation with Korea. Korea should find something different from other countries. Korea pursues a win-win strategy that could bring some positive impact to Korea when it comes to ODA. It should be more focused on pursuing mutual benefits.

The Korean government has policies called "Selection and Concentration" for ODA activities which shows that projects could be more carefully selected and focused as it could improve aid effectiveness. Rwanda was one of the countries chosen to get heavy engagement in Korean ODA projects especially in ICT areas. Rwanda is a small country in terms of territory and population compared with other neighboring countries. Rwanda is now equipped with the best ICT infrastructure in Africa. Korea's ODA should be focused on S&T cooperation including education, R&D, policy, and industrial technology. These can be done through the holistic approach as a model of ODA which will develop the African continent.

Notes

1. Korea's development since the 1960s was one of the best in the world after World War II. The Korean economy was completely transformed from poverty to an advanced industrial economy.
2. Five countries, notably, Norway, Sweden, Denmark, the Netherlands and the UK spent more than 0.7% of gross national income (GNI) on Official Development Assistance (ODA).
3. OECD (2008) stated that the Korean government announced to increase the share of GNI 0.25% by 2015.
4. Seo (2016) studied the relationship between political corruption and ODA in Africa.

5. The total amount of ODA includes the Korean government's contribution to UN agencies and multilateral development banks such as World Bank as well as regional development banks, for instance, African Development Bank, Asian Development Bank, and Inter-American Development Bank.
6. https://www.brookings.edu/blog/africa-in-focus/2017/05/18/africa-and-the-world-poverty-clock/.
7. http://stat.wto.org/CountryProfile/WSDBCountryPFView.aspx?Country=KR&Language.
8. Yoon and Moon 2014: 279.
9. There were a handful of recommendations on various subjects. There was a strong suggestion to collaborate with other donors, which Korea had already executed projects with, such as the Japan International Cooperation Agency (JICA) of Japan and the *Gesellschaft für Internationale Zusammenarbeit* (GIZ) of Germany.
10. Korea enacted the Framework Act on International Development Cooperation, and the Presidential Decree came into force in 2010, which was the basic principle of the Committee for International Development and Cooperation—CIDC (ODA Korea 2018).
11. The Ministry of Education (MOE) has its own ODA budget, and eligible to execute projects.
12. Korean fiscal year starts in January 1.
13. Until 1973, Korea had a one-Korea policy which did not allow having the two Koreas in Africa.
14. The early years of Korea's diplomatic relations with African countries were dedicated to get supports from African countries to become a member of the United Nations (Veras 2018).
15. Korea's interest in Africa was also a reaction to the increasing economic activities among China, Japan, India, Turkey, Brazil, and Russia in recent years (Yoon and Moon 2014).
16. https://news.joins.com/article/20777115.
17. The Saemaul Undong initiative was used as a soft power export by Korea in the hopes of closer partnerships in Africa. Rwanda had a big project on the Saemaul Undong, and this was linked to rural community development project in 2015 (Seitz 2017).
18. Country Partnership Strategy (CPS) reports are prepared for priority countries. Park et al. (2013) insisted that there are too many priority countries for Korea's ODA, and there is no clear justification for the selection.
19. There were 24 CPS countries that were selected in 2016. Asia had 11, Latin America 4, the Middle East and Commonwealth of Independent States (CIS) 2, and Africa 7.
20. https://www.un.org/ldcportal/when-should-concessional-loans-be-reported-as-oda/.

21. Japan keeps high proportion of concessional loans than European and North American countries. Japan supported many developing countries in Asia with concessional loans since the 1960s and receiving back their loans which Japan is topping up the repaid loans to other ODA projects in recent years.
22. Cohen et al. had an empirical study and found that loans could bring better results than grants.
23. Grants aid to Africa was distributed to 47 countries, that is, 87% of the total number of African countries, whereas concessional loans covered 20 countries, that is, 37% of African countries.
24. This is partly because many African patients do not take meditation when they are under the treatment. The mobile application will remind the patient to take medicine.
25. There are numerous numbers of ODA proposals from many developing countries. Each ministry has its own selection processed within its budget.
26. The other two countries were recommended to promote their agricultural sectors, but not listed in the priority sector.
27. Garcia et al. (2008) found that early childhood education would improve learning capacity in later age.
28. For more detailed activities of the NEPAD, see Akokpari et al. (2009).
29. Mabaya 2018.
30. OECD 2018.
31. Ayuk and Marouan (2007) state that research results are not effectively linked to policymakers in sub-Saharan countries. Korean ministries have government-sponsored research institutions that provide policies to the subject ministry and have managed to accumulate knowledge.

References

Akokpari, J., Ndinga-Muvumba, A., & Murithi, T. (2009). *The African Union and Its Institutions.* Cape Town: Fanele-Jacana & Centre for Conflict Resolution.

Amoako, K. Y. (2000). *Perspectives on Africa's Development.* Addis Ababa, Ethiopia: United Nations Publication.

Aye, M. A., & Lee, J. S. (2018). Foreign Aid on Economic Growth in Africa: Does Its Effect Vary from Low- to Middle-Income Countries? In G. Tesar et al. (Eds.), *Marketing Management in Africa.* New York and London: Routledge.

Ayuk Elias, T., & Marouani, M. A. (2007). *The Policy Paradox in Africa: Strengthening Links between Economic Research and Policymaking.* New Jersey: International Development Research Center, Africa World Press.

Broadman, H. G. (2007). *Africa's Silk Road: China and India's New Economic Frontier.* Washington, DC: The World Bank.

Chun, H. M., Munyi, E. N., & Lee, H. K. (2010). South Korea as an Emerging Donor: Challenges and Changes on Its Entering OECD/DAC. *Journal of International Development, 22*, 788–802.

Collier, P. (2005). *The Bottom Billion: Why the Poorest Countries Are Failing and What Can Be Done About it.* Oxford: Oxford University Press.

Easterly, W. I. (2007). *The White Man's Burden.* Oxford: Oxford University Press.

Darracq and Neville. (2014). South Korea's Engagement in Sub-Saharan Africa: Fortune, Fuel and Frontier Markets, *Research Paper*, Chatham House, The Royal Institute of International Affairs, London, UK.

Garcia, M., Pence, A., & Evans, J. L. (2008). *Africa's Future, Africa's Challenge: Early Childhood Care and Development in Sub-Saharan Africa.* Washington, DC: The World Bank.

Golubski, C. (2017). Africa and the World Poverty Clock. Brookings Institution. Retrieved December 27, 2018, from https://www.brookings.edu/blog/africa-in-focus/2017/05/18/africa-and-the-world-poverty-clock/.

Iimi, A., & Ojima, Y. (2005). *Complementarities between Grants and Loans, Japan Bank for International Corporation,* Working Paper No. 20. Tokyo, Japan. Retrieved December 29, 2018, from https://www.jica.go.jp/jica-ri/IFIC_and_JBICI-Studies/jica-ri/english/publication/archives/jbic/report/working/pdf/wp20_e.pdf.

International Monetary Fund. (2019). *World Economic Outlook Database (GDP based on Purchasing Power Parity).* Retrieved January 19, 2019.

Kim, T. H. (2014). South Korea's Strategic Relationships with Sub-Saharan Africa: Energy Security and Beyond, *Discussion Paper*, Deamen College.

KOEXIM. (2018). Korean Africa Development Partnership, paper presented at *the International Conference on Seoul Dialogue* Organized by the Korea Africa Foundation, Dec 2018, Seoul, Korea.

KOICA. (2016). *International Development and Cooperation: In Depth Study.* Korea: Sigong Media.

KOICA. (2018). Korean Africa Development Partnership, paper presented at *the International Conference on Seoul Dialogue* organized by the Korea Africa Foundation, Dec 2018, Seoul, Korea.

Lee, Y. H., & Lee, J. S. (2015). *Strategies of Korea-Africa Partnership: New Approach for Science and Technologies,* Discussion paper on Korea Africa Relations, Duksung Women's University, Seoul, Korea.

Mabaya, Edward. (2018). A Call for Investment in Africa, paper presented in a conference the *Seoul Dialogue on Africa*, Dec 2018, Seoul, Korea.

Marx, A., & Soares, J. (2013). *South Korea's Transition from Recipient to DAC Donor: Assessing Korea's Development Cooperation Policy,* International Development Policy, pp. 107–142.

Moyo, D. (2007). *Dead Aid: Why Aid is Not Working and How There is a Better Way for Africa.* New York: Penguin Press.

ODA Korea. (2018). *White Paper of Korea's ODA in 2017,* Seoul, Korea.

OECD. (2008). *Development Co-operation of the Republic of Korea*, DAC Special Review.
OECD. (2017). *Development and Cooperation Report 2016, The Sustainable Development Goals as Business Opportunities*. Paris: OECD.
OECD. (2018). *The DAC's Main Findings and Recommendations: OECD Development Co-operation Peer Review Korea 2018*. Paris: OECD DAC.
Park, B. Y., Lee, H. S., & Koo, J. W. (2013). *A Study of Selection Process and Methods of Priority Countries*, Policy Research Series, 2013-03. KIEP.
Prime Minister's Office. (2017). Korea's ODA White Paper, Korea.
Sachs, J. (2005). *The End of Poverty: Economic Possibilities for Our Time*. New York: Penguin Press.
Seitz, Martin. (2017). South Korea's Saemaul Unodong in Africa. The Diplomat. Retrieved December 12, 2018, from https://thediplomat.com/2017/10/south-koreas-saemaul-unodong-in-africa/.
Seo, S. H. (2016). ODA and FDI Impacts of Political Corruption: Case of Africa. *Korea Journal of African Studies, 49*, 97–130.
Ulku, H., & Cordella, T. (2004). Grants Versus Loans, *IMF Working Paper No. 04/161*, Washington DC. Retrieved December 18, 2018, from https://www.imf.org/en/Publications/WP/Issues/2016/12/31/Grants-Versus-Loans-17576.
Veras, O. (2018). Unpacking South Korea's Engagement with Africa. Retrieved December 15, 2018, from https://www.howwemadeitinafrica.com/unpacking-south-koreas-engagement-with-africa/62140/.
Yoon, M. Y., & Moon, C. S. (2014). Korean Bilateral Official Develop Assistance to Africa Under Korea's Initiative for Africa's Development. *Journal of East Asian Studies, 14*, 279–301.

INTERNET SOURCES

Retrieved December 18, 2018, from http://www.odakorea.go.kr/ez.main.ODAEngMain.do.
Retrieved December 14, 2018, from http://www.oecd.org/dac/financing-sustainable-development/development-finance-data/aid-at-a-glance.htm.
Retrieved December 28, 2018, from http://www.odakorea.go.kr/eng.etc.HLF-4.do.
Retrieved December 18, 2018, from http://stat.wto.org/CountryProfile/WSDBCountryPFView.aspx?Country=KR&Language.
Retrieved December 12, 2018, from https://www.un.org/ldcportal/when-should-concessional-loans-be-reported-as-oda/.
Retrieved November 30, 2018, from https://news.joins.com/article/20777115.
Retrieved November 30, 2018, from https://odakorea.go.kr/eng.result.overview.do.

CHAPTER 5

Korea–Ethiopia Relations Since the Korean War

Eun Kyung Kim and Mark W. DeLancey

INTRODUCTION

We set out to write a chapter in this book on Korea's engagement with Africa in order that our readers realize the notability of the Ethiopian case and that country's participation in the Korean War in 1950. Though Ethiopia was an extremely poor country at that time, it had a great cause to protect another weak nation, the Republic of Korea (ROK), from outside forces. Our purpose in writing this chapter is to give some insight into current relationships between the two countries, which are seemingly cooperating ever more. With respect to Official Development Assistance (ODA), for example, Ethiopia has received the most ODA from Korea among African states since 2012. While there are no previous studies on

---

E. K. Kim (✉)
Institute of African Studies, Hankuk University of Foreign Studies (HUFS), Yongin-si, South Korea

M. W. DeLancey
University of South Carolina, Columbia, SC, USA

Sookmyung Women's University, Seoul, South Korea

© The Author(s) 2020
Y. Chang (ed.), *South Korea's Engagement with Africa*, Africa's Global Engagement: Perspectives from Emerging Countries, https://doi.org/10.1007/978-981-32-9013-6_5

Korea–Africa relations dealing with how the old wartime memories influence the present situation of Korea–Ethiopia engagements, we argue for their significance. In this chapter, we briefly review Ethiopia's participation in the war, its motives, and actions, and then examine how this participation has impacted relations between the governments and peoples of Ethiopia and South Korea, the ROK.

Background: The Korean War and Ethiopia's Participation

At the end of World War II, the Korean Peninsula was divided into two areas, the ROK in the south under United States' influence and the Democratic People's Republic of Korea in the north under Soviet Russian influence. Relations between the two states, commonly referred to as South and North Korea, were hostile and frequently conflictual.

Real war began on June 25, 1950, when an artillery barrage opened from the north and more than 70,000 of its troops crossed into South Korea. Some estimates place this figure at 100,000. These forces had the backing of the People's Republic of China and the Soviet Union. Their advance was rapid as the northern forces were better armed and better trained than those of the south. The United States, under the leadership of President Harry S. Truman, immediately pledged US support to South Korea.

The United Nations (UN) became the setting for the approval and go-ahead for military support to South Korea. On the same day as the invasion began, June 25, the UN Security Council passed Resolution 82 demanding an end to the North's invasion. The North rejected this and continued advancing. On June 27, the Security Council passed Resolution 83 declaring that the North's action was a breach of the peace. This stated that members of the UN were asked to provide military help to the South and "furnish such assistance to the Republic of Korea as may be necessary to repel the armed attack and to restore international peace and security in the area," an action frequently defined as an example of collective security. Such UN resolutions were possible because at that time the Soviet Union was boycotting the Security Council and thus was not present to use its veto power.

The response from members of the UN was quick and significant. Recall that as of 1950, the UN had only 60 members, seven of which were under Russian domination or influence. Of the remaining 53 members, 16 provided military assistance,[1] and five provided medical support personnel.[2] Several other countries provided non-military support. Of the members of the UN at that time, there were only four African countries—Egypt, Ethiopia, Liberia, and South Africa. The remainder of the continent was then under colonial rule. Ethiopia and South Africa provided military forces.[3] Liberia offered supplies.

Ethiopia (formerly known as Abyssinia) is an ancient country, certainly the oldest in continuous existence in Africa and one of the world's most ancient. Ethiopians are and have long been a predominantly Christian people with a large Muslim population too. Estimates vary, but today about 65–75% are Christians, the majority of whom are Orthodox, and 34% Muslim (Pew Research Center). Ethiopia has been a Christian country since the Emperor declared the Orthodox faith as the state religion in AD 341. Ethiopia is also a complex ethnic mosaic. The Oromo are the largest group, with the Amhara second. Other groups include Somalis, Tigray, and Sidama, with several much smaller groups. Traditionally, the Amhara has been the dominant political group.

In more modern times, Ethiopia's existence as an independent state was confirmed on March 1, 1896 at the battle of Adowa when its troops under the leadership of Emperor Haile Selassie I overwhelmingly defeated an Italian invasion and attempt to colonize the country. The Italians invaded again on October 3, 1935, and this time succeeded in conquering Ethiopia. Emperor Selassie was forced in to exile in 1936, only to return in 1941 with the aid of British troops who drove the Italians out. The events surrounding this Italian conquest of Ethiopia are instrumental in understanding why, two decades later, Ethiopia, still under the leadership of Emperor Selassie, was eager to support the UN in the war between the two Koreas.

Of those countries participating, several were what we would now define as underdeveloped or Third World. Columbia, the Philippines, South Africa, Thailand, and Turkey fell into this category, but Ethiopia was the least developed of these. In a ranking by per capita income of 52 countries in 1950, Ethiopia was last, number 52, with a per capita income of $277 (NationMaster n.d.).

In 1950 Ethiopia had a population of about 18.4 million people. It was a poorly educated population: data from the 1960s indicate rural literacy rates of less than 1% for females and about 2% for males; in urban areas it was about 27% but for the country as a whole 6.1% (Inquai 1969: 58). Modern health care was inadequate and in many places unavailable; for example, the estimated infant death rate in 1950 was 205.22 deaths per 1000 live births (Knoema n.d.). It was an agrarian society, with the vast majority of its people dependent upon agriculture and there was little industrial development in this largely subsistence economy. Coffee represented slightly more than 46 % of exports; the United States was its major purchaser. Oil seeds, pulses, and hides and skins were other major exports. Why would Ethiopia, a proud but rather poor and not powerful country, take up this challenge?

Ethiopia was a founding member of the League of Nations, set up on January 10, 1920 after the end of World War I to provide, among many other things, the prevention of war by means of collective security, dispute settlement, and disarmament. Sadly, as we now know, the League failed in its primary mission and that failure was first made obvious by the history of Italy's 1936 invasion of Ethiopia. As noted, an earlier invasion by Italy in 1895 had been soundly defeated, but in 1936, a more modern Italian army attacked. In spite of numerous appeals by Emperor Selassie for the implementation of collective security, the League failed to take serious action. Salt in the wound was the proposed Hoare–Laval Pact between Britain and France which would have partitioned Abyssinia (the Ethiopian Empire) and made it an Italian colony. Though never signed, news of this total betrayal of the League's collective security concept was shocking to many. Condemnations against the invasion were made, some economic sanctions were imposed (but petroleum products, so critical to warfare, were exempted), but no country was willing to take the necessary military action, the promised and reliable threat of which is the basic foundation of collective security.

Italy invaded with 400,000 troops, used mustard gas and other items of chemical warfare, and poisoned water supplies while the world stood by, watching and acquiescing. Thus, the people of Ethiopia and their Emperor learned the hard way that collective security only works when the peaceful nations are willing to go to war in order to maintain the peace. The threat is either real and perhaps it will work, or unreal and thus clearly it will fail. In 1936 it had indubitably failed.

When North Korea invaded the south on June 25, 1950 and the UN called for action, the memory of the failure of the League of Nations was still raw in the minds of Ethiopia's leaders. As a firm believer in the content of the UN Charter, Emperor Haile Selassie was quick to respond, sending $100,000 in medical supplies immediately and beginning preparations to send troops to aid the UN forces in Korea. As the first of those troops were about to depart, the Emperor spoke of the failure of the League of Nations and of Ethiopia's faithfulness to the responsibilities involved in collective security:

> You are departing on a long crusade in defense of that very principle for which we have so long fought ... Precisely fifteen years ago this very month, your Emperor and Commander-in-Chief, addressed from the battlefield a pressing appeal to the League of Nations for the respect and application of the principle of collective security ... But in the same month, fifteen years ago today, the Council of the League of Nations finally and formally declared its inability to meet these essential requirements of collective security ... We are being faithful today, to ourselves and to our obligations [by unhesitatingly responding to the appeal for collective assistance launched by the UN following the aggression in Korea] which we conceive to be the most high and solemn duty, not alone of the present hour, but of the present century. (Scordiles 1954: 4)

More bluntly, he went on: "Isn't it right that a small country which did everything to defend itself take collective security as the last resort for survival? A collective security system must be responsive and absolute. Any small country with companionship, any democratic country, or any person must be protected by the collective security of the UN" (Won 2012: 56). Now for the first time, an action within the definition of 'collective security' was to be undertaken, and Ethiopia was to be a part of that undertaking!

An additional factor may have been the relationship between the United States and Ethiopia at that time. The United States had assisted Ethiopia during World War II and a positive relationship was maintained after that war. The United States was the main buyer of Ethiopia's coffee exports and both shared a growing abhorrence of communism. During the Korean War, the United States provided most of the funding, equipment, and much of the training for the Ethiopian forces, and those forces were attached to the US 7th Army in the field. The relationship between the two states was thus strengthened and would after the war lead to US support for significant aims of Ethiopian foreign policy, particularly in respect of its competition with Somalia, which developed a Soviet Russia relationship, and Ethiopia's desire to maintain control of the territory of Eritrea (Marcus 1983).

Forces and Actions in the War[4]

All the Ethiopian soldiers who came to Korea were volunteers; all were drawn from the Emperor's personal guards. It is also reported that all were six feet tall or taller. The battalions were named the Kagnew Battalions, variously translated as "to bring order out of chaos" or "to overthrow" (Scordiles 1954: ix). A second explanation for the selection of this name is that it was the same as that of a famous warhorse used by the Emperor's father in the First Italo-Ethiopian War. Officially in the US military documents, this unit was known as the Ethiopian Expeditionary Force–Korea.

Under the command of Brigadier General Mulugetta Bulli, a plan and then an operational unit was established. After receiving several months' training in modern weapons and warfare, the first battalion departed from Djibouti on April 16, 1951 on a United States troop ship, the USNS *General J. H. McRae*, and arrived in Pusan (now Busan) harbor on May 7, 1951. After further training, these troops went into combat at the end of July under the command of Lt. Colonel Teshome Irgetu. They were replaced by a second contingent of Ethiopian soldiers in June 1952 under the command of Lt. Colonel Asfew Andargue. This battalion was in turn replaced on April 16, 1953 after its arrival in Pusan on another US troop ship, the USS *General R. M. Blatchford*. Lt. Colonel Wolde Yohannis Shitta commanded this third Kagnew Battalion. Each battalion contained between 1110 and 1200 men (Won 2012: 63). In total, slightly more than 6000 Ethiopian soldiers, nurses, and support personnel were deployed to Korea.

During the period of combat, a small detachment of nurses was sent to Korea and Japan (where the best hospitals were located) by the Ethiopian Red Cross to tend to the wounded; language problems made it difficult for medical personnel of other nations to treat Ethiopian wounded (Omer 2015).

That the Ethiopians fought well was acknowledged by many observers and supervising officers. Numerous citations and medals were awarded by the US and Korean authorities. The Ethiopian government awarded two medals, the Korean government awarded seven, and the US government awarded 21 medals to individuals in recognition of bravery, and the Korean and US authorities issued one unit citation each (Korean War Medals n.d.). An example of this bravery is the story of Lt. Mamo Habtewold, who in May 1953 led a small detachment on patrol. A force of Chinese troops much larger (estimated ratio of 20:1) than the Ethiopian unit attacked. Every Ethiopian and one US soldier attached was wounded or killed, but the Chinese were driven off. Habtewold was wounded several times but persisted, encouraging his troops; he led them well. He received medals from the US and Ethiopian governments (BBC World Service 2012).

Another example, among many, is the story of Private Gifar. On August 15, 1951 a small patrol of Ethiopian soldiers under the command of 2nd Lt. Begresus came under heavy enemy fire. An Ethiopian soldier, Private Figar, was killed and his comrade, Private Gifar, raced 50 meters through enemy fire to protect the dead man's body and evacuate him to a safe place. Gifar received the Bronze Star medal for his bravery (Won 2012: 68–69).

A total of 238 (some reports indicate 253) battles or 'actions' were fought by the Ethiopians and, additionally, numerous patrols and smaller missions were undertaken. The most well known of the major battles are Pork Chop Hill during the spring and summer of 1953 (Marshall 1953);[5] Triangle Hill from October 14 until November 25, 1952; Heartbreak Ridge during September and October, 1951;[6] Mt. Jeoggeun (for which a permanent memorial was constructed on the site); Hill 602; the Punchbowl (August 31 to September 21, 1951); and Yoke-Uncle Hill. There were 121 combat deaths and 536 Ethiopian soldiers were wounded (Scordiles 1954: viii).[7] Indicative of the valor of the Ethiopian soldiers, not one was ever taken prisoner and no dead were left behind during combat. Several reports suggest that never seeing a dead Ethiopian soldier and never managing to take one prisoner was quite mystifying to the Chinese and North Korean soldiers, leading to rumors that the Ethiopians were superhuman.

Although to this day the war has not formally ended, an armistice was signed on July 27, 1953, and fighting stopped. The third battalion returned to Ethiopia soon after, in April 1954. A small detachment remained to help monitor the armistice agreement. These troops were regularly rotated back to Ethiopia, with the last detachment leaving in March 1956. On January 3, 1965, the last Ethiopian soldier deployed to the armistice monitoring team departed. Upon their return, the members of the Kagnew Battalion were welcomed and honored by their government and the people of Ethiopia. But years later in 1974, when the communists under Mengistu Haile Mariam overthrew the Emperor and his government, the veterans were seen as pro-capitalist and were badly treated by communist supporters. According to one source:

As part of its aid package, North Korea demanded Mengistu officially disavow the Kagnew battalion, which he did. The Kagnew veterans were stripped of all military decorations and had their pensions revoked. Many were harassed by Mengistu's secret police, and some fled abroad. The Kagnew veteran's association was banned, and monuments to the battalion were destroyed. In Ethiopian school textbooks, the nation's participation in the Korean War was erased from history. (WordPress 2016; allaboutETHIO n.d.)

Once the last Ethiopian soldier was gone, did the relationship between the wartime allies, the ROK and Ethiopia, today known as the Federal Democratic Republic of Ethiopia, prosper or wither? In what ways has this relationship altered over time? As the ROK has moved from being a poor, underdeveloped country to being one of the world's wealthiest and most modern economies, has that bond formed of blood in wartime dissolved or become stronger?

Korea's Engagement with Ethiopia Since 1991

The second part of this chapter examines the Korean government's current approach to Ethiopia. Ethiopian troops' participation in the Korean War was a laborious and uncommon effort to be made by an African country. That endeavor to fight with South Korea in the past has been brought to light after the Cold War, and started to yield favorable diplomatic outcomes in the relationship with South Korea. Two former Korean presidents visited Addis Ababa, one in 2011 and the other in 2016, while promising to provide substantial support for Ethiopia's economic development and growth. In recognition of Ethiopian soldiers' contribution to the Korean War, the Korean government in 1996 decided to grant these veterans pensions for the rest of their lives (in essence, restoring the Ethiopian government pensions removed by the communist government during the period of the Derg) and, in 2007, built a memorial hall/museum for the Kagnew Battalions in Chuncheon city, which was the heart of their military operation. We explore such Korean government moves to shape strong friendship ties with Ethiopia in three ways: (1) exchanges of leading officials; (2) Korea's ODA to Ethiopia; and (3) commemoration and rewards for Korean War veterans and their descendants. Korea's engagement with Ethiopia, however, is not limited to the three aforementioned types of governmental activities and events—there are also trade relations, intercultural exchange, international broadcasting, and private-sector investment that contribute to shaping Korea–Ethiopia relations. We introduce some of these public–private collaborative works when relevant in order to understand their mutual effect on the construction of the two countries' relations. Overall, the aim of this section is to trace the patterns of the Korean government's policies and actions in improving the bilateral relationship with Ethiopia and to offer speculative discussion of Korea's diplomatic strategy for Ethiopia as part of its general approach to Africa.

Exchanges of Governmental Officials

As with any relationship between two states, meetings between officials of the two governments often imply some sort of attempt to establish or reinforce a partnership between the two countries to render security, stability, and development within their territories and in their neighboring countries. Especially, the types of offices held by and the rank of the personnel on a given tour show the importance and intent of the visit. With regard to Korea–Ethiopia relations, their bilateral interactions became more significant after Mengistu Haile Mariam's communist regime collapsed in 1991—as we see from the more frequent contacts between the two countries' public figures.

Figure 5.1 shows a timeline of Ethiopian and Korean officials' visits to each other's countries, distinguishing between ministries and levels of government by different types of marker. To explain the visits from the bottom of the plot, a hollow circle represents a trip made by a head of the state or by an official from the office of the president or prime minister. A solid square indicates that, in a specified year, a minister or a deputy minister of Foreign Affairs and Trade had a meeting in their counterpart's country. A solid diamond shows a visit made by a member of congress or a congress leader. Next, a solid circle includes a visit by either an interior (deputy) minister or a province-level government leader. A cross sign means the presence of a defense (deputy) minister; a solid triangle represents a visit by a minister or deputy minister responsible for finance or investment; a hollow triangle is for a highest-ranking official's visit representing the ministries related to matters of energy, water, or environment; and hollow squares indicate trips made by leading officials in charge of development-related ministries such as industry, construction, technology, transport, communication, and health.

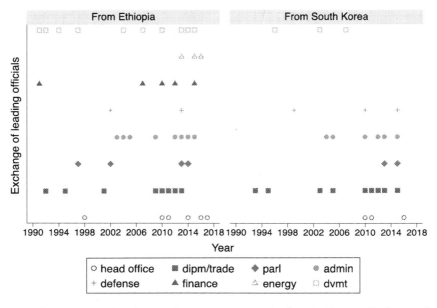

Fig. 5.1 Personnel exchanges between Korea and Ethiopia (Source: Embassy of the Republic of Korea in the Federal Democratic Republic of Ethiopia; Embassy of Ethiopia in Seoul, the Republic of Korea; and Won (2012))

As shown in Fig. 5.1, beginning anew in 1991 after the Cold War, the exchange of leading officials has proliferated over time. Some of the early visits by Ethiopian officials were made even before the new Transitional Government of Ethiopia (TGE) was inaugurated in July 1991: in the same year, Minister of Public Health Gizaw and Head of the Joint Investment Office Gubaie visited Seoul in February and April, respectively. Again, in October 1991, a few months after the TGE was launched, Minister of Construction Aagaw was sent to Seoul as a presidential envoy. Two more officials—Minister of Industry Bekele and Minister of Foreign Affairs Seyoum Mesfin—visited South Korea shortly after. It was thus Ethiopians who made visits to Korea before a Korean delegation made its first trip to Ethiopia in June 1993 after the end of the Cold War. Here, it appears that it was the Ethiopian government that first contacted South Korea to open a new phase of the relationship, while Ethiopia was perhaps in search of new friends and allies that could give the fledgling regime political and economic assistance. As a result of the Ethiopian officials' visits, the

Economic and Technology Cooperation Agreement was made in 1992 to promote trade, investment, and other areas of economic cooperation, and Desta Erifo was appointed as the first Ethiopian ambassador who would be stationed in Korea in 1992. In return, a 1993 visit by Korean officials was made by a civil-government delegation group led by Ambassador Bong-kyu Kim in pursuit of economic cooperation. Two years later, in June 1995, a local office of the Korea International Cooperation Agency (KOICA) was established in Addis Ababa, the first such office in sub-Saharan Africa (See Appendix 1 for details about personnel exchanges).[8]

We also can note several other interesting patterns in Fig. 5.1. First and foremost, Korea's official visits to Ethiopia seem to have focused on long-term diplomatic objectives rather than at obtaining direct economic benefits. By looking at the types of offices responsible for the trips to Ethiopia, we recognize that they are mostly the presidential office, the Ministry of Foreign Affairs and Trade, KOICA, the Korean Veterans' Association, and local government such as Chuncheon city mayor's office, all of which tried to strengthen diplomatic ties with Ethiopia by, with every visit, emphasizing and rewarding the efforts of the Korean War veterans from Ethiopia in many different ways rather than just blatantly asking for permits for minerals and energy development. Although there have been Korean attempts to enhance interstate trade relations, with economic and trade delegations sent to Ethiopia, the outcome is as yet immaterial—only 1.4% of Korea's total exports go to Ethiopia and Ethiopian products consist of only 1% of Korea's total imports as of 2016 (KITA 2017). With respect to South Korea's engagement in sub-Saharan Africa, Darracq and Neville (2014) argue that the Korean government builds relationships with African counterparts—governments and business enterprises—in pursuit of the expansion of trade opportunities and food and energy security. Unlike their claim, though, it seems Korea is making friends based on the past wartime relationship with Ethiopia. as we see from the types of officials mostly sent to Ethiopia.[9] They may be taking a long-term approach for possible benefits that can be drawn from the African nation's great potential, but not directly from its excavated natural endowments.[10]

By contrast, Ethiopian personnel that have been sent to Korea vary in their position and duties. In addition to diplomatic posts, officials from various ministries closely connected to the national development plan (or development planning) such as energy, industry, health, and technology departments have made trips to Korea.

Personnel exchanges have become more frequent in recent years in both directions, culminating in the visits of the heads of the states. In July 2011, President Myung-bak Lee made a state visit to Ethiopia (Embassy of the Republic of Korea in the Federal Democratic Republic of Ethiopia 2010). The importance of his Ethiopian trip is not just that he is the first South Korean president to visit, but that it was a turning point in the two country's relations as a way to make the relationship more cooperative and mutually supportive. The key things on his to-do list during his three-day-visit can be summarized into three. First, Lee met with Ethiopian Korean War veterans through several events such as a veteran appreciation meeting and dedication of a wreath at the Korean War Memorial. In those meetings with the veterans, he expressed gratitude for their participation in the war and promised to give their descendants opportunities to come to Korea for technological training. Another interesting aspect of his itinerary was that the President himself joined in volunteer work to build public bathrooms and clinics and help with disinfection in slum areas near Addis Ababa as a gesture of Korea's willingness to offer development assistance and share its development experiences. Indeed, Korea has become more active in aid and development cooperation with Ethiopia after President Lee's visit, which is delineated in greater detail in the next section. Third, during the summit talks with Ethiopian Prime Minister Meles Zenawi, Korea and Ethiopia agreed to create an environment attractive to Korean and other international private businesses to invest in the areas of agriculture, electricity, renewable energy, and information technology in Ethiopia. More talks about the investment continued when Meles visited in November 2011 (Appendix 2 exhibits the Korean companies currently doing business in Ethiopia).

Meles' 2011 visit was not his first. He had been to Seoul twice before, in 1998 with 57 private-sector representatives for economic cooperation and in 2010 as a guest for the G20 summit meeting. In November 2011, Meles made appeals to the Korean government for Korean corporations' investment in Ethiopia, particularly in the textile and leather industrial sectors and for training youth in knowledge and skills for economic development. After these exchanges by the heads of state, about 200 officials and leaders from Ethiopia including Addis Ababa mayor Kuma Demeksa and the presidents of Ethiopia's 12 major universities visited Seoul in 2013. Through these consecutive personnel exchanges, both countries expressed a strong willingness to cooperate, while acknowledging each other's diplomatic value.

Former Korean President Park Geun-hye also visited Ethiopia in May 2016 and discussed construction of a textile industrial complex for Korean companies and other infrastructure programs for Korean government and corporations to participate in. While Korea showed its willingness to provide a US$500 million loan to Ethiopia between 2016 and 2018 so that Korean companies invest in Ethiopia, Ethiopia considered offering tax benefits to Korean textile companies to attract investments. Discussion of investments in the textile business has continued after the presidential visit. In December 2018, a textile and apparel investment forum was held in Addis Ababa aiming to enhance mutual understanding and advantages of investing in the industry between Ethiopia and South Korea (Allafrica 2018; Ethiopia Online 2016). As we see from Appendix 2, there are already several Korean companies engaged in the textile and garment industry in Ethiopia.

Park also announced that the government would invite 6000 students to obtain job training and tertiary education, send 4000 Korean volunteers to Ethiopia, and launch a soft loan program called Economic Development Cooperation Fund (EDCF), which set aside US$500 million for 2016–2018 (Korea.net 2016a). In addition, cultural exchanges and medical treatment services were provided during her visit, while she also paid tribute to the Korean War veterans in a meeting with surviving veterans and their family members (Korea.net 2016b). Taken together, the exchanges of leading officials between Ethiopia and Korea show their diplomatic willingness and various strategies to promote Korea–Ethiopia relations.

Korea's Official Development Assistance to Ethiopia

The primary objective of the Korean government's development assistance to Ethiopia is to help solve economic and social problems of the recipient country within the larger framework of the Sustainable Development Goals. There are two main government ministries involved in developing ODA policies and two related agencies operating such programs under the supervision of the ministries: The Ministry of Foreign Affairs and Trade and its executing agency, KOICA, is responsible for grant aid programs and the Ministry of Strategy and Finance and the EDCF are planning and implementing concessional loan policy. Moreover, some 30 more ministries, agencies, and local governments are involved in giving development aid to poverty-ridden countries.

Traditionally, Korean aid assistance had chiefly focused, in terms of geographic regions, on Asia and, in terms of its purpose, increasing economic returns and maintaining security alliances rather than on poverty reduction (Chun et al. 2010; Kim 2011). Since the early 2000s, however, the Korean government has begun to expand the international development assistance and allocate more to Africa. In line with this trend of raised Korean ODA to Africa, Korean aid to Ethiopia has grown significantly. Figure 5.2 represents the surge observed since the late 2000s.

In comparison with the other African states and other non-African recipient countries, Table 5.1 lists African states among the top 20 recipient countries to which ROK provides most ODA. Up until 2008, besides Egypt, which had been the sole African recipient showing up in the top 20 list while constantly supported by Korea, Korea's assistance to Africa had been inconsistent in terms of its recipients and the amounts (not shown in the table). But since 2008 with President Lee's ascendance, Ethiopia has become one of the top recipients of Korean ODA, and after Lee's visit to Ethiopia in 2011, it has received the most ODA from Korea among African states.

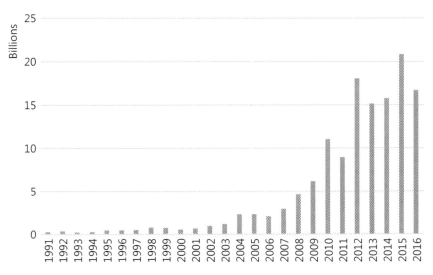

Fig. 5.2 Korea's ODA to Ethiopia since 1991 (Source: Korea International Cooperation Agency)

Table 5.1 African states in the list of top 20 recipient countries Korea provides most ODA (by within-Africa ranking; Unit: KRW)

Year	Rank 1	Rank 2	Rank 3	Rank 4	Rank 5
2016	Ethiopia (16,680,821,632)	Rwanda (12,677,154,573)	Uganda (11,726,589,055)	Tanzania (10,202,674,934)	
2015	Ethiopia (20,818,731,574)	Rwanda (15,884,853,799)	Tanzania (11,148,712,165)	Uganda (11,086,372,869)	
2014	Ethiopia (15,749,787,922)	Rwanda (14,501,614,749)	Senegal (10,377,738,166)		
2013	Ethiopia (15,141,586,540)	Rwanda (10,085,997,417)	Uganda (9,247,628,902)	Tanzania (7,990,885,758)	
2012	Ethiopia (18,038,908,191)	Tanzania (11,397,106,614)	Ghana (7,562,360,132)	Rwanda (7,151,027,009)	
2011	Tanzania (9,815,598,820)	Ethiopia (8,946,119,941)			
2010	Tanzania (11,137,912,767)	Ethiopia (11,035,560,315)	Rwanda (7,051,404,227)		
2009	Tanzania (10,211,673,768)	Egypt (7,244,192,414)	Kenya (7,018,889,446)	Senegal (6,893,715,912)	Ethiopia (6,172,619,969)
2008	Egypt (8,290,628,937)	Ethiopia (4,654,470,704)			

Source: Korea International Cooperation Agency

Interestingly, we may notice from Table 5.1 that the top African recipients of Korean ODA are mostly East African countries, including Ethiopia. While Tanzania has been a favored recipient ever since the early 1990s, recently Rwanda and Uganda are also preferred by the Korean government. At the same time, none of these nations is a major oil-producing country. Considering its choice of ODA recipients, the Korean government perhaps attempts not only to seek paths to markets but also to make friends in Africa by associating itself with the common national traits with Ethiopia such as resource-poor settings, military regime background, Korean War participation, and linguistic homogeneity.

With respect to the sectors to which development assistance is supplied, some scholars paid particular attention to Korea, which was once an ODA recipient and has gone on to become a Development Assistant Committee (DAC) member, as to which model it would adopt as a donor—the DAC model, the developing country model of Brazil, Arabic states, and China, or something else (Marx and Soares 2013; Walz and Ramachandran 2010). Figure 5.3 shows the share of Korean aid to Ethiopia by sector over the period between 1991 and 2016. To interpret the bar graph, we find some clearly distinguished patterns. A large portion of the aid was

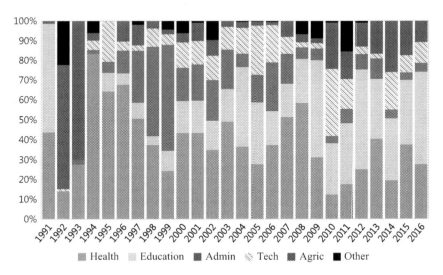

Fig. 5.3 Korea-to-Ethiopia ODA trend by sector (Source: Korea International Cooperation Agency)

funneled into the agriculture, forestry, and fishery sectors (noted as *Agric* in Fig. 5.3) in 1992 and 1993, and they have been refocused after 2010. What followed in 1994 was a rise in aid to the health sector, which has been reduced in its share after that, but maintained its significance until recently. Assistance for public administration increased in the second half of the 1990s and onwards, while the technology, environment, and energy sectors (noted as *Tech*) have been supported consistently at varying degrees. Also noticeable is an increase in the share of support for the education sector since 2000. That the ODA from Korea emphasized food and health sectors in the early 1990s, administrative assistance in the late 1990s, and education support lately shows its flexibility to meet the needs of the recipient country.

To identify whether these sectoral patterns that have emerged in Korean ODA to Ethiopia are particularistic practices or compatible with broader trends in Korea's ODA to Africa, Fig. 5.4 compares the sectoral shares of Korean ODA between Ethiopia and the other African recipients since 2008, when Ethiopia began to appear in the top 20 recipient list. The health and education sectors are presented in solid colors in contrast to the

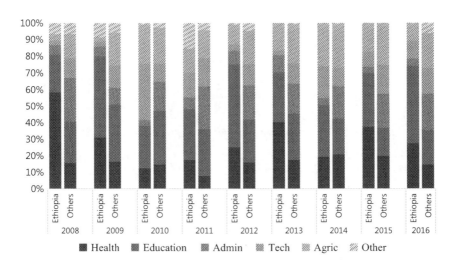

Fig. 5.4 Korea's ODA to Ethiopia versus other African countries by sector (Source: Korea International Cooperation Agency. Note: African countries categorized as "Others" vary by year, but "Others" comprise of all the African states receiving ODA from Korea in each corresponding year)

other sectors in the slashed area. Except for the year 2010, Ethiopia has received proportionally more aid resources for health and education over the past decade. In some years, such as 2008 and 2016, the share of health and education ODA for Ethiopia was almost double that for the other African countries. According to Marx and Soares (2013), Korea, in general, concentrates its ODA funds on education, health, and transport and storage across countries and regions as a way to increase the effectiveness of the assistance programs. Even considering this general trend of emphasizing such sectors, the allocation of Korean aid within Ethiopia favors the health and education sectors to a great extent.

To introduce the KOICA programs that have been implemented, there are six types of involvement aiming to help development in Ethiopia. Humanitarian aid was delivered in 1992–2009 to relieve distress caused by natural disasters such as food shortages, while small grants were granted in the forms of office supplies such as computers and printers and vehicles in 1992–2004 (See Table 5.2). In contrast to this cash- and goods-based support, the remaining four types of assistance are more robust and interactive interventions. Through the KOICA Fellowship Programs, the agency organizes seminars and workshops where attendants attend lectures on various development-related topics including promotion of industries and trade, policy management, and reforms in the fields of environment, gender, health, and education, and some vocational training. The fellowship programs have evolved to meet more diversified demands and socioeconomic realities over time. When the fellowship program began in the early 1990s, the programs mostly focused on industrial and

Table 5.2 KOICA's humanitarian aid and small grants to Ethiopia

	Humanitarian Aid (US$)	*Small Grants* (US$)
1992	1,477,150	9,517,720
1994	728,123	–
1999	–	3,512,658
2000	512,943	–
2001		3,545,252
2002	3,001,617	11,278,351
2003	–	44,615,128
2004	–	67,742,502
2008	10,878,829	–
2009	7,455,182	–

Source: Korea International Cooperation Agency

rural development, trade promotion, and economic planning. But it expanded to environmental protection, educational training and reforms, development of diplomatic partnership, and promotion of criminal justice in the late 1990s. In the 2000s and onwards, it has introduced new topics for the fellowships such as women's health and empowerment, World Trade Organization agreement implementation, election management, cybercrime investigation, intellectual property protection, and airport operation. As the fellowships provide workshops on modern technologies and effective strategies for advancing the economy, the numbers of personnel involved in the programs have increased remarkably from one person in 1991 to 624 and 596 in 2015 and 2016, respectively (KOICA Annual Reports).

The operations under project-type cooperation are carried out to deal with the issues of water and electricity supplies, health, rural development, and education. Some similar projects are also executed in collaboration with Korean NGOs, universities, hospitals, and business corporations. These KOICA projects and multilateral cooperation were both launched in 2007. The project type cooperation, in particular, has grown dramatically since 2010 regarding the number of projects and the amount of the relevant aid, as Table 5.3 shows.

Further, sending trained volunteers is an important task of development assistance. Every year, an increasing number of volunteers in the fields of science, technology, medical care, sports, and education serve to improve the quality of life in Ethiopia. Following Korea's general ODA patterns, the volunteer program has grown significantly since 2010 (See Fig. 5.5). Overall,

Table 5.3 KOICA's project type cooperation

Year	No. of projects	Amount (US$)
2007	1	1,735,475
2008	2	3,162,711
2009	1	1,582,417
2010	3	6,029,814
2011	3	2,803,197
2012	4	8,251,956
2013	7	7,843,768
2014	7	7,843,768
2015	7	9,492,107
2016	10	9,078,111

Source: Korea International Cooperation Agency

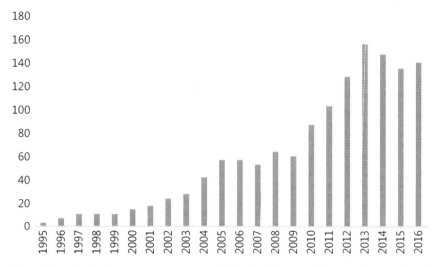

Fig. 5.5 KOICA volunteers to Ethiopia (Source: Korea International Cooperation Agency)

an enormous increase in Korea's ODA to Ethiopia is seen during the Myung-bak Lee administration and its aftermath, which coincides with frequent Ethiopia visits by leading Korean officials in the 2010s. Korea offers the most official development assistance to Ethiopia out of anywhere in Africa.

Support for Korean War Veterans

To be clear, the matter of honoring and rewarding Ethiopian Korean War veterans constitutes a substantial part of Korea's relationship with Ethiopia. As we see from the aforementioned events and activities involving the two countries, commemorating the sacrifices of the Kagnew Battalion in the Korean War always accompanies any bilateral diplomatic engagements. This section considers government efforts to work with charity organizations to help the surviving veterans and their descendants.

In 1996, the Korean War Veterans Foundation was established in Korea to support the veterans and their families and to promote their self-sustainability and welfare, and in turn to contribute to the country's overall growth. The Foundation's work is largely threefold: providing medical services, offering funding for better education, and improving housing conditions. Its projects are usually conducted in collaboration with other Korean and government agencies. Its members visit Ethiopia every year to facilitate relevant development projects and to give assistance to veterans and their families. Other groups and organizations have provided assistance, too. For example, in 2017 a group of active-duty Korean soldiers donated part of their allowances each month to an NGO, Good Neighbors, in order to assist Ethiopian veterans.

Chuncheon city, which was the hub of Ethiopian military operations during the Korean War, has had a partnership with the city of Addis Ababa since Chuncheon city mayor Jong-su Yu and Addis Ababa mayor Arkebe Oqubay exchanged visits to each other's countries in 2004. Together with Korea's Ministry of Patriots and Veterans Affairs and the Korean War Veterans Foundation, Chuncheon city founded the War Participation Monument and the Memorial Hall in Addis Ababa in 2006. Also established in 2007 in Chuncheon city, the Ethiopian War Participation Memorial Hall plays a role in improving people's understanding of the history of Ethiopians' war participation and about Ethiopia in general. The first floor of the hall is used as a museum about the veterans, and on the second floor, works of Ethiopian art and culture are displayed. Chuncheon city has also donated used computers, fire engines, and ambulances to Addis Ababa.

The Scholarship Program for Descendants of UN Korean War Veterans was established by the Ministry of Patriots and Veterans Affairs in 2010 on the 60th anniversary of the Korean War. In the first year of the program, the fund was collected through many different people's and organizations' donations. Then, in 2012, an international NGO, World Together, which has its office in Addis Ababa, took over responsibility for allocating funds for the veterans' descendants, especially those who are attending elementary or middle school. So far, there have been 6236 beneficiaries of the scholarship program, each of whom has received 30,000 won (about 440 Birr) every other month (Won 2012).

KOICA runs programs to assist the veterans as well. In 2011, the agency provided mobile medical service to the veterans and their families while training Ethiopian doctors and nurses. In addition, an education project that started in 2012 supports their offspring's vocational capacity building with a budget of US$9 million for a six-year period. Expanding this education project, KOICA, in collaboration with LG, one of Korea's largest conglomerates, organizes a scholarship program for veterans' descendants, whereby education fees and living expenses are offered for three years. This program, currently sponsoring approximately 100 pupils, is targeted to students preparing for high school entrance (2017 KOICA Annual Reports).

Conclusion

The relationship between Korea and Ethiopia, which commenced a little earlier than the other Korea–Africa relations, started with Ethiopians' Korean War participation from 1950. Ethiopia under the leadership of Emperor Selassie was eager to support the UN in the war between the two Koreas because it believed that an international institution must collectively take action to protect small and weak countries from any attack on their sovereignty. Ethiopia's excruciating memory of the League of Nations' failure to prevent the Italian conquest made it quick to respond, sending troops and medical supplies to aid the UN forces in South Korea. Despite their honorable service, the Ethiopian Korean War veterans were badly treated by the communist government under Mengistu Haile Mariam in the Cold War era. The Kagnew veterans' association was banned and monuments to the battalion were destroyed. At that time North Korea was Ethiopia's close ally, giving the country aid and urging it to renounce the Kagnew veterans. Here, changes in the norms and power relations in international politics seem to have considerably affected Ethiopia–Korea relations.

After the collapse of the Soviet Union, the capitalist globalized era provided a great opportunity to bring about changes in ways to make friends and foes between states. From the 1990s, many countries realized the importance of cooperation and integrity for national economic development and governance capacity building. In this chapter, we have investigated the Korean government's efforts to (re)engage itself with an old ally in a new context. Since the Myung-bak Lee administration starting in 2008, Korea has significantly increased its ODA to Ethiopia which became the biggest recipient of Korean aid among African states from 2012 onwards. The delivery of aid also has become more highly diversified and better institutionalized to meet the needs of the recipient country. Ethiopia is not a mineral-rich land; Ethiopia–Korea trade is not intense. In that case, why has Korea increased Africa's portion of its ODA, with a special focus on Ethiopia? We are mindful of such factors as investment potentials in Ethiopia, other countries' influence, and geopolitical benefits that may affect Korea's diplomatic strategy in Ethiopia. Nevertheless, examining the dialogues, attitudes, and actions Korea has taken to engage with Ethiopia, we find that the fact that Ethiopia dispatched its troops to fight for South Korea as part of the UN mission is a major influence on the Korean government's calibration of its foreign policy positively toward

Ethiopia. The Korean government has established institutions and policies to commemorate and reward the Ethiopian veterans and works with charity organizations to help surviving veterans and their descendants. The two former Korean presidents' visits to Ethiopia always involved meetings with Ethiopian Korean War veterans and dedication of a wreath at the Korean War Memorial. In conclusion, in a world where each state makes freer choices, less constrained by the international power structure than during the Cold War, Korea chooses Ethiopia as a partner for cooperation in Africa. The past relationship in the hard times sowed the seeds of stronger ties between the two countries in preparing for an uncertain future.

APPENDIX 1: TIMELINE OF OFFICIAL VISITS

Yr. Mo.	From Ethiopia	Yr. Mo.	From Korea
1991. 2	Gizaw, Minister of Public Health	1993. 6	Civil-government delegation for economic cooperation
1991. 4	Gubaie, Executive of the Joint Investment Office	1995. 5	Si-young Lee, Deputy Minister of Foreign Affairs
1991. 10	Aagaw, Presidential envoy, Minister of Construction	1996. 1	Joon-yun Jung, President of KOICA
1992. 4	Bekele, Minister of Industry	1999. 7	Tae-wan Jang, President of Korean Veterans' Association
1992. 11	Seyoum Mesfin, Minister of Foreign Affairs	2003. 5	Woong-kyu Cho and two others, members of the reunification, trade, and diplomacy committee in congress
1994. 11	Duri Mohammed, Minister of Development and Economic Planning	2003. 7	Hyo-seung Ahn, Special envoy of Foreign Affairs
1995. 11	Tamrat Layne, Deputy prime minister	2003. 12	Suk-hyun Kim, President of KOICA
1997. 4	Ethiopian People's Revolutionary Democratic Front (EPRDF) members	2004. 5	Jong-su Yu, Chuncheon city mayor
1997. 10	Haile Assegedie, Minister of Construction	2005. 5	Jin-kook Kim, Chuncheon city deputy mayor
1998. 10	Meles Zenawi, Prime Minister	2005. 6	Tae-sik Lee, Deputy Minister of Foreign Affairs
2001. 6	Fantaye Biftu, Executive of Export Promotion Office	2007. 1	Jang-bum Shin, President of KOICA
2002. 5	Dr. Workneh Gebeyehu, Executive of the Federal Police Agency	2010. 2	Yong-jun Lee, Assistant Secretary of Foreign Affairs

(continued)

(continued)

Yr. Mo.	From Ethiopia	Yr. Mo.	From Korea
2002. 7	Vice chair of lower chamber	2010. 6	Young-jun Park, Deputy Minister of State Affairs
2003. 5	Enwoy Gerbremedhin, Chair of Anti-corruption committee	2010. 6	Representatives of Foreign Affairs
2004. 5	Haile Assegide, Deputy Minister of Infrastructure	2010. 6	Presidential administrative officials
2004. 6	Arkebe Oqubay, Addis Ababa mayor	2010. 10	Presidential administrative officials
2005. 5	Abai Tekle, Chair of Ombudsman committee	2010. 12	Yang Kim, Minister of Patriots and Veterans Affairs
2007. 5	Dr. Kasu Yilala, Minister of Development and Economic Planning	2011. 7	Myung-bak Lee, President
2007. 6	Representatives of Finance Ministry	2011. 4	Sung-hwan Kim, Minister of Foreign Affairs
2009. 6	Kuma Demeksa, Addis Ababa mayor	2012. 3	Kwan-yong Kim, Governor of Gyeongbuk province
2010. 4	Tekeda, Deputy Minister of Foreign Affairs	2012. 9	Sung-hwan Kim, Minister of Foreign Affairs
2010. 6	Assefa Kessito, Presidential aide	2013. 1	Sung-hwan Kim, Minister of Foreign Affairs
2010. 9	Sufian Ahmed, Minister of Finance	2013. 1	Byung-suk Park, Deputy chair of parliament
2010. 9	Juneydi Saddo, Minister of Science and Technology	2013. 7	Chang-hee Kang, Chair of parliament
2011. 6	Yaekob Yala, Minister of Trade	2013. 9	Kwan-yong Kim, Governor of Gyeongbuk province
2011. 11	Meles Zenawi, Prime Minister	2013. 12	MPs
2012. 6	Abay Woldu, Governor of Tigray state	2015. 2	Woo-yeo Hwang, Deputy Prime Minister
2012. 10	Ambassador Berhane Gebrekristos, Deputy Minister of Foreign Affairs	2015. 3	Jong-sub Chung, Minister of Government Administration and Home
2012. 10	Sufian Ahmed, Minister of Finance	2015. 3	Nak-hoe Kim, Chair of Customs Service
2013. 6	Dr. Tedros Adhanom, Minister of Foreign Affairs	2015. 7	Byung-se Yoon, Minister of Foreign Affairs
2013. 6	Abadula Gemeda, Leader of lower chamber	2015. 12	Seung-chun Park, Minister of Patriots and Veterans Affairs
2013. 7	Muktar Kedir, Minister of Government Administration	2016. 5	Park Geun-hye, President

(*continued*)

(continued)

Yr. Mo.	From Ethiopia	Yr. Mo.	From Korea
2013. 7	Siraj Fegessa, Minister of Defense		
2013. 10	Alemayehu Tegenu, Minister of Water Energy		
2013. 11	Demitu Hambisa, Minister of Science and Technology		
2014. 2	Abadula Gemeda, Leader of the lower chamber		
2014. 4	Dr. Mulatu Teshome, President		
2014. 6	Gedu Andargachew, Governor of Amhara state		
2014. 7, 10	Muktar Kedir, Governor of Oromia state		
2014. 10	Abay Woldu, Governor of Tigray state		
2014. 10	Dr. Debretsion Gebremichael, Minister of Information and Communication		
2014. 12	Demeke Mekonen, Deputy Prime Minister		
2015. 1	Dessie Dalke, Governor of Southern Nations Nationalities and People (SNNPR) state		
2015. 2	Ahmed Abetew, Minister of Industry		
2015. 2	Demitu Hambisa, Minister of Science and Technology		
2015. 6	Mekuria Haile, Minister of City Planning and Development		
2015. 10	Dr. Debretsion Gebremichael, Minister of Information and Communication		
2015. 10	Dr. Workneh Gebeyehu, Minister of Transportation		
2015. 11	Mekuria Haile, Minister of City Planning and Development		
2015. 11	Abdulaziz Mohammed, Deputy Minister of Finance		

(*continued*)

(continued)

Yr. Mo.	From Ethiopia	Yr. Mo.	From Korea
2016. 3	Dr. Shiferaw Teklemariam, Deputy Minister of Forestry and Climate Change		
2016. 5	Dr. Arkebe Equbay, Prime Minister Aide		
2017. 2	Bereket Simon, Prime Minister Aide		

Source: Embassy of the Republic of Korea in the Federal Democratic Republic of Ethiopia; Embassy of Ethiopia in Seoul, the Republic of Korea; and Won (2012)

APPENDIX 2: KOREAN COMPANIES IN ETHIOPIA (2018–2019)

No.	Company name	Sector	Details
1	Samsung Electronics East Africa, Co., Ltd.	Manufacturing	Electronics
2	Wooam Co., Ltd	Construction	–
3	BM Ethiopia Garment & Textile S.C.	Manufacturing	Textile and apparel
4	LG Electronics Co., Ltd	Service	Science and technology
5	Keangnam Enterprises, Ltd.	Construction	–
6	Daewoo Engineering & Construction Co., Ltd.	Construction	–
7	Dohwa Engineering Co., Ltd	Service	Business support
8	Myungsung Medical Center Addis Ababa, Ethiopia	Service	Health and welfare
9	Byucksan Power Co., Ltd	Construction	–
10	Shints ETP Garments PLC.	Manufacturing	Textile and apparel
11	Access Bio Ethiopia, Inc.	Manufacturing	Chemicals and medicine
12	E-Kos Co., Ltd.	Manufacturing	Metals
13	Hyosung Heavy Industries Corporation	Construction	–
14	Kunhwa engineering & consulting	Service	Business support
15	EJIAN Logistics PLC	Service	Logistics
16	PUNGKOOK ETHIOPIA BAG MANUFACTURING, PLC.	Manufacturing	Textile and apparel

Source: Korea Trade-Investment Promotion Agency (KOTRA)

NOTES

1. The countries that provided military assistance are Australia, Belgium, Canada, Ethiopia, France, Greece, Luxembourg, Netherlands, New Zealand, Philippines, South Africa, Thailand, United Kingdom, and the United States (Won 2012: 187–188).
2. Denmark, India, Italy, Norway, and Sweden provided medical support personnel (Ibid.: 188).
3. South Africa provided a fighter-bomber squadron with a total of 826 personnel over the period of engagement (Ibid.: 188).
4. For thorough discussion of the roll of the Ethiopians in the Korean War, see Won (2012), Marshall (1953), and Scordiles (1954).
5. This was made into a Hollywood film in 1959 titled, *Pork Chop Hill*, starring Gregory Peck.
6. A Hollywood film, *Heartbreak Ridge*, starring Clint Eastwood was produced in 1986.
7. The names of the decreased are listed in Won (2012: 193–198).
8. KOICA is a governmental organization, which undertakes Korea's development aid (or Official Development Assistance [ODA]) programs for developing countries. Its main mission is to develop and implement strategies to effectively facilitate the development programs and thus maintain and strengthen diplomatic relations with the partner countries.
9. The subsequent sections provide more evidence of this argument that Korean government's engagement with Ethiopia tends to be geared toward strengthening its diplomatic ties with Ethiopia.
10. Ethiopia has small reserves of minerals including gold and copper, but its uncultivated arable land and water resources are great potential for farming and energy production.

REFERENCES

allaboutETHIO. (n.d.) Ethiopia in the Korean War. Retrieved November 15, 2018, from https://allaboutethio.com/hwkorea.html.

Allafrica. (2018, December 7). Ethio-South Korea Textile, Apparel Investment Forum Held in Addis. Retrieved January 14, 2019, from https://allafrica.com/stories/201812070492.html.

BBC World Service. (2012, September 25). An Ethiopian Hero of the Korean War, Written by Alex Last. Retrieved November 8, 2018, from https://www.bbc.com/news/magazine-19639459.

Chun, H., Munyi, E. N., & Lee, H. (2010). South Korea as an Emerging Donor: Challenges and Changes on Its Entering OECD/DAC. *Journal of International Development, 22*(6), 788–802.

Embassy of the Republic of Korea in the Federal Democratic Republic of Ethiopia. (2010, November 1). President Lee Myung-bak Made a State Visit to Ethiopia. Retrieved January 14, 2019, from http://overseas.mofa.go.kr/et-en/brd/m_10269/view.do?seq=668637&srchFr=&srchTo=&srchWord=&srchTp=&multi_itm_seq=0&itm_seq_1=0&itm_seq_2=0&company_cd=&company_nm=&page=6.

Ethiopia Online. (2016, May 28). Ethiopia to Create Textile Industrial Complex for South Korean Companies. Retrieved January 14, 2019, from http://onlineethiopia.net/2016/05/ethiopia-create-textile-industrial-complex-south-korean-companies/.

Inquai, S. (1969). Adult Literacy in Ethiopia-A Profile. *Journal of Ethiopian Studies, 7*(1), 55–63.

Kim, S. (2011). Bridging Troubled Worlds? An Analysis of the Ethical Case for South Korea Aid. *Journal of International Development, 23*(6), 802–822.

Knoema. (n.d.). Ethiopia-Infant Mortality Rate. Retrieved November 5, 2018, from https://knoema.com/atlas/Ethiopia/topics/Demographics/Mortality/Infant-mortality-rate.

Korea International Trade Association. (2017). http://www.kita.org/kStat/byCount_SpeCount.do.

Korea International Cooperation Agency. Annual Statistical Reports (for various years). https://www.koica.go.kr/koica_en/3497/subview.do.

Korea.net. (2016a, May 27). Korea, Ethiopia to Expand Cooperation on Economy, Development. Retrieved January 14, 2019, from http://www.korea.net/NewsFocus/policies/view?articleId=136690.

Korea.net. (2016b, May 29). Korea Will Forever Remember Sacrifices Made by Ethiopian Veterans. Retrieved January 14, 2019, from http://www.korea.net/NewsFocus/policies/view?articleId=136795.

Korean War Medals. (n.d.). Ethiopia. Retrieved November 12, 2018, from http://www.korean-war-medals.com/ethiopa/medal_1.shtml.

Marcus, H. G. (1983). *Ethiopia, Great Britain, and the United States, 1941–74: The Politics of Empire*. Berkeley, CA: University of California Press.

Marshall, S. L. A. (1953). *Pork Chop Hill: The American Fighting Man in Action, Korea*. New York: Morrow.

Marx, A., & Soares, J. (2013). South Korea's Transition from Recipient to DAC Donor: Assessing Korea's Development Cooperation Policy. *International Development Policy|Revue internationale de politique de développement, 4*(4.2), 107–142.

NationMaster. (n.d.). Economy > GDP Per Capita in 1950: Countries Compared. Retrieved November 11, 2018, from http://www.nationmaster.com/country-info/stats/Economy/GDP-per-capita-in-1950.

Omer, A. H. (2015). Profile of Aster Ayyana and Berqnäsh Käbbädä: Two Pioneer Nurses in the Third Kagnew During the Korean Peace Keeping Mission

(1953–1954). *Annales d'Ethiopie*. Retrieved November 16, 2018, from https://www.persee.fr/doc/ethio_0066-2127_2015_num_30_1_1593.
Pew Research Center. Global Religious Futures Project. http://www.globalreligiousfutures.org/countries/ethiopia#/?affiliations_religion_id=0&affiliations_year=2010&ion_name=All%20Countries&restrictions_year=2016.
Scordiles, K. (1954). *Kagnew: The Story of the Ethiopian Fighters in Korea*. Tokyo: Radiopress.
Walz, J., & Ramachandran, V. (2010). *Brave New World: A Literature Review of Emerging Donors and the Changing Nature of Foreign Assistance*. Working Paper 273.
Won, T. J. (2012). *The Eternal Partnership: Ethiopia and Korea*. Seoul: Republic of Korea. Ministry of Patriots and Veterans Affairs.
WordPress. (2016, August 18). Ethiopians in the Korean War: WWII Gear Used. Retrieved November 15, 2018, from https://wwiiafterwwii.wordpress.com/2016/08/18ethiopians-in-the-korean-war-gear-used/.

CHAPTER 6

Dynamics of Korea-Africa Cultural Engagements

Suweon Kim

INTRODUCTION

In an era marked by 'Looking East' in Africa, understanding Asia's engagement with Africa has become increasingly critical. The increasing engagement is witnessed on all fronts: military, foreign policy, trade, investment, development cooperation, migration, tourism, and regional organizations. Less studied is cultural engagement, which can be understood in the context of 'soft power'. Soft power is the ability to attract people to our side (Nye 2008). Soft power brings about voluntary actions and, therefore, its impact lasts longer and spills over more broadly. In an era of global consumption and migration, soft power produces a favorable image and reputation and has become more significant than hard power—using military and economic superiority (Gilboa 2008).

Although there is a growing body of literature on cultural engagement between Asia and Africa, the regional focus has been limited to China's engagement in Africa (Zhang et al. 2016). Based on China's cultural engagement in Benin, Gilbert suggests that cultural engagement is viewed

S. Kim (✉)
University of the Western Cape, Cape Town, South Africa

© The Author(s) 2020
Y. Chang (ed.), *South Korea's Engagement with Africa*, Africa's Global Engagement: Perspectives from Emerging Countries, https://doi.org/10.1007/978-981-32-9013-6_6

as the most positive dimension of China-Africa relations (Gilbert 2017). Even though Korea's cultural engagement in Africa has been overlooked and captured under the broad brushstroke of 'Asia', the pattern of Korea's cultural engagement is distinctive from that of other Asian countries, China in particular. The Chinese understanding of soft power includes the coercive use of economic power, with China using its growing economic prowess to win the hearts and minds of Africans (Kurlantzick 2007). In regard to target audience, China tends to focus on the African elites and policymakers. Korea, on the other hand, sticks to the conventional sources of soft power: culture, political value, and legitimacy of foreign policy. In the Korea-Africa context, Korea, an aspiring middle power, relies mostly on culture due to the geopolitical constraints in the Korean peninsula. This chapter discusses the patterns of growing cultural engagement between Korea and African states. It examines the reception of Korean pop culture in Africa and Korea's development projects in the cultural sector, and highlights the Korean government's understanding of cultural engagement as public diplomacy.

The chapter has three main parts. The first part provides a theoretical framework by explaining the concept of soft power and public diplomacy in more detail. The second part discusses a history of Korea's cultural engagement with Africa. Rather than simply revisiting the events in chronological order, this part aims to explain the political economy of Korea's cultural engagement with Africa in the particular context of the geopolitical rivalry between North and South Korea over the states of Africa. The third and main part explores the current state of cultural engagement. The state-led cultural engagement, which remains the main form of cultural engagement between Korea and Africa, has achieved a degree of success but has also made a number of significant errors. The chapter concludes with thoughts on Korea's cultural engagement in the African context in light of the changing dynamics of global soft power and enduring global imbalance.

Soft Power

Soft power is the ability to attract people to our side (Nye 2008). In an era marked by global connectedness (both physically and virtually), great soft power has become increasingly pivotal to the prosperity and security of states (Melissen 2013). To build greater soft power, governments resort to public diplomacy, which refers to 'an instrument used by states, associations of states, and some sub-state and non-state actors to understand cultures, attitudes, and behavior; build and manage relationships; and influence thoughts and mobilize actions to advance their interests and values' (Gregory 2011: 353). Public diplomacy has long been a means of promoting soft power, although the term itself is relatively new in a long history of foreign policy and diplomacy. The term public diplomacy was coined in 1965 and began to garner academic attention in the early 1990s. Today in diplomatic studies, no other type of diplomacy attracts more academic attention than public diplomacy (Melissen 2013: 192–194). A goal of public diplomacy is to engender a favorable image and reputation in audiences abroad. To achieve this goal, instead of relying on force or incentives, a state uses various public instruments.

In traditional public diplomacy, sending messages to a foreign public, rather than to a small diplomatic elite, took a substantial budget, which was affordable only to a limited number of wealthy countries in Europe and America. Most conventional, traditional public diplomacy took the form of sending informative messages in local languages through mass media; for instance, the *BBC* in Arabic and the *Voice of America* in Spanish. Wealthy countries also opened cultural institutions in foreign countries such as the Alliance Française and the Goethe Institute worldwide. Still, the US is the hegemonic soft power in terms of the volume of export in media products, and world periphery areas are mostly on the receiving end (Gunaratne 2005; Thussu 2014).

Nevertheless, the source of soft power has been increasingly shifting to alternative and lesser hegemonic states. While the expanded soft power of hegemonic countries is often perceived as cultural oppression by foreign audiences (Bátora and Van de Craen 2006), the cultural transfer of small and medium-sized countries is freer from the claims of hegemonic motivations. Furthermore, minor foreign cultures are often perceived as 'cool' to the youth in foreign audiences who try to differentiate themselves from the familiar majority. In addition, the advancement of information and communications technology (ICT) contributed to the shift by enabling the public to gain direct access to foreign cultural products, bypassing official institutions and channels which are costly to maintain for the government. Decades ago, for instance, Ghanaians were able to learn French or German and watch European movies in Alliance Française or the Goethe Institute located in Accra, but it was not easy for them to learn Korean or Korean culture, since a small and less wealthy country like Korea was not able to set up and maintain cultural centers in a country 20 hours away from Seoul by plane. However, today, learning Korean or watching Korean movies in Ghana is just a click away.

The advancement of ICT changed the role of foreign audiences as well. In traditional public diplomacy, senders and receivers were distinctively differentiated as domestic constituencies and foreign public. The foreign public in diplomatic studies was referred to as the foreign audience in Mass Communications/Public Relations, and targets or consumers in International Marketing. Today, however, with the advancement of ICT, the distinct identification and nomenclature has become increasingly blurred. Those who used to be considered on the receiving end are not a passive public, audience, or mere consumers any more in today's global mediascape, where foreign content is transferred not only from top to bottom but also from bottom to top and side to side. In current public diplomacy studies, the erstwhile passive foreign public is considered salient policy participants who proactively select the message that they would like to listen to or watch. If they like it, they recommend and forward the message to those who have not received it and, more importantly, to those who are not easily reached by the primary initiators. In the process, the proactive receivers become secondary senders, which makes them secondary stakeholders in public diplomacy (Zaharna 2010).[1] Compared to the principal stakeholders or domestic constituencies who share a policy sponsor's goals, however, the secondary stakeholders do not necessarily share the goals of the original senders, which makes them fluid and risky to rely on, despite being of importance in the process of public diplomacy. They can be catalysts in both constructive and destructive ways, and therefore, identifying and understanding them is critical to the success of public diplomacy. This makes public diplomacy in Africa more challenging than in regions with which Korea is more familiar. Korea's engagement in Africa is relatively recent compared to its engagement in other continents, and therefore understanding the audiences or secondary stakeholders takes more research and trial and error. While engagement between the Republic of Korea and the independent states of Africa has come relatively late, the history of connection between them is surprisingly old, and, indeed, the oldest in some senses.

A History: The Koreas and Africa

Kangnido (short for *Honil gangni yeokdae gukdo jido*), the oldest world map depicting the complete form of the African continent for the first time, was made in 1402 during the Joseon dynasty (1392–1879). It was drawn up a century earlier than European maps, which were drawn only after the explorations of the late 1400s, and it also predated Zeng He's travels to Africa. However, the map was not made for the purpose of a cross-continental voyage. Rather, the creation of the map was a symbolic gesture to show the cultural power of the new dynasty of Joseon, locally and internationally, by drawing the world as precisely as possible at the time and placing the new kingdom in it (Oh 2016: 131–132). Without physical contact or connections with Africa, Joseon virtually connected with Africa by establishing both Korea and Africa in the world. A half millennium later, the Joseon dynasty lost its sovereignty to Japan, and a half century after that, at the end of World War II, the surrender of Japan and international politics tore the old Joseon dynasty into two Koreas (the Democratic People's Republic of Korea (DPRK), or North Korea, and the Republic of Korea (ROK), or South Korea). Still, *Kangnido* and the two Koreas' engagement with Africa share a critical similarity in the area of cultural modus operandi in pursuit of national aspirations and legitimacy.

In the beginning, North Korea appeared to inherit the cultural legacy in its pursuit of diplomatic relations with Africa, although its cultural initiation should be understood in the context of inter-Korean rivalry. The independence of most African states came later than that of the Koreas, but African states became members of the UN, while the Koreas were still trapped in the Cold War dynamics between the US and the Union of Soviet Socialist Republics (USSR), competing to gain international legitimacy by acquiring UN membership. Initially, North Korea overwhelmingly outperformed South Korea in building diplomatic relations with African countries. Newly independent and radical African states, such as Tanzania, were instinctively attracted to North Korea's anti-imperialist rhetoric. In the 1960s, most independent African states built close bonds with socialist countries, including North Korea. North Korea actively engaged with Africa bilaterally and multilaterally as a vocal member of the Non-Aligned Movement. Even though both Koreas tried to isolate the other from the international community, South Korea's initial engagement with Africa was dormant and passive compared to that of the North. South Korea even severed existing diplomatic ties with any country that had diplomatic ties with the North, thus excluding many African countries from its diplomatic radar. On the other hand, North Korea did not push African countries into a 'either North or South' dilemma, and, instead, sought to build diplomatic ties with any African state willing to develop relations with them. Consequently, while North Korea was expanding its diplomatic spheres in the continent, the rigid anti-Communist policy of the South cost diplomatic relations with a number of African states, including Mauritania and Congo Brazzaville in 1964 and 1965, respectively, due to their newly cemented diplomatic relations with the North. Since its rigid stance only helped the North's expansion in the continent, South Korea reversed the policy at the end of the 1960s.

North Korea needed African states for its 'anti-Seoul' campaign and to 'steer clear of the Sino-Soviet quagmire' (Owoeye 1991: 631), and used cultural policy as a strategic tool to cultivate African support. The North's appreciation of cultural policy and public diplomacy came from its close observance of the Soviet model; the Stalin apparatus treated 'cultural education' as seriously as organizing a socialist economy and performed the task 'on the greatest of scales' (Bahro 1978: 39). Having observed and learned, the government in North Korea embarked on using culture to propagate its political ideology and legitimacy, even before its government was officially established. In the 1950s, however, its cultural diplomacy mostly targeted Communist Europe, China, and the USSR in an effort to collect funding to sustain the three-year-long Korean War (1950–1953). In regard to Africa, North Korea's cultural engagement began in the 1960s. North Korea signed a series of cultural agreements, entailing cultural and educational exchanges, the provision of material for broadcasting and filmmaking, together with economic, technical, and military assistance with multiple African states, including Mali (1961), Niger (1964), Mauritania (1965), and Ghana (1966).

The main form of North Korea's cultural engagement in the 1960s was propagating *Juche*, through supporting *Juche* study groups in newly decolonized African countries, which became more active in the 1970s. *Juche* is roughly translated as 'self-reliance'. Despite its ideological debt to Maoism and Stalin-Leninism, *Juche* was propagated among Africans as a political philosophy created by Kim Il-sung, independent from socialist ideologies in China and the Soviet Union (Lee 2003). African leaders and officials were invited to North Korea and experimented with *Juche* ideology. While the presence and influence of *Juche* study groups appeared to be 'quite small and marginal', the activities of the groups were broadcast in North Korea in detail for domestic propaganda (Young 2015: 105). Even though most of the *Juche* study groups were dissolved in the mid-1990s, when North Korea could not afford financially sponsoring the study groups due to its economic hardships, Alhassan Mamman Muhammed, Chairman of the Nigerian committee for the study of the *Juche* idea, argues that thousands of *Juche* supporters still exist in Nigeria (Byrne 2014).

Another pillar of North Korea's public diplomacy in Africa was hosting students from Africa in universities in North Korea. According to anecdotes[2] from students who spent time in North Korea (Young 2015), it is uncertain whether the ultimate purpose of the policy was to nurture pro-North Korean elites in Africa, which is the conventional goal of the practice of inviting students or opinion leaders to study abroad. Rather, the students were invited as a gesture of gift-giving to celebrate various diplomatic events between North Korea and African states. Still, it was an impressive act of public and cultural diplomacy that about 200 students from across Africa were invited and studied in North Korea in the 1980s.

In addition, North Korea initiated art-oriented diplomacy. In post-independence Africa, socialist realism gained ground in lieu of imperialist modernism, and against this background, North Korea started the Mansudae Overseas Projects,[3] building socialist monuments in Africa. The project started with the Tiglachin Monument in Ethiopia in 1974, and North Korea offered similar statues or monuments to Madagascar, Togo, and Guinea as gifts, without charging anything for diplomatic interests. Aesthetically, the North Korean statues and monuments lack African qualities and display North Korean socialist realism, representing the *Juche* Art (Che 2014), or 'a new subjectivity in the process of modernization' (Lee 2015). Politically, the cultural gifts were part of Kim Il-sung's efforts to buy votes from African countries, while the two Koreas were still vying for a seat in the UN. Across Africa, the Mansudae Overseas Project has built faux Soviet Socialist mega-sized statues or structures in over 20 countries. However, the statue diplomacy of North Korea did not gain much attention before 2010, when the statue 'African Renaissance', built by the Masudae Overseas Project, was revealed in Dakar, Senegal. The statue is 50 meters high, which made it bigger than the Statue of Liberty in New York; it took 60 North Korean workers two years to complete and cost USD 25 million, with half of this paid to North Korea. The African Renaissance statue, as well as a number of giant statues built by the Mansudae Overseas Project in recent years, shows the cultural diplomacy of North Korea. They were presented to strengthen bilateral bonds and have now become a source of hard currency for North Korea. The initial cultural engagement of North Korea with Africa has indeed transformed to a harder form of diplomacy, including military cooperation or illicit diplomatic practices such as trafficking wildlife, counterfeit cigarettes, and counterfeit notes.

On the other hand, initially, South Korea's engagement with Africa demonstrated little in the way of cultural diplomacy. In contrast to the Soviet Union's presence in the North, the US Military Government initially did not have a keen interest in supporting culture in the South or using culture to propagate its democratic ideology. It was only after the Korean War that the US Military Government realized the necessity of cultural diplomacy both to Koreans and audiences outside the US. The Korean War became an opportunity for the US to learn that there were a significant number of communist sympathizers in the South, which became a turning point in the US government's use of public and cultural diplomacy after World War II. On its own, the South Korean government practiced various forms of public diplomacy in the form of cultural diplomacy, but the government only recently officially recognized the importance of cultural and public diplomacy for national interests. The government designated 2010 as the first year of public diplomacy and identified it as one of the three pillars of diplomacy, along with state diplomacy and economic diplomacy. The increased interest and enacted legislation can be understood as part of South Korea's attempt to become an emerging middle power.[4] Even though South Korea had already used culture in the form of public diplomacy, it is only in 2016 that its first ever public diplomacy act took effect. The Korean government defines public diplomacy as 'diplomacy activities through which the State enhances foreign nationals' understanding of and confidence in the Republic of Korea directly or in cooperation with local governments or the private sector through culture, knowledge, policies, etc' (Public Diplomacy Act 2016). The next section discusses the Public Diplomacy Act in the context of Africa.

In the context of Africa, Korea's diplomatic engagement started relatively late compared to the engagement of its East Asian neighbors such as China, Japan, and North Korea. In large part, its diplomatic practices emulated those of its neighboring countries. Upon gaining its independence in 1945, Korea's diplomacy was predominantly US-focused, since the US was the primary aid donor to Korea. As mentioned earlier, only after the abolition of the rigidly anti-Communist Hallstein Doctrine in 1973 did Korea actively begin to build diplomatic ties with a number of African countries. In 1982, in the midst of competition against North Korea for accession to the UN, Korea's president visited Kenya, Nigeria, Gabon, and Senegal—the first ever presidential trip to the African continent. However, once Korea gained membership of the UN, its interest in Africa soon lapsed, and the South Korean government closed down 11 embassies in Africa in four years.

Korea's re-engagement with Africa began with the second presidential visit by Roh Moo-hyun (2003–2008) in 2006. With the visit, the government launched Korea's Initiative for African Development, which set out its international development cooperation plan specifically to Africa in highlighted areas: to triple its Official Development Aid (ODA) to Africa by 2018, to share development experience, and to establish regular meetings between Korean and African ministers and heads of state.[5] Based on the pledge taken in the Summit, in 2015 more than USD 122 million of Korea's ODA was transferred to Africa, accounting for more than 20% of its total aid, a significant rise from 2.7% in 2002.[6] Again, however, the re-engagement coincided with Ban Ki-moon's election campaign for the position of UN Secretary General. Along with its engagement in other sectors, cultural exchange between South Korea and various states in Africa has been growing. Based on this historical understanding, what follows focuses on current forms of cultural engagement between the Koreas and Africa, led mainly by South Korea.

Public Diplomacy

Since public diplomacy is the main form of Korea's cultural engagement in Africa, the newly enacted Public Diplomacy Act needs to be discussed in a little more detail here. The Act defines public diplomacy as 'diplomatic activities through which the State enhances foreign nationals' understanding of and confidence in the Republic of Korea directly or in cooperation with local governments or the private sector through culture, knowledge, policies, etc. for improving the Republic of Korea's image and prestige in the international community' (Public Diplomacy Act 2016). With the enactment of the Act, the budget doubled to USD 12.8 million from 2013, when the government set a stand-alone budget for public diplomacy for the first time.

Table 6.1 Number of embassy projects in public diplomacy by continent

	Asia	America	Europe	Middle East and North Africa	Sub-Saharan Africa	Total
Number of projects (percentage)	152 (30%)	135 (27%)	160 (31%)	36 (7%)	28 (5%)	511 (100%)

Source: Ministry of Foreign Affairs (2015)

In terms of regional distribution of the budget, although one of the three basic principles of public diplomacy proclaims that 'no public diplomacy activities shall be disproportionately concentrated in any specific region or country', a dominant share of the budget is directed to areas with strong traditional diplomatic ties with Korea (Public Diplomacy Act 2016). Interestingly, public diplomacy projects by the Korean government appear to be more effective in developing countries where a lower budget has been directed (Paik 2017: 14). Table 6.1 shows a number of government projects carried out by Korean embassies and official institutes abroad as part of public diplomacy in 2014. Only 5% of overall projects were conducted in Africa. The small proportion of African projects looks even slimmer, considering that, despite the increase in public policy budget, the size of the overall public diplomacy budget is insignificant compared to that of other regional actors; Japan's budget allocated to public diplomacy is almost 40 times that of Korea's.

While the volume of public diplomacy practices initiated by regional municipalities and civil society has been rapidly growing, Korea's public diplomacy is mainly led by the central government. Similarly, in Africa, cultural exchange is mainly led by Korean embassies.[7] The government's drive toward cultural diplomacy in Africa is centered around Korean embassies, with cultural events including taekwondo competitions, the screening of Korean films, and the promotion of Korean foods (the Taste of Korea program).

Regular cultural activities are usually led by Korean Cultural Centers, which date back to the Korean Culture and Information Service of 1971.[8] Currently, there are 32 overseas Korean Cultural Centers around the world. In sub-Saharan Africa, the first and (at present) the only Korean Cultural Centre opened in Abuja, the capital of Nigeria, in May 2010, marking the 30th anniversary of Korea-Nigeria diplomatic ties and the

50th anniversary of Nigeria's independence. In celebration, Korean performance teams went to Nigeria in exchange for a visit by Nigerian performance teams to Korea. With the opening of the Centre, an exhibition of Nigerian modern paintings was held in Seoul and, in exchange, the first Korean movie festival was held in Abuja. Prior to the opening of the Centre, there was little cultural exchange between the two countries except for a few events; a team of Korean traditional dancers performed in Nigeria to celebrate a state visit by Korea's president to Nigeria in 1982, and a private broadcasting company, AIT, aired the first Korean TV drama, *Dae Jang Geum* (Jewel in the Palace) in Nigeria in 2008. The Korean Cultural Centre in Nigeria has continued to provide a number of Korean TV dramas since 2010, and the first Korean movie festival was held in Abuja in 2010, becoming an annual event. Since then, the cultural exchange between the two countries has expanded into a variety of areas, and in 2012 the two governments signed an agreement of 'culture and education cooperation'. The Centre currently offers classes teaching taekwondo, K-pop, the Korean language, and *Jang-gu* (traditional Korean percussion).

Among these classes, the promotion of taekwondo is one of the main strategies of Korea's global public diplomacy (Ministry of Foreign Affairs 2016a). Promoting taekwondo is undertaken as part of sport diplomacy, which involves diplomatic activities undertaken by sports people to create a better image and to meet the foreign policy goals of the country (Murray 2012). Sport diplomacy, as part of cultural and public diplomacy, is a relatively new subject in International Relations, despite the fact that the Ancient Olympic Games are deeply related to both war and peace. In 2017, the first World Taekwondo Championship, the Ambassador's Cup, took place in Kukkiwon (the world taekwondo headquarters) in Seoul, hosted by the Ministry of Foreign Affairs. The Ambassador for Public Diplomacy announced the beginning of the championship by reflecting on the government's understanding and use of taekwondo as part of public diplomacy. In total, 52 athletes from 25 countries participated in the event, with athletes enjoying a five-day visit to Korea and engaging in various activities that promoted Korean culture. After the Championship, the government announced that it would 'continue to increase cultural diplomacy which allows foreign taekwondo practitioners from all walks of life to directly participate in it and thereby to develop an interest in Korean culture and spirit' (Ministry of Foreign Affairs 2017).

Taekwondo is particularly popular in a number of African countries. In Côte d'Ivoire, taekwondo became the second most popular sport after soccer after Cheick Sallah Cissé won a gold medal in the 2016 Rio Olympics—the first ever gold medal achieved in any sport by Côte d'Ivoire. Currently, there are more than 30,000 belt-holders in the country. Nigeria is another African country with a growing interest in taekwondo. In total, 300,000 Nigerians currently practice taekwondo, including 15,000 belt-holders, and Nigerian taekwondo Olympian Chika Chukwumerije won bronze in the 2008 Beijing Olympics. The Nigerian government selected taekwondo as one of its five strategic sports, together with soccer, boxing, wrestling, and track-and-field sports. In 2018, 41 athletes graduated from a taekwondo course at the Korea Culture Centre in Abuja.

Both North Korea and South Korea share the cultural heritage of taekwondo. North Korea has long been active in North Korean taekwondo in Africa; however, while taekwondo was initially taught by North Koreans as a form of military assistance and public diplomacy, currently, South Korea is leading in taekwondo diplomacy. North Korea signed a Memorandum of Understanding on Bilateral Co-operation in the Field of Sport and Recreation with South Africa in 2007. The South Korean government, on the other hand, dispatches taekwondo performing teams and masters and provides taekwondo facilities in a number of African countries.

Hallyu

Besides taekwondo in sport, one of the most widely influential source of Korea's soft power is its popular culture, called *Hallyu*. *Hallyu*, coined by Chinese news media in 1998, refers to the craze of Korean pop culture abroad. Initially, the export of Korean screen products was driven by international capitalism against the background of the financial crisis in Asia (Cho 2005), but after the Kim Dae-jung administration (1998–2003) designated the media and entertainment sector as one of its key growth industries, the government of Korea has played an essential role in promoting *Hallyu* worldwide. The Korean government sees *Hallyu* as a form of cultural diplomacy and has stepped up its drive of using *Hallyu* to strengthen its soft power. The production and export of popular cultural products is as institutionally supported by the Korean government as the industries of electronics and cars once were in Korea (Kim 2007: 124). Currently, the size of *Hallyu* export has reached USD 7.03 billion (KOTRA/KOFICE 2016), and its fandom is found across the world, including Scandinavian Europe, South America, Arab countries and sub-Saharan Africa, in addition to its traditional terrain of Asia and North America (Kim 2018; Elfving-Hwang 2013; Hübinette 2012; Ko et al. 2014; Oh 2009). The growing and positive reception of Korean pop culture in the form of music, TV series, films, and food indicates the emerging soft power of a semi-periphery country, representing an alternative to hegemonic American pop culture.

In addition, the government supports the dubbing and captioning of Korean dramas into local languages and provides them for free in CIS[9] and Africa. The risk of promoting Korean popular culture in developing countries, particularly in Africa, is that the government has a blurry understanding of the difference between cultural promotion and development cooperation. A *Hallyu* strategy paper submitted to the government recommends the strengthening of cultural ODA as one of multiple strategies to promote *Hallyu*; it recommends expanding cultural ODA projects, building cultural leadership to establish Korea's cultural stature in international society, and initiating a 'culture and development' agenda (Han 2012). The promotion of Korean pop culture, often presented as a patriotic government affair, lulls the Korean government into believing that it is engaged in effective diplomacy, and that it is acceptable and appropriate to play Korean pop music as part of ODA.

The government's obsession with 'developmental soft power' and greater cultural soft power led to the ill-designed Korea Aid, an ODA project undertaken in Ethiopia, Kenya and Uganda (Kim 2019). When Korea Aid was launched during Park Geun-hye's state visits to these countries, the Korean government extolled the project as a 'new complex mobile development cooperation meeting two combined goals of ODA and cultural diplomacy' (Ministry of Foreign Affairs 2016b). The project comprised ten vehicles delivering K-medic, K-meals, and K-culture to each country; three medical vehicles (one medical check-up truck and two ambulances), four food trucks (three trucks with cooking facilities and one refrigerator vehicle), one truck with a projection screen, and two supporting sport utility vehicles (SUVs). K-medic was intended to provide basic medical services, particularly to girls in remote areas. The vehicle with a projection screen played a four-minute exercise video and a video clip encouraging girls to go to school and teaching proper ways of washing hands and coughing. The screen's primary mission was to promote K-culture through the playing of K-pop and the screening of videos on Korean tourism and the PyeongChang Winter Olympics to African people.

Four K-meal vehicles introduced Korean food such as bibimbab (a traditional Korean dish of rice and vegetables). K-meals also provided two different rice products to locals: a rice cookie for infants and rice powder for pregnant or young women. Originally, the ten trucks were to visit remote areas in each country once a month from 2016 to 2017.

The government extolled the project as a new Korean model combining cultural diplomacy and development assistance, but in fact it was ill-designed, conceived without any understanding of the cultural and developmental contexts of Ethiopia, Kenya or Uganda. Recently, similar concerns have been raised in other developing countries; regarding *Hallyu* in Laos, Ainslie argues that the aggressive promotion of *Hallyu* is perhaps of little benefit to local consumers. According to Ainslie (2016: 25), the narrative used by the Korean government with regard to *Hallyu* is one-directional and commercially directed, while Korean representations of Laos are based on a 'position that constructs South Korea as inherently culturally superior and benevolent in terms of the civilized influence that it can offer the new-Orientalized and much more primitive Laos'. This troubling approach is observed in the government promotion of *Hallyu* in Africa; the head of the Korean Culture Centre in Abuja once wrote an opinion piece in a newspaper entitled The saga of expanding *Hallyu* to Africa, a culturally marginalized region. In the article, he writes 'although Hallyu in Nigeria is still not significant, keeping the potential of growth of this country in mind, I think we need to make arduous efforts to sow seeds of Hallyu from now on' (Han 2017).

Despite the government's blunders, Korean cultural products are increasingly received by secondary stakeholders in Africa. According to Kim's research in Ghana, Korean TV dramas are becoming popular among a particular socio-economic bracket in the country (Kim 2018). The Korean government initially provided African broadcasting companies with Korean TV dramas free of charge, with most viewers in Ghana first watching Korean screen products on TV. The current form of cultural engagement, however, often bypasses traditional TV channels, since a growing number of African audiences directly research and choose what they want to watch and listen to using IT.[10] The current pattern of Korean TV drama consumption requires an infrastructure and income level that is not always accessible to people in Ghana, such as screen devices, reliable electricity and Internet, a sufficient level of education to follow subtitles provided in European languages, accumulated experience of watching foreign screen products, and sufficient leisure time to enjoy such screen products. Korean TV dramas are becoming popular among a network of young people who can afford these prerequisites, but they create a barrier to others, confining *Hallyu* to a particular network in Ghana. Students of prestigious universities and their families in urban areas are among those who actively receive Korean screen products.

These findings are derived from a case study conducted in Ghana, and are therefore not generalizable to the media-scape of sub-Saharan Africa. For instance, in South Africa, the reception of Korean screen products and pop music is distinctively differentiated along racial lines. Even though South Africa has rather peculiar socio-economic conditions compared to other African countries, its reception of *Hallyu* still yields a valid point— that Africa should not be approached as a monolithic entity. Africa is diverse, and each country, and more often various actors at sub-country level, must be approached with different analytical sets. Nevertheless, it appears that the reception of Korean pop culture in Africa has been continuously growing,[11] with the growth fairly limited. Gray's (2011: 107) ethnographic research on Malawi's video market suggests that Korean films are found only in the university town of Zomba and not in the stalls and stores of other towns.

Cultural Official Development Assistance

The project of building the National Museum of Congo is noteworthy here because it is not only an ODA project in the cultural sector, but, more importantly, it also reflects the changing international dynamics that Africa must contend with in an increasingly multi-polarized world order. The Korean International Cooperation Agency (KOICA), an international development cooperation agency of the Korean government, agreed to build the National Museum of Congo in 2013. The project, costing about €20 million, was initiated at the request of Joseph Kabila, the President of the Democratic Republic of the Congo (DRC). For the Korean government, it was the first project of its kind in Africa, even though the government had assisted with managing and preserving cultural heritage sites in South Asian countries such as Laos, Cambodia, and Bangladesh. The project had multiple challenges. According to Sim, the project manager, it was a unique project because Korea, which shares almost no similarities with the DRC in terms of culture and religion, built a national museum showcasing the DRC (Sim 2014). The most challenging task, she considers, was a lack of understanding of the culture and language of the DRC by the Koreans; the team struggled to understand about 60,000 artifacts in the museum, most of which lacked documentation, so that her staff were forced to rely on oral explanations.

Yet the project served as an opportunity to deepen and expand mutual understanding between the two countries. The project is currently ongoing. In 2018, the Korea Cultural Heritage Foundation invited 20 government officials and researchers of Congolese national heritage to participate in training, as part of the ODA project in preparation for the opening of the museum in 2019 (Gang 2018). Building a national museum as part of ODA was appreciated as a fresh approach by officials in the DRC and scholars of African culture. Caleb Wandera Obwora, a Kenyan researcher on African culture, notes that a handful of cultures, such as that of Maasai, predominantly represent diverse African cultures due to their commercial value. While China and Japan approach African culture from an economic perspective, he perceives that the Korean government's culture-oriented position, as observed in the National Museum of Congo project (Obwora 2014).

The museum has drawn attention since its construction coincided with the re-opening of the Africa Museum in Belgium and a statement by Emmanuel Macron, the President of France, regarding the reinstitution of African art. Macron's 2017 speech in Ouagadougou, the capital of Burkina Faso, had serious repercussions for a number of museums in former European colonies, which still hold massive quantities of African art and documents: 'I cannot accept that a large part of the cultural heritage of several African countries is in France', he said (Maclean 2018). The African Museum in Belgium, whose former name was the Royal Museum for Central Africa, holds one of the largest collections of African artifacts. According to Joseph Ibongo, Director of the National Museum of Congo, the inventory of artifacts in Kinshasa is roughly one-tenth the size of that in Brussels (O'Donnell 2014). On the other hand, Guido Gryseels, the Director of the Africa Museum in Belgium—located close to the former 'human zoo', which held hundreds of Congolese people as part of an African exhibition, on the orders of King Leopold—said that the incapacity of the Congolese government to keep the artifacts would be one of the main issues to be dealt with in discussions on the repatriation of African art.[12] After the re-opening of the Africa Museum in Belgium and with the opening of the National Museum of Congo in Kinshasa, Joseph Kabila is seeking to bring the artifacts back from Belgium to hold them in the brand new museum funded by the South Korean government (Boffey 2018).

National museums are, of course, more than just buildings. Yet the architecture of public buildings have symbolic meaning, as do the contents and the location of such buildings. Furthermore, the presence of a national museum reaffirms the identity of a country and symbolically legitimizes the country as a state. In this sense, Korea's museum project in Congo reveals the changing dynamics in global cultural engagements with Africa. An Asian emerging donor with no historical burden is building the national museum, digitalizing the cultural heritage and training museum staff and officials, supporting Africa's call for the repatriation of its stolen artifacts. Sarah van Beurden, a Belgian historian of modern Africa in Ohio State University, reads Korea's message as follows: 'The story they (Koreans) tell about themselves is about a formerly colonized country that has overcome its past to become a highly successful developed nation … and they're using that image to say to the Congolese, you don't need to work with your old colonial overlords, you can work with us instead' (Brown 2018). Some commentators point out that Korea has commercial interests in the DRC, since the country is rich in cobalt, a precious mineral in telecommunication, in which Korea is vying to expand its global market.

Nevertheless, the cultural engagement of Korea is changing long-standing post-colonial dynamics. The change does not necessarily imply that Africa is merely replacing Europe with Korea, or with any other country aiming to expand their engagement with Africa, particularly from Asia. This binary approach is not mutually constructive in the long run for any of the states involved, in this case either for Korea or the DRC, or even for Belgium, for that matter. The lesson learned from the National Museum of Congo project is noteworthy in this regard. According to the project director, a successful museum project calls for three different levels of cooperation: first, academic cooperation is required to understand the culture of Francophone Africa, the history of art, and the history of museums; second, intergovernmental cooperation is required between cultural institutes; and, third, Korea can benefit from international cooperation with European countries which have established cultural knowledge on Africa, such as France and Belgium (Sim 2014).

Conclusion

This chapter has discussed Korea's cultural engagement with Africa by looking closely at embassy-initiated cultural activities, taekwondo, *Hallyu*, and a museum project. In concluding this chapter, I would like to introduce a few cases of Korea's cultural engagement with Africa that took place within Korea, in order to offer another dimension of Korea-Africa cultural connection. Korea's cultural engagement with Africa has been growing; not only regarding Korean influence in Africa but also regarding African influence in Korea, with an interesting difference in terms of stakeholders. In contrast to Korea's cultural engagement in Africa, which has been mainly led by the government of Korea, African cultural events taking place in Korea have been initiated by civil society at the initial stage. Even though Korea has recently experienced a burgeoning interest in Africa, the interest is still at a nascent stage, and the size of the cultural events are yet insignificant; funding seems to be a constant challenge; and attempts to hold regular long-term events often end after an event or two. Nevertheless, there have been a number of events worth noting due to their political and cultural significance in the context of changes in Korea's understanding of Africa and the people of Africa.

The first African movie festival in Korea was held in Busan in 2014 and repeated in 2015, organized by Africa-related NGOs and private institutes on a small scale. A number of African movies were played and African arts and crafts were sold at the venue. However, after two years, the festival was discontinued. The most successful African cultural event initiated by civil society, at present, would be the Seoul Africa Festival. It has been held annually from 2016, organized by academic institutes and NGOs, including the Institute of African Studies at Hankuk University of Foreign Studies, Africa Insight, and World Together. Beginning with about 3000 participants in the first year, the festival has been growing in terms of both volume and content. For instance, the second festival in 2017 introduced foods, drinks, art, music, and fashion from Africa and opened marketplaces to buy and sell African products. There were sessions to share travel experiences to countries in Africa and to learn Korea-Ethiopia relations. The festival included an African fashion show and African movies. Participants could attend classes teaching African traditional musical instruments and dance, and the Ghanaian and Cameroonian embassies participated by sending their dance teams to perform at the festival.

Among the initial drive and growing participation by civil society, the government organized the most comprehensive Korea-Africa cultural event, introducing Africa's culture, history, and life to Koreans. The event took place in 2018 when the 53rd annual meeting of the African Development Bank was held in Busan. The meeting focused on accelerating Africa's industrialization, with an expectation of 6000 participants joining the meeting from 80 regional and non-regional member countries of the African Development Bank. The Korean government organized a variety of cultural events to mark the meeting across the city of Busan, the second largest city of South Korea (YTN 2018). The cultural festival was designed around the theme of 'blending nature, human and culture'. The African Cultural Festival took place as a participatory event, offering opportunities to experience the culture and life of Africa; for instance, there was a 'coffee-drinking' session with storytelling about Kaldi, a legendary Ethiopian who discovered the coffee plant, and a story about the Queen of Sheba and King Solomon. The Busan Museum had a special exhibition on Africa, in which 200 African artworks were on display, including *Kangnido*. Cine Park in the city played six African movies, and the Busan Museum of Art hosted an exhibition of the works of Yinka Shonibare MBE, who had already exhibited with success in Daegu Art Museum in 2015.

Besides events, there are a number of museums holding African artifacts in Korea. All are privately run. The Museum of African Art was opened in Seoul by a private collector in 1998 and later moved to Jeju Island in 2004. The construction of the new building was modelled after Djenne Grand Mosque, the world's largest mud-brick building in Mali. The museum shows photos and artworks from 30 countries in Africa. Another museum, Africa Museum of Original Art in Pocheon, Gyeonggi Province, focused more on a general experience of the African continent. The Museum once provided dance performances from Burkina Faso and artworks from Zimbabwe, until 2014, when the team of artists was dissolved after a racism and human rights abuse scandal involving the owner, Hong Moon-jong, a member of parliament. The passports of artists were confiscated by the employer, and they were forced to work from 9 am to 6 pm every day, violating the original contract which stipulated three hours of performing per day. In addition, they received only two-thirds of the legal minimum wages. Yet they were told by their employer: 'I gave you an opportunity; you would not make this much money in your home country' (YTN 2017). The 'slave labor' scandal revealed the reality of Korea, where Africans or darker-skinned laborers in general struggle against racism and exploitation. After the scandal, one of the dancers chose to stay in Korea, teaching Mandingo dance from Burkina Faso. In 2017, he choreographed and danced in a show to deliver a message that 'we are all humans, measured by pain only', entitled *Degesbe*, meaning, 'What are you looking for? There is nothing there' in one of languages of Burkina Faso (Sohn 2017).

In conclusion, Nye, who coined the term 'soft power' in 1990, asserts that the soft power of South Korea as a middle-ranked country is growing due to its greater role in international politics and rich cultural resources (Nye 1990, 2009). Since the 1990s, the Korean government has adopted a global strategy that could translate its economic clout into international political influence, and it has begun to make institutional efforts to become a middle power with soft power, particularly in the area of culture and development cooperation. Against this background, Africa became a strategic destination of Korea's cultural products and development projects. Korea's cultural engagement with Africa will increase due in part to the current government's philosophy and in part to the place Korea now occupies in its economic and political development. The Moon Jae-in administration has placed cultural public diplomacy at the top of five core public diplomacy strategies in the First Basic Plan on Public Diplomacy (2017–2021), which will serve as a guideline for the government. However, the Moon administration's understanding of international development cooperation as part of public diplomacy strategy tends to echo the self-praise and misadventure of Korea Aid, run by the disgraced Park Geun-hye administration (Democratic Party 2017).

Historically, even though North Korea initially outperformed South Korea in regard to cultural diplomacy in Africa, current cultural engagement is predominantly conducted by the South. This is, in part, because North Korea's diplomatic engagement in Africa has become mainly elusive and sometimes illicit, casting a shadow over any engagement of note in terms of cultural diplomacy (Rademeyer 2017).[13] This does not mean that there is no cultural engagement between North Korea and states in Africa. Even though North Korea's diplomatic engagement is relatively hard to observe due to its elusive nature, it appears that the North continues to use its culture as a diplomatic tool in Africa.[14] On the other hand, South Korea has become a significant actor in the context of public diplomacy and soft power in the increasingly multi-polar world, backed by its growing economic prowess and policies supporting its global expansion.

While the Korean government initiated cultural diplomacy with Africa by offering Korean screen products for free, lately, commercial activities using existing cultural markets are more frequently observed; in 2017, a private company exported a Korean TV drama, 'Bridal Mask', to Cameroon for the first time (KBS 2017). In broader terms, growing cultural engagement between Korea and Africa benefits Korea. Cultural proximity is regarded as playing a positive role in the volume of trade conducted (Felbermayr and Toubal 2010: 279). Such cultural proximity will work in favor of Korea due to current trade patterns between Korea and most African countries. Against this background, concerns are being expressed by African governments regarding the protection of Africa's cultural industry from increasing Eastern influence. However, a sense of the need for cultural protection is observed; according to the Korea Foundation's findings, although there is no entry barrier for *Hallyu* in Africa, at present, it is expected that laws and regulations will be put in place to protect domestic cultures. The cultural exchange should start from an understanding and respect of mutual cultures to prevent the impression that Korean culture is unilaterally advancing in Africa (Korea Foundation 2017: 25). Even though the volume of cultural engagement has been increasing, with other dynamics in trade and distribution of cultural products enduring, the question as to which side will benefit from the increase remains.

Notes

1. A stakeholder in public diplomacy refers to 'an individual or group that has the ability to enhance or constrain a nation's ability to accomplish its mission' (Fitzpatrick 2012: 424).
2. According to Young's interview with students who studied in North Korea in the 1980s, the African students were segregated from North Korean students, female students in particular, in North Korea's efforts to keep the North Korean biological linage clean and pure. They were constantly spied on and were subject to racism, and interactions with North Korean students were extremely limited.
3. North Korea's statues and monuments are designed and made by Mansudea Art Studio, located in Mansudae Street in Pyeongyang.
4. The debate on how to define a middle power is beyond the scope of this chapter. Despite the variety of approaches to middle power, Korea is regarded as an emerging middle power country based on how its political and diplomatic behaviors have been undertaken.
5. The structure of aid was announced in the Korea-Africa Forum. The summit, which started in 2006 following the format of the Tokyo International Conference on African Development (since 1993) and the Forum on China-Africa Cooperation (since 2000), became a flagship of Korea's diplomacy in Africa.
6. Korean International Cooperation Agency (KOICA), 'Statistics 2016'.

7. Ghana, Gabon, Nigeria, South Africa, Rwanda, Madagascar, Mozambique, Senegal, Sudan, Angola, Ethiopia, Uganda, Zimbabwe, Cameroon, Kenya, Côte d'Ivoire, Democratic Republic of the Congo, and Tanzania. Half of the embassies either opened for the first time or re-opened after closure since the 1990s, and a third opened in the 2000s.
8. After several changes in name, the Korean Culture and Information Service was changed to the Korean Culture and Information Service in 2008. It falls under the Ministry of Culture, Sports, and Tourism and has 'the mission of promoting the values of Korean culture around the world and helping to upgrade the country's national image' (KOCIS 2019). The primary duty of KOCIS is to provide support for Korean arts and cultural activities overseas and to correct misinformation on Korea.
9. CIS is an acronym for the Commonwealth of Independent States, an alliance of former Soviet republics. They include Armenia, Azerbaijan, Belarus, Georgia, Kazakhstan, Kyrgyzstan, Moldova, Russian Federation, Tajikistan, Turkmenistan, Ukraine, and Uzbekistan.
10. Nigeria, South Africa, and Kenya have a number of online *Hallyu* fan clubs (Korea Foundation 2017).
11. For instance, a K-pop dance festival was first held in Nigeria in 2012 and aired on Nigerian Television Authority (NTA), the biggest national broadcaster in the country. A Nigerian K-pop dance team, Pacific Starz, won grand prize in 2015 and another Nigerian team, Supreme Track, won best performance in 2016 in the Changwon World K-pop Festival.
12. A speech given by Guido Gryseels for a group of African/Asian Studies scholars, including the author, who visited the Africa Museum in Tervuren as a part of events at the 5th CA/AC Conference: China-Africa in Global Comparative Perspective (Brussels 27–29 June 2018).
13. North Korean diplomats are involved with wildlife trafficking in Africa. In May 2015, a North Korean diplomat working at the North Korean Embassy in South Africa was arrested in Mozambique while moving 4.6 kilograms of rhino horn, which he and his accomplice had purchased from poachers on Mao Tse Tung Avenue in Maputo. North Korean diplomats are thought to be involved in illegal rhino horn trade on a regular basis (Wildlife News 2015). North Korean diplomats send the horns to their colleagues in Vietnam or China, where demand for rhino horn is high. Kan and others name this type of active state engagement in illicit international activities 'criminal sovereignty' (Kan et al. 2010).
14. Animation is one of the few areas in which North Korea enjoys international competitiveness. When the North Korean government found that the controversial movie 'Interview' was being sold on the black market of Nigeria, along with registering official complaints to the Nigerian police and the National Film and Video Censors Board (NFVCB), North Korea

warned Nigeria that the circulation of the movie could hurt the long-standing friendship between the two countries and hinder future cooperation in animation production in Nigeria. Nigeria, which aims to extend its Nollywood to animation for children, was expecting a visit by North Korean animation experts and promised that proper measures dealing with the circulation would be put in place. It was relieved by the assurance by North Korea that there would be no change in the cooperation for animation production (*Frist Africa News* 2015).

REFERENCES

Ainslie, M. J. (2016). Korean Overseas Investment and Soft Power: Hallyu in Laos. *Korea Journal, 56*(3), 5–32.

Bahro, R. (1978). *The Alternative in Eastern Europe* (D. Fernbach, Trans.). Thetford, Norfolk: Lowe & Brydone Printers Ltd.

Bátora, J., & Van de Craen, F. (2006). Public Diplomacy Between Home and Abroad: Norway and Canada. *The Hague Journal of Diplomacy, 1*(1), 53–349.

Boffey, D. (2018, December 8). Belgium's Revamped Africa Museum Triggers Request by DRC. *The Guardian*. https://www.theguardian.com/world/2018/dec/08/belgium-revamped-africa-museum-demands-congo-kabila.

Brown, R. L. (2018). In Congo, a New National Museum Renews Quest to Reclaim History. Retrieved December 7, 2018, from https://www.csmonitor.com/World/Africa/2018/0427/In-Congo-a-new-national-museum-renews-quest-to-reclaim-history.

Byrne, L. (2014). Interview: Thousands of North Korea Juche Supporters Exist in Nigeria. Retrieved December 5, 2018, from https://www.nknews.org/2014/06/interview-thousands-of-north-korea-juche-supporters-exist-in-nigeria/.

Che, O. (2014). Media City Seoul. Retrieved February 13, 2016, from http://mediacityseoul.kr/2014/en/participating_artists/exhibition/che-onejoon/.

Cho, H. J. (2005). Reading the "Korean Wave"as a Sign of Global Shift. *Korea Journal, 45*(Winter), 147–182.

Democratic Party. (2017). Election Pledges by Democratic Party (the 19th Presidential Election) (in Korean). Retrieved December 26, 2018, from http://theminjoo.kr/autoalbum/page/minjoo/view.html?extweb=true.

Elfving-Hwang, J. (2013). South Korean Cultural Diplomacy and Brokering 'K-Culture' Outside Asia. *Korean Histories, 4*(1), 14–26.

Felbermayr, G. J., & Toubal, F. (2010). Cultural Proximity and Trade. *European Economic Review, 54*(2), 279–293.

Fitzpatrick, K. R. (2012). Defining Strategic Publics in a Networked World: Public Diplomacy's Challenge at Home and Abroad. *The Hague Journal of Diplomacy, 7*(4), 421–440.

Frist Africa News. (2015, September 14). North Korea Angry with Nigeria Over "Provocative Film" Sale. *Frist Africa News.* http://www.firstafricanews.ng/index.php?dbs=openlist&s=28059.

Gang, G. (2018). Korea Cultural Heritage Foundation, Sharing Its Know-How to Manage National Museum with DRC (in Korean). Retrieved December 6, 2018, from http://kocis.go.kr/koreanet/view.do?seq=10615&RN=5.

Gilbert, C. (2017). Chinese Literature in Africa: Meaningful or Simply Ceremonial? Retrieved December 7, 2018, from https://theconversation.com/chinese-literature-in-africa-meaningful-or-simply-ceremonial-63416.

Gilboa, E. (2008). Searching for a Theory of Public Diplomacy. *The Annals of the American Academy, 616*(March), 55–77.

Gray, J. (2011). Mobility Through Piracy, or How Steven Seagal Got to Malawi. *Popular Communication, 9*(2), 99–113.

Gregory, B. (2011). American Public Diplomacy: Enduring Characteristics, Elusive Transformation. *The Hague Journal of Diplomacy, 6*(3–4), 351–372.

Gunaratne, S. A. (2005). Public Diplomacy, Global Communication and World Order: An Analysis Based on Theory of Living Systems. *Current Sociology, 53*(5), 749–772.

Han, G. (2012). *A Study for Hallyu Promotion.* Seoul: Ministry of Culture, Sports and Tourism.

Han, S. (2017, October 6). The Saga of Expanding Hallyu to Africa, a Culturally Marginalised Region (in Korean). *The Korea Economic Daily.* Retrieved from http://snacker.hankyung.com/life/73194.

Hübinette, T. (2012). The Reception and Consumption of Hallyu in Sweden: Preliminary Findings and Reflections. *Korea Observer, 43*(3), 503–525.

Kan, P. R., Bechtol, B. E., & Collins, R. M. (2010). *Criminal Sovereignty: Understanding North Korea's Illicit International Activities.* Carlisle, PA: U.S. Army War College, Strategiv Studies Institute.

KBS. (2017, April 12). Export: Cameroon TV Air Korean Drama 'Bridal Mask' (in Korean). *KBS News.* Retrieved from http://news.kbs.co.kr/news/view.do?ncd=3462383.

Kim, Y. (2007). The Rising East Asian 'Wave'. Korean Media Go Global. In D. K. Thussu (Ed.), *Media on the Move: Global Flow and Contra-Flow* (pp. 121–135). London and New York: Routledge.

Kim, S. (2018). Who Watches Korean TV Dramas in Africa? A Preliminary Study in Ghana. *Media, Culture & Society, 40*(2), 296–306.

Kim, S. (2019). The Misadventure of 'Korea Aid': Developmental Soft Power and the Troubling Motives of an Emerging Donor. *Third World Quarterly,* 1–25.

Ko, N. C., No, S., Kim, J.-N., & Simões, R. G. (2014). Landing of the Wave: Hallyu in Peru and Brazil. *Development and Society, 43*(2), 297–350.

KOCIS (Korean Culture and Information Service). (2019). Vision and Mission. Retrieved July 29, 2019, from http://www.kocis.go.kr/eng/openVision.do.

Korea Foundation. (2017). 2017 Global Hallyu IV (in Korean). Retrieved November 10, 2018, from http://www.kf.or.kr/archives/ebook/ebook_view.do?p_cidx=2544&p_cfidx=30738.

KOTRA/KOFICE. (2016). *Research on the Economic Impact of Hallyu (in Korean)*. Seoul: KOTRA/Korea Foundation for International Culture Exchange.

Kurlantzick, J. (2007). *Charm Offensive: How China's Soft Power Is Transforming the World*. New Haven and London: Yale University Press.

Lee, G. (2003). The Political Philosophy of Juche. *Stanford Journal of East Asian Affairs, 1*(3), 105–112.

Lee, Y. (2015). *Rethinking Contemporaneity in Asia-Africa Through Contemporary Art*. Accra: Africa-Asia, A New Axis of Knowledge.

Maclean, R. (2018, November 21). France Urged to Change Heritage Law and Return Looted Art to Africa. *The Guardian*. Retrieved from https://www.theguardian.com/world/2018/nov/21/france-urged-to-return-looted-african-art-treasures-macron.

Melissen, J. (2013). Public Diplomacy. In P. Kerr & G. Wiseman (Eds.), *Diplomacy in a Globalizing World: Theories and Practice* (pp. 192–207). New York: Oxford University Press.

Ministry of Foreign Affairs. (2015). 2014 Public Diplomacy by Overseas Agencies I & II (in Korean). Retrieved November 21, 2018, from http://www.prism.go.kr/homepage/theme/retrieveThemeDetail.do?leftMenuLevel=110&cond_brm_super_id=NB000120061201100059686&research_id=1262000-201500039.

Ministry of Foreign Affairs. (2016a). Plan for Korea's Public Diplomacy, 1 (2017–2021). Retrieved November 20, 2018, from http://www.mofa.go.kr/www/brd/m_4075/down.do?brd_id=234&seq=366226&data_tp=A&file_seq=1.

Ministry of Foreign Affairs. (2016b). 'Korea Aid', New Korean Style Development Cooperation Model, Visits Africa (in Korean). Retrieved June 8, 2017, from http://www.mofa.go.kr/news/pressinformation/index.jsp?mofat=001&menu=m_20_30.

Ministry of Foreign Affairs. (2017). 1st World Taekwondo Championship of Ambassador's Cup Takes Place Successfully(12.6). Retrieved November 20, 2018, from http://www.mofa.go.kr/eng/brd/m_5665/view.do?seq=319551&srchFr=&srchTo=&srchWord=&srchTp=&multi_itm_seq=0&itm_seq_1=0&itm_seq_2=0&company_cd=&company_nm=&page=1&titleNm=.

Murray, S. (2012). Commentary: The Two Halves of Sports-Diplomacy. *Diplomacy and Statecraft, 23*, 576–592.

Nye, J. S. (1990). Soft Power. *Foreign Policy*, (80), 153–171.

Nye, J. S. (2008). Public Diplomacy and Soft Power. *The Annals of the American Academy, 616*(March), 94–109.

Nye, J. S. (2009). South Korea's Growing Soft Power. Retrieved May 10, 2017, from https://www.project-syndicate.org/commentary/south-korea-s-growing-soft-power.

O'Donnell, J. (2014). Colonial Ghosts Haunt Belgium as Africa Museum Eyes Change. Retrieved December 7, 2018, from https://www.reuters.com/article/us-belgium-congo-museum/colonial-ghosts-haunt-belgium-as-africa-museum-eyes-change-idUSBREA1N07K20140224.

Obwora, C. (2014). Apro. Retrieved December 6, 2018, from http://mkor.theapro.kr/index.asp?pageNo=3&ord=1&ordt=1&state=view&idx=407&sub_num=14.

Oh, I. (2009). Hallyu: The Rise of Transnational Cultural Consumers in China and Japan. *Korea Observer, 40*(3), 425–459.

Oh, S. H. (2016). The Current Discourse on 「Honil gangni yeokdae gukdo jido」 and Reassessment of the Map (in Korean). *Journal of the Korean Geographical Society, 50*(1), 117–134.

Owoeye, J. (1991). The Metamorphosis of North Korea's African Policy. *Asian Survey, 31*(7), 630–645.

Paik, W. (2017). A Study of Strategies and Policies of Public Diplomacy in Korea: Conceptualisation of Basic Patterns (in Korean). *National Strategy, 23*(3), 5–31.

Public Diplomacy Act. (2016). *Act No. 13951*. The Government of Korea.

Rademeyer, J. (2017). *Diplomats and Deceit: North Korea's Criminal Activities in Africa*. Geneva: Global Initiative Against Transnational Organized Crime.

Sim, J. (2014). Apro. Retrieved December 6, 2018, from http://mkor.theapro.kr/index.asp?pageNo=3&ord=1&ordt=1&state=view&idx=407&sub_num=14.

Sohn, G. (2017, November 21). African Dancer Talks About 'Human Dignity' with His Body in Kore: Interview (in Korean). *Media Today*. Retrieved from http://www.mediatoday.co.kr/?mod=news&act=articleView&idxno=139884.

Thussu, D. (2014). *De-Americanizing Soft Power Discourse?* Los Angeles: Figueroa Press.

Wildlife News. (2015). North Korean Diplomat Arrested with Rhino Horn. Retrieved September 17, 2015, from http://wildlifenews.co.uk/2015/06/north-korean-diplomat-arrested-with-rhino-horn/.

Young, B. (2015). The Struggle for Legitimacy: North Korea's Relations with Africa, 1965–1992. *BAKS Papers, 16*, 97–116.

YTN. (2017, December 14). African Dancer Work in Korea Making 2500 Won a Day (in Korean). Retrieved from https://www.ytn.co.kr/_ln/0103_201712141530066859.

YTN. (2018, May 16). AfDB Annual Meeting to Be Held in Busan Next Week. Retrieved from https://en.yna.co.kr/view/AEN20180516008300320.

Zaharna, R. (2010). The Public Diplomacy Challenges of Strategic Stakeholder Engagement. In A. Fisher & S. Lucas (Eds.), *Trials of Engagement: The Future of US Public Diplomacy* (pp. 201–230). Leiden: Martinus Nijhoff Publishers.

Zhang, X., Wasserman, H., & Mano, W. (2016). *China's Media and Soft Power in Africa: Promotion and Perceptions*. London: Springer.

CHAPTER 7

South Korea's Civil Engagement with Africa

Sookhee Yuk

INTRODUCTION

When many of the African countries became independent in the 1960s, South Korea accelerated official diplomatic relations with African nations starting with the establishment of diplomatic ties with Cote d'Ivoire in 1961. The early stage of Korea's engagement with Africa from the 1970s until the 1990s focused on the security issues and economic cooperation. To that effect, Korean private entities have had a business path to Africa. Over the past 30 years, the activities of Korean civil organizations have surpassed the influence of Korean companies on Africa. Before elaborating on South Korea's civil societies' engagement in African countries, it is crucial to understand the characteristics of Korean civil society organizations as represented by not-for-profit organizations (NPOs) or non-government organizations (NGOs).[1]

Internationally, the 1970s and 1980s were when donor countries stressed the purpose of developing foreign aid. During this period, the rising oil prices in the early 1970s led to a series of debt and economic crises in developing countries and famine in Africa, which led to a growing interest in foreign aid. It was a time when the size of non-governmental

---

S. Yuk (✉)
Graduate School of International Area Studies, Hankuk University of Foreign Studies (HUFS), Yongin-si, South Korea

© The Author(s) 2020
Y. Chang (ed.), *South Korea's Engagement with Africa*, Africa's Global Engagement: Perspectives from Emerging Countries, https://doi.org/10.1007/978-981-32-9013-6_7

organizations in developed countries increased as development objectives were stressed in foreign aid. They did not simply stay as a provider of support services but also promoted the need for development assistance. At a time when Western civil society's active involvement in international affairs was prominent, the Korean civil society began to remain calm at the same time. South Korea began its civil society culture in 1987 as citizens began a nationwide wave of protests against decades of authoritarian politics. Since then, the Korean civil society has seen an explosive growth with the tide of democratization. There are various opinions on the origin and history of Korean civil society, but considering the meaning of Korean civil society in terms of modern perspective, it can be seen as around the end of the 1980s when civil society was actively dynamic.

The study focuses on distinguishing organizations related to Africa among Korean civil societies based on the core values of Korean civil society and the strategies and definitions of the development NGO of David Corten (1990). Previously, mainly studies were conducted on the activities and status of Korea's development non-government organizations or civil society organizations (CSOs). With that in mind, it is meaningful that none of Korea's CSOs or NGOs engaged with Africa has been studied on a particular continent. In this chapter, there are four main types of organizations that represent civil society. First, the NGOs that implement projects directly on the continent of Africa called development NGOs or development CSOs; among them, there are a religious-based organizations called faith-based organizations (FBOs). A policy monitoring organization that monitors the Korean government's ODA policy, which is directly and indirectly related to the African continent. Other NGOs are divided into advocacy-focused NGOs aimed at improving perception of Africa. The analyses focused on the case of policy monitoring and advocacy organization, reflecting the characteristics of Korean civil society rather than on the project cases of development NGOs conducted mainly.

BACKGROUND OF THE KOREAN CIVIL SOCIETY

Today, the concept of civil society is understood as an area where social activities voluntarily take place to build public trust and community, apart from the logic of the state and market.[2]

Around the world, civil society has significantly grown since the 1980s. The democratization of Eastern Europe, Latin America, Asia, and South Africa is all indicative of the growth of civil society as citizenship and community take on greater importance. In the process of institutionalizing democracy, civic action is expanding into economic and social areas. On the other hand, in the developed world, traditional political participation, such as elections and political parties and trade unions, is growing and new civic-led activities are being created. Huntington described the process of democratization worldwide since the mid-1970s as a 'third wave'. With the culmination of the Cold War and democratization taking place around the world, increased globalization and communication have brought an opportunity for the growth of the global sense of citizenship.

The term NGO was first used in 1953 as a neutral term for the Organization of Other Categories by the United Nations, which consists of government organizations (GO).[3] Since the early 1970s, the term NGO began to be widely used as private organizations participated in international conferences organized by the United Nations and held NGO forums. Collective organizations that operate in the sphere of civil society include the voluntary association and the social movement organization, whose names are NGOs from participating in the work of the United Nations. However, civic activists around the world are against the term NGO. Although NGOs refer to all organizations that do have diplomatic status as national team members in the United Nations, they use the alternative term CSO, a civic group (Kim 2010). Civil Society Organization (CSO) is also called the third sector because it aims to adhere to the principles of non-profit, non-government, and non-artisan, and it acts in areas that are distinct from the activities of the state and market (Jung 1995).

Private organizations in Korea also expressed their determination to implement the power of civil society to realize the universal values of humanity and to ensure the shared future of humanity only by strengthening the strength of the civil society and activating the international solidarity of private organizations, in 1995, when they participated in Copenhagen's Social Summit. This growth in civil society has opened up new spaces for NGOs to operate. It was not until 1992 when the term NGO became widely known in Korea, as private organizations participated in the Rio Environment Conference, followed by the Copenhagen Social Development Summit in 1995, and the Women's Conference in Beijing.

The terms NGO and CSO have been the centerpiece of Western aid donors' policies and efforts. However, the use of clearly defined development NGOs and development CSOs in Korea has been mixed. In a study by Jang (2012), development NGOs were seen as one of the organizations within the CSOs. In other words, CSO includes non-market and non-governmental organizations and covers the scope of member-centric CSO, casual-oriented CSO, and service-oriented CSO. It also includes community-based organizations (CBO) or village committees, environmental groups, women's human rights groups, peasant associations, faith-based organizations, trade unions, professional associations, commerce meetings, independent research institutes, and non-profit media. The Asian Development Bank labels CSO as a third sector, separate from the government or business, and includes NGOs, CBOs, mass organizations, professional associations, trade unions, private research institutes, universities, foundations, and social movement groups, just like the Organisation for Economic Co-operation and Development—OECD (ADB 2011).

In this research, NGO primarily refers to non-governmental organizations participating in international development cooperation. In addition to development NGOs, various civic and social actors, including women's organizations, environmental groups, volunteer groups, medical and health groups, and human rights groups, are participating in international development cooperation, and the use of the term Civil Society Organization (CSO) is used to cover these groups. In Korean society, various CSOs have been categorized as development NGOs, focusing on international development cooperation activities. In this study, CSO is used to refer to voluntary and independent civil society organizations, including both development NGO and advocacy NGOs and is used in parallel with NGOs.

NGO is a general expression referring to organizations operating in the civil society area, not the realm of the state and market. Development NGOs refer to organizations that participate in international development, while CSOs cover groups of various characteristics within civil society, inducing NGOs. Recently, the term CSO has become more widely used as a more accurate representation of activities (Sohn and Han 2014).

A total of 43 government agencies and local governments manage the NPOs or NGOs in Korea, and it is difficult to identify the current status of civic and social groups associated with Africa.[4] According to the *Act on the Establishment and Operation of Public Interest Corporations in 1976*, the religious organizations, educational facilities, social welfare corporations, medical corporations, public utilities, arts, and cultural organizations are treated as public corporations. Currently, the number of non-profit corporations and non-profit organizations registered with related government departments in Korea is estimated at 33,689. Given that most organizations that carry out overseas projects must register with the Ministry of Foreign Affairs and Trade, it is estimated that 741 organizations are implementing overseas projects (*ibid*). Considering that faith-based organizations registered with other ministries are also interested in overseas projects, it is possible to predict that the number of civil society organizations directly or indirectly active in not only Asia but also Africa is increasing.

The Role and Classification of Civil Society

In this chapter, Korean CSOs that operate directly or indirectly with Africa are considered wide-ranging development NGOs. Based on existing research on the development NGOs studied by Clark and Corten, the CSOs engaged with Africa are to be distinguished.

John Clark (1991) divided the development NGOs into six types by reflecting the historical development process. The first is the Relief and Welfare Agencies. Second, the pioneer Technical innovation organizations with new and improved approaches to solving the development problem. Third, Public Service contractors which are commissioned to implement part of the Official Development Assistance (ODA) program in developed countries because they are more effective than the government. Fourth, popular development organizations focused on self-help and social development. Fifth, grassroots development organizations in the Southern Hemisphere, whose members are the poor and oppressed. Moreover, the last, it is the advocacy groups and networks that do not do business on-site and do education and lobbying for the primary purpose.

On the other hand, David C. Corten (1990) has classified activity types of development NGOs into four generations by observing the core activities of NGOs that have changed gradually. The first generation of NGOs carried out activities for emergency relief and welfare improvement, mainly supporting individuals or families affected by the disaster. However, since these activities have to be done immediately at the scene of the disaster, they focused their activities on logistics management of goods to quickly deliver relief to the disaster victims. However, the activities of these NGOs have always been hampered by a lack of resources. Moreover, as one of the solutions to these problems, they have focused on starving children for development education and promotional activities. The second-generation NGOs actively promoted projects aimed at specific areas or villages to prevent disasters and address poverty through humanitarian emergency relief efforts. Therefore, the focus of their activities was on managing the project successively, and they served as the main actors with common responsibilities for NGOs and communities. In order to solve the community's lethargy, they focused on development education and public relations activities on strengthening the self-reliance capacity of the community. The third-generation NGOs are tasked with developing a long-term and sustainable social, economic system for a relatively wide range of regions or countries beyond emergency relief or disaster prevention. To this end, specific policy and institutional changes are pursued because these changes must be preconditioned to achieve justice, sustainability, and comprehensive development. Not only NGOs but also the state and local governments, public institutions, and residents all participated as joint actors, focusing on strategic management of long-term development programs for rebuilding the failed economy and restoring the social system. Therefore, the focus of development education and public relations activities was also on the improvement of the system that hindered development. The fourth-generation NGOs seek change at national or global levels. Thus, decentralized actions for human-centered development will be strengthened to a larger scale than the second- and third-generation NGOs, thus focusing on autonomous management of integrated and vital networks beyond individual organizations.

Based on the distinction between Clark and Corten, Korean civil society, which is directly or indirectly related to Africa, can be divided into a religious-based organization belonging to the first generation in the fetal age and development NGOs and policy monitoring advocacy institutions that can belong to the second and third generations.

It is still tricky to tell if there are CSOs related to the continent of Africa that belong to the fourth generation. However, compared to a decade ago when the Korean NGOs and CSOs were concentrated in the first and second generations of Corten, it can be noted that these days, the activities of organizations focusing on policy monitoring and advocacy campaigns are becoming prominent.

Defining CSOs or NGOs of Korea Engaged with Africa

Initially, government aid agencies focused on poverty and unemployment in the 1970s, expanding the activities of development NGOs toward rural development and education, and efforts were made to expand the operations and provide supplemental government support to NGO development activities at small scales. Furthermore, religious missionary organizations initially devoted to missionary work in Africa tend to expand and convert into development NGOs.

According to the report issued by Korea NGO Council for Overseas Development Cooperation (KCOC), in 2015, 59 of South Korea's CSOs carried out 700 projects in 39 countries in Africa. The organizations mostly targeted the areas of education, health, social welfare, agricultural development, water, and hygiene at the grassroots levels.

As Koreans gained access to information on African countries through the media, NGOs engaged in poverty reduction activities in African countries or advertisements for fundraising activities. As of 2017, the number of foreign residents living in Korea stood at 2.18 million, up 72% from 1.57 million in 2013. During the same period, the number of residents from African countries increased by about 60% from 10,880 to 18,198 in 2017. Compared to the total number of foreigners residing in Korea, only about 0.8% of foreign residents are from African countries, making African residents a tiny sliver even within the minority communities of Korea. Since opportunities for Koreans to know and acquire the knowledge about African countries directly from an African foreign resident in Korea are nearly impossible, most Korean rely heavily on the media and NGOs' activities to receive the information about African-related issues.

One of the most common terms for using non-governmental organizations on the continent from the perspective of the third parties or donors is 'NGOs' or 'CSOs'. The definition of civil society as defined in the field of international development cooperation has been and is most widely used in the mainstream society of donor countries and international organizations.

According to the OECD DAC,

> [CSOs] can be defined to include all non-market and non-state organizations outside of the family in which people organize themselves to pursue

shared interests in the public domain. Examples include community-based organizations and village association, environmental groups, women's rights groups, farmer's associations, faith-based organizations, labor unions, co-operatives, professional associations, chambers of commerce, independent research institutes and the not-for-profit media.[5]

Based on the understanding of the definition and background of modern Korean civil society, one can find the fundamental reason why Korean civil society has entered the country of sub-Saharan African countries with some purpose and motive.

The development of history and the socio-economic background of Korea led to the emergence and importance of development NGOs and CSOs taking different paths. After the devastation of the Korean War, the country was an aid-recipient country; however, after rapid economic growth, Korea emerged as a donor when it joined the OECD as a member of the DAC in 2009.

The total size of the Korean ODA in 2018 was 932.8 billion KRW, with the ODA/GNI ratio of 0.086%. However, according to the International Development and Cooperation Comprehensive Implementation Plan, which is 12 years later, the ODA size (budget) of 2018 was about 3.48 trillion KRW, the world's 16th most significant in terms of total growth among OECD member countries.

ODA: The Momentum of Korea CSOs' Entry into Africa

Korea's development has been effective in overcoming challenges in the early stages as poor local conditions amid a lack of experience and limited finance created significant learning opportunities, where now an increasing number of NGOs are reaching a certain status granted by the United Nations in recognition of their achievements internationally. Since Korea's NGOs have only a short history of development cooperation, they often lack in experience, financing, and size of membership compared to more advanced NGOs in other donor countries. In a relatively short period, Korean NGOs have shown considerable progress given their short history, elevating their status within the broader global NGO community. Furthermore, the Korean government is also supporting development NGOs. The government has allocated a budget for international cooperation development NGOs since 1995, and to help this system, a private partnership department within the KOICA was established.

In February 1999, the KCOC was officially launched, consisting of 26 NGOs from Korea's overseas Civil Aid Organizations, facilitating Korea's international cooperation projects. It also strengthened ties between NGOs through the exchange of information and development of joint plans. Furthermore, it has become a vital policy dialogue channel with the government. From 1995, the government has been providing aid to developing countries through NGOs through KOICA support for 18 private aid organizations.

As the government expanded the ODA budget to support various programs in African countries, civil society began to establish its role in supporting the development and humanitarian projects. They also participated in the creation of an agenda for poverty and development in Africa and assisted in planning effective programs. The government-funded KOICA has pioneered development and cooperation programs in Africa in partnership with various private organizations. For example, the Korean Committee of UNESCO has planned a bridge project and has established and operated a regional learning center since 2010 to strengthen its literacy skills by sending Korean activists to six African countries. As part of KOICA's first public-private partnership project, the Bridge Program is designed to contribute to the eradication of illiteracy in Africa by combining KOICA's financial and administrative support, Samsung Electronics' resources and local infrastructure, and the expertise of UNESCO Korea Committee. And moreover various civil groups from religious backgrounds are also stepping up their volunteering work in Africa and sending young activists to short- and long-term programs. (Han 2013).

Table 7.1 shows the scale of the ODA to development CSOs and ODA through the development CSOs. ODA through development CSOs is that NGOs are participating in programs that are developed and held responsible by donor governments. This is an example of the growing importance of public-private cooperation in aid projects aimed at developing countries.

Table 7.1 Aid for civil society organizations 2010–2016 in Korea (USD million, disbursements, Constant 2015 prices)

	2010	2011	2012	2013	2014	2015	2016
ODA channeled to CSOs	1	1	1	1	2	1	4
ODA channeled through CSOs	18	23	25	27	31	38	34
ODA channeled to and through CSOs	19	23	27	28	33	39	39

Source: OECD (2018)

Table 7.1 shows that the size of ODA through CSOs is about eight times larger than that of the ODA to CSOs in 2016. From 2010 to 2016, the amount of ODA through CSOs has almost doubled. This implies that the importance of policy harmony with government agencies such as KOICA, which is in charge of grant-type aid, is also increasing. Korea's CSOs in the field of international development and cooperation regarding ODA can no longer be seen as a third party unrelated to the government.

In the field of international development cooperation, research on collaboration between the Korean government and NGOs began in the early 2000s (Chang 2001; Lee 2004) and increased in real earnest as of 2010 with Korea's accession to the OECD Development Assistance Committee (DAC). Most of the studies analyze the systems and support cases of advanced donor countries of the OECD DAC and present the challenges and improvement measures compared to domestic cases (Sohn et al. 2011; Sohn 2011; Jang 2012). It also analyzed the governance model of Japanese and German governments and NGOs horizontally and vertically (Kim and Park 2010), as well as the research on the process of institutional change in the case of joint fundraising in the Netherlands (Sohn and Han 2014) has been conducted. Alternatively, qualitative research was done to analyze the cooperation, supplementation, and supplemental relationships between the government and the development NGOs (Lee and Lee 2017). Quantitative analysis, however, has been done only by some studies (Kim 2010; Lee 2015).

According to the 2017 KOREA International Development Cooperation CSO book released by KCOC, the number of projects running in Asian countries was more than double the number of projects in African countries. The following Table 7.2 shows that unlike the number of projects conducted by region, Africa received only slightly more in total project expenses. This is believed to be due to the relatively large-scale projects implemented in Africa.

Despite the geographic advantage of Korean CSOs in geographically carrying out their projects in Asian countries, the more significant and important unit projects are shifting to Africa. Eight of the top ten countries, Vietnam, Bangladesh, Cambodia, Nepal, Mongolia, Myanmar, Philippines, that have received the highest number of implemented overseas projects belong to Asia, but only about half of the total project expenses are of the projects in Asia.

In 2015, the Korean government selected the second major strategic partner countries based on the income level and aid environment of developing countries, and economic and diplomatic relations with it's own coun-

Table 7.2 Project Expenses by continent (Unit: 1 million KRW)

	Self-Finance		Government Grant		Total Expenses	
	Amount	Proportion	Amount	Proportion	Amount	Proportion
Asia	114,246	24.8%	18,500	38.8%	132,746	26.1%
Africa	127,490	27.7%	18,849	39.5%	146,339	28.8%
Latin America	17,421	3.8%	1618	3.4%	19,039	3.7%
Middle East	7222	1.6%	545	1.1%	7767	1.5%
Oceania	less than 1 M	0.1%	–	–	Less than 1 M	0.1%
Europe	3982	0.9%	–	–	3982	0.8%
Multiple Nations	83,188	18.1%	5734	12.0%	88,922	17.5%
Other	106,815	23.2%	2440	5.1%	109,255	21.5%
Total	460,364	100%	47,686	100%	508,050	100%

The Board of Audit and Inspection. 2011 [Request for Disposal of Audit Results: Status of Implementation of Public Development Assistance (ODA)]. The Board of the Board of Audit and Inspection. 2012. [Audit Results Report: Audit of the Ministry of Foreign Affairs and Trade's press release]

Source: 2017 KCOC Korean International Development Cooperation CSO Statistics Handbook p. 21

Table 7.3 African Countries where Korean CSOs operate

No of Active Countries	Active Countries where Korean CSOs operate their projects
36	Ghana, Guinea, Guinea-Bissau, Nigeria, South Sudan, South Africa, Niger, Liberia, Rwanda, Madagascar, Malawi, Mali, Morocco, Mozambique, Benin, Burundi, Burkina Faso, Senegal, Somalia, Sudan, Swaziland, Sierra Leon, Eritrea, Ethiopia, Uganda, Egypt, Zambia, Central Africa Republic, Zimbabwe, Chad, Cameroon, Kenya, Cote d'Ivoire, Democratic Republic of the Congo, Tanzania, and Togo

Source: Edited by author based on 2017 KCOC Korean International Development Cooperation CSO Statistics Handbook p. 39

try as indicators; a total number of 24 countries were selected for support. Currently, seven African countries out of pro countries that are selected are Ghana, Rwanda, Mozambique, Senegal, Ethiopia, Uganda, and Tanzania. According to the report by KCOC in 2017, 23 of 96 states where the Korea Development CSOs carried out the projects in 2017, while the top 10 countries ranked second with Ethiopia (19,011 million KRW), Uganda (15,360 million KRW) and Tanzania (10,689 million KRW) showed that Korea's CSO is operating in the poorest countries (Table 7.3).

Development NGOs

Development NGOs have supported economic and social development in developing countries by providing humanitarian assistance and activities for regional development through private funds and government grants. While the early NGO's development activities were limited by a lack of resources and technology, the government has continually expanded the size of aid, significantly affecting economic growth in developing countries, including sub-Saharan Africa.

Kwon Kyung-im (2016) classified CSOs which are active in the international development cooperation sectors into seven types. First, the organizations used to be a foreign private aid organization transformed to donor organizations such as World vision, Korea Committee of UNICEF, Children's Foundation, and Save the Children. Second, the organizations that had carried out poverty reduction projects in Korea and transferred their knowledge to developing countries, including The Population Health and Welfare Association, The Korea Health Management Association, and Korea Saemaul Undong Center. Third, religious-based NGOs that were founded on a religious basis. Fourth, Korean self-reliance development NGOs, which were founded in Korea by Koreans, such as Good Neighbors, Global Civic Sharing, COoperation and Participation In Overseas NGOs (COPION)[6]. Fifth, professional-based organizations such as medical, legal, and agricultural organizations whose members were professionals in each area. Sixth, civil society organizations carrying out international development cooperation such as Korea YMCA and Peace Asia, and, lastly, the traditional social welfare institutions, which expanded their business to overseas, including Angel's Haven for Children, Heart to Heart International.[7]

Most of the NGOs mentioned earlier were registered as members of the KCOC to implement their projects in Africa. In a 2017 handbook published by KCOC, Korea Development CSOs were classified into three major categories. The handbook lists 121 Korean self-reliance organizations[8] (86.4%), 18 International NGO partner organizations (12.9%), and one other organization (0.7%). Among the most notable development NGOs such as World Vision, Save the Children, and Good Neighbors for the history and scale of their experience in running the project of self-reliance organizations and International NGO partner organizations have been carrying out various projects for a long time in African countries. As these development NGOs are registered as social welfare corporations in Korea, they are carrying out domestic and overseas projects. Also, the amount of donations is enormous as they carry out active number of projects in developing countries. According to the top ten organizations in terms of the scale of donations by public released by Guide Star Korea[9], as of the business year 2017, there are six corporations with 30 billion KRW or more in donation income. Among them, the corporations with more than 100 billion KRW in donations were World Vision and ChildFund Korea. A leading International NGO (INGO), Save the Children Korea also had 56.1 billion KRW as their donation income and a representative self-reliance NGO, Good Neighbors, also had 17.5 billion KRW.

The World Vision is a leading development NGO, and their work can be summarized in three significant projects: Emergency Relief, Transformational Development, and Advocacy. In 2014, a total of 871,219 people were supported.[10] The support was extended not only to victims of acute disasters, which have become a major international issue such as Typhoon Haye, Syrian refugees, and the Gaza Strip, but also to people suffering from chronic disasters in 27 countries including Somalia, Congo, Sudan, South Africa, Uganda, and Zimbabwe.

The advocacy project is similar to other policy monitoring and civic group activities. In general, there have been advocacy campaigns to identify the structural causes of poverty and to change policies, institutions, and customs.

> As part of this effort, the World Vision Korea carried out campaigns such as the aid transparency campaign, activities to propose the Overseas Humanitarian Assistance Policy, Campaign against child labor and policy-making activities, Post-2015 development proposal activity and the global children's Health campaign. (Child Health Now)[11]

As of 2017, Save the Children International actively carried out its project in 117 countries, while Save the Children Korea was active in 20 countries. Among them, Save the Children Korea operated its projects in eight African countries: Niger, Liberia, Sierra Leone, Ethiopia, Uganda, Zambia, Kenya, and Cote d'Ivoire. Main activities are child sponsorship services abroad, maternal health project, protection and support for refugee children, primary education, and drought response projects related to environmental issues which are underway in Kenya and Ethiopia (Save the Children 2017).

Good Neighbors was founded in March 1991 to research and promote welfare both locally and globally based on the spirit of Christianity. This is meaningful in that Good Neighbors is the first development NGO established in Korea by a Korean. Starting with aid and development assistance to Bangladesh, they have started full-fledged relief activities. In 1996, the UN Economic Council granted the General Consultative Status, which is the highest NGO status to Good Neighbors. The organization has two divisions. One of them is called 'Social welfare foundation Good Neighbors', which provides specialized welfare services within Korea, and the other division that operates as the 'Good Neighbors International' carries out overseas relief development projects and aid project for North Korea. Through continued development, the organization is currently implementing overseas relief development projects at 212 workplaces in 35 countries as of February 2019. They are currently active in 15 Asian countries, 5 Latin American countries, and 12 African countries[12].

These major NGOs are doing a variety of projects in Africa, not only in most of the priority partner countries selected by the Korean government but also in the most needed African countries.

As for the field, they have not only carried out direct projects in education or health sectors but also campaigns to raise awareness about civil society. However, they are not limited to the African region, and they rather deal with issues such as children's rights or girl's education.

FBOs in Africa

The international community's interest and support for 'Faith-Based Organization' have recently increased. In particular, in Western society, FBO is recognized as a significant NGO group doing good to the socially vulnerable with an attitude of divine love and devotion and being an essential participant in society. Also, expanding financial support for religious faith-based NGOs and establishing cooperative partnerships are also increasing.

In the international development cooperation sector, 'Faith-Based Organizations (FBO)' is an organization with different religious backgrounds as a religious NGO which carries out development and relief work at the national, regional, and international levels. The United States Agency for International Development (USAID) defines FBO as 'a group of individuals with spiritual or religious systems that guide them to work together' (Green 2003).

FBO stipulates that organizations sponsored or organized by believers of confident religions, such as Christianity, Judaism, Buddhism, Catholicism, and Islam, organizations established or motivated by religious believers, founders or boards of directors, and religiously established motivations in the mission statement (Ferris 2005: 6).

The conceptual intent for religious belief-based NGOs is diverse. Among these, the Faith-Based Organization (FBO) is the most commonly used concept in recent major research reports on international development and policy. Specifically, the Joint United Nations Programme on HIV/AIDS (UNAIDS), an international organization dealing with AIDS, defined religious faith-based NGOs as FBO and described them as 'an organization that performs development and relief projects at national, regional and international levels'. (UNAIDS 2009). Clarke and Jennings (2007) referred to FBO as 'an organization that has been guided or inspired by their activities from theological school or specific interpretations or principles or teachings of the faith'.

In Korea, in the late nineteenth and early twentieth centuries, Christian missionaries not only established and operated various modern schools, hospitals, orphanages, and nursing homes before the government but also helped break down the feudal class society and promote greater equality and humanism. During religious periods, international NGOs, such as the World Vision, entered Korean society to spearhead the beginning of Korean NGOs, and the scope of their activities has also expanded to all areas including social services, education, political advocacy, and relief. Especially in the field of international development cooperation, they have the advantage of participating from a committed position based on doctrines and extensive experience in carrying out missionary and relief work in developing countries. Besides, FBOs often cultivate communal and civic life with clear doctrinal lessons about neighborhood love.

In the field of international development cooperation, the history of development NGOs in Korea began in the 1950s with the support of foreign private aid organizations assisting in the aftermath of the Korea War. Since then, in the 1960s and 1970s, there has been a government-related institution addressing population and health problems, while the country expanded socially and economically, and in the 1980s, FBOs were mainly engaged in development and relief activities related to overseas missionary work.

However, according to the CSO handbook of the KCOC 2017, the proportion of organizations that responded to the survey that the purpose or activity of the organization was not related to a particular religion has steadily increased since 2011, reaching 60% in 2017. This shows that faith-based organizations still account for a significant portion, but as time goes by, secular affiliations are growing to demonstrate the universal values of civil society and maturation of Korean CSOs.

Korean Catholic Church

The Korean Catholic Church participates in overseas projects through their official foreign aid organization, the Korea Caritas International. Caritas Korea is actively involved with 165 members of the international Caritas, and unlike Buddhist faith-based organizations which are regionally skewed toward Asia, in 2017, the organization supported refugees from Nigeria, Niger, South Sudan, Bhutan, Myanmar, Syria, Sudan, and the Democratic Republic of the Congo, and Iraq. Korea Caritas International is focused mostly on emergency aid and development cooperation. As of 2018, they have carried out projects supporting livelihoods, support for children's education, and medical support in 14 countries. The total amount of overseas assistance from 1993 to 2018 by the Korea Caritas International was 53.2 billion KRW.[13] In 2018 alone, the Catholic FBO provided 3.9 billion KRW (3.4 million USD) for 50 projects in 33 countries. Also, some 20 organizations, including the ONE BODY ONE SPIRIT under Seoul Archdiocese, Gwangju Foundation for Human Rights and Peace, and the Joy Sharing Foundation, are working together. The Korean Catholic Church has been laying the foundation for information exchange and cooperation among aid agencies through 'Catholic Overseas Aid Network' since 2011.[14]

Buddhism NGO in Africa?

Buddhist Development NGO has started to work widely and actively in earnest in the international development cooperation sector since the early 1990s, and the Korean Join Together Society (JTS) began with relief work for the untouchable people in India. Over the past 20 years, about 20 out of 30 Buddhist NGOs in Korea are currently active in international development cooperation. Since the 2000s, the Korean Buddhist community has begun a more active engagement at the grassroots level in the international cooperation sector. By breaking the practice of collecting donations and delivering them to the government authorities, emergency relief units were dispatched to the scene, and by launching related restoration and regional projects, they have sought and implemented more professional approaches in their aid relief, working more closely with direct victims and aid recipients (Lee 2015).

The Buddhist-based activities include operating orphanages, kindergartens, local children's centers, and implementing water and irrigation projects, establishing hospitals and health centers, and other projects to improve the health and environment of the communities they assist. Although Buddhist NGOs have recently entered specialized fields such as supporting fair trade and spreading appropriate technologies, it is still considered insufficient to address international problems, including poverty effectively. According to Table 7.4, among many Buddhist-based development NGOs, about five significant groups are actively running their projects in developing countries, including Korea JTS, Good Hands, Lotus World, and The Promise.

Among Korea's major development NGOs, some organizations such as World Vision Korea and Good Neighbors are widely recognized as Christian-based organizations. Although FBOs belonged to the existing first-generation defined by Corten, it was able to witness an increasingly developed form, not focusing on one-dimensional fundraising campaigns and relief efforts. The proportion of FBOs operating in Africa and other developing countries is high in Christianity, while the Buddhist-based organizations were active in major Asian developing countries similar to cultural background and belonging to the Buddhist cultures.

Table 7.4 List of Buddhist-based organizations in the development sector

Name of Organizations	Oversea Projects Countries
Join Together Society (JTS)[a]	North Korea, India, Philippines
Good Hands[b]	Cambodia, Myanmar, Laos, Mongolia, Kenya
Lotus World[c]	Cambodia, Myanmar, Laos,
The Promise[d]	Nepal, East-Timor, Marshall Island, Malawi, Myanmar, India, Bhutan, North Korea, India, Vietnam, Sri Lanka, Haiti, China

Source: Reconfigured by the author based on the information on the each organizations' each official web page

[a]https://www.jts.or.kr/
[b]http://goodhands.or.kr/main/main.php
[c]http://www.lotusworld.or.kr/
[d]http://www.thepromise.or.kr/

Aid Policy Monitoring CSOs

According to the Encyclopedia of Korean Culture[15], civil society organizations are defined as non-governmental organizations that continually represent opinions of civil society. Although it does not have any coercive power, it has secured supporters of civil society through commenting and exerting influence on the government, businesses, and the media through it.

The Citizen's Coalition for Economic Justice (CCEJ) and People's Solidarity for Participatory mainly focus on the monitoring and efficiency of ODA government policies. The activities of CCEJ widely cover the economic justice in terms of policy issues, and People's Solidarity for Participatory instead focuses on Asia in terms of regional level and intensely working and monitoring democracy and human rights issues as well as Korean ODA policies.

The civil society movement in Korea began with the birth of the Citizen's Coalition for Economic Justice in 1989 and took place in various fields, including politics, economy, administration, environment, education, women, media, culture, and consumers. However, since 2010 South Korea's civic groups have relatively weakened their performance compared to the 2000s, and the number of times that civic groups' claims have been reported to the media has decreased, but the direction of the reports and citizen's perception of civil society have also changed negatively. The main reason is that the government has accepted many of the demands of civic groups and as a result, public's support for civic groups has declined.

The Citizens' Coalition for Economic Justice was created by a group of citizens voluntarily with 0% of government subsidy. And it is a non-governmental organization focused on the movement for economic inequality and economic justice in Korea, including the eradication of real estate speculation, the introduction of the real-name financial real-name system, and raising the minimum wage. As the amount of foreign aid increased, the CCEJ analyzed the OECD DAC Peer Review Report, commented, and consistently raised on international social issues.

Although the CCEJ does not directly conduct business in African countries, it is trying to encourage public campaigns and civic participation that are not directly related to political or economic factors toward the efficiency and resource allocation of the aid delivered by civil society. In particular, due to the lack of short history and philosophy of international development cooperation in the situation where the ODA budget has been increased, the number of corruptions mobilized by the previous regime has been steadily increasing. Each time, African countries are the most closely related to Korean ODA policy directly or indirectly as the target area selected as a policy of resource diplomacy or the countries that decided to follow the development model of Korea by inheriting the spirit of 'Saemaul Movement'.

The Korean government has used ODA as a means of resource diplomacy as an aid for companies to advance overseas and develop overseas resources. According to the third Basic Plan for Overseas Resource Development (2007–2016) written at the end of the Roh Moo-hyun administration, it is necessary to mobilize available diplomatic means for strategic resource diplomacy, and especially to support ODA to create a favorable atmosphere before entering the country. It was around the middle of the Myung-bak Lee administration that the plan to link ODA to resource diplomacy became full-fledged. The Myung-bak Lee administration's resource diplomacy is an overseas resource development project that started with the aim of securing resources stably in Korea, which lacks natural resource. Especially, considering the situation where the African countries have abundant resources but the resource development performance is low due to the unstable situation, the Korean government encouraged the packaged resource development such as building power plants and social overhead capital (SOC) for the African region by utilizing ODA. Therefore, the government chose to build roads or schools or hospitals in order to create a favorable environment in exchange for acquiring mineral mining rights or joint development projects in connection with resource diplomacy and ODA. However, the government has provided mineral resources exploration and investigation projects themselves as a form of aid. About eight of the African countries (Ghana, Nigeria, Libya, Mozambique, Algeria, Uganda, Kenya, and the Democratic Republic of Congo) received free aid in the name of technical cooperation in mineral exploration with ODA funds. The Myung-bak Lee administration had a policy intention to focus more on mineral exploration than the previous government and actively utilized the grant project to investigate minerals. Civic groups criticize the Myung-bak Lee administration's intention to investigate the amount of mineral resources reserves in other countries for the economic benefit of donor countries for the purpose of acquiring resources whether it was pure intentions of international development. CCEU and People Power21 criticized the resources diplomacy scandal of the Myung-bak Lee and raised the question of effectiveness and transparency in the regime's ODA policies.

The movement for Saemaul is no exception, as the underlying theme of international development is suggested on an impromptu basis whenever the regime changes. CCEJ also raised questions about the Saemaul Movement[16] which Park Geun-hye government actively pursued the primary basis of the international development cooperation policy. They argue that for the Saemaul Movement to become a global village development program, it should look at the outcome and its attributes as well. People Power 21 raised the issues as well that the core of critical evaluation of the Saemaul Movement in the 1970s was the 'National-led mental reform movement to maintain the dictatorial regime'. However, the 'International Expansion Plan of the Saemaul Movement' adopted by the Park Geun-hye government in 2016 also emphasizes 'reform of the residents' consciousness in the mental aspect'. While it is desirable for Korea to contribute to rural development and poverty eradication in developing countries, People Power 21 criticizes that it is not to globalize the uniform and nationalist mental reform movement during the past Korean development dictatorship by adhering to the political cause of spreading the Saemaul Movement. And they strongly criticize the Saemaul ODA of the Park Geun-hye government as a one-sided idea that ignores the capacity and consciousness level of the residents of the developing countries. They also urged the government to reconsider the 'Globalization of Saemaul Movement' strategy and to conduct proper verification and evaluation work on Saemaul ODA in the presence of civil society, academia, and experts.

ODA Watch/People's Initiative for Development Alternative[17]

CCEJ's international committee was formed on June 2, 2006 as a department under CCEJ, but in March 2009, the task of monitoring the policy within the international committee was reborn as ODA (Our Development Alternative) Watch as a completely independent policy NGO from CCEJ. The rebranded organization was launched as a full-scale policy monitoring movement while providing advocacy. Within the early stages of ODA Watch, the organization provided research and networked professional execution committee members and former and current NGO working institutions to monitor and research policies for development projects carried out in Africa resulting in a monthly ODA Watch Letters (OWLs).

The Webzine ODA Watch letter was launched in November 2006, and a total of 115 monthly issues were produced until September 2016. This webzine is relaunched as a Development Alternative PIDA every other month when ODA watch met for their 10th anniversary and re-named it to People's Initiative for Development Alternative (PIDA). To the public, the content of the webzine covers a wide range of topics and not just in African countries but also various areas of development and cooperation not only in African countries.

People's Solidarity for Participatory (People Power 21)[18]

In 1996, the International Solidarity Committee of the People's Solidarity for Participatory integrated the international Solidarity Committee and the Human Rights Commission and established a new International Committee in 2000. With a focus on human rights issues in Asia and ODA policy monitoring, the organization also works on the promotion of human rights and democratic solidarity in Asian countries.

The organization published the 'Global Citizen's Society and Issues' in May 2002 and began to monitor policies such as ODA in the second half of 2002. In 2005, a campaign to monitor international development and cooperation policies was launched to provide greater depth. The International Committee prepared the International Development Charter in 2005; interpellated ODA at the inspection of the administration; published newsletters for ODA policy monitoring in the global community; and held many rallies, debates, and news conferences.

The People's Solidarity for Participatory only has a few activities directly related to the issues related to African countries since the organization is geographically engaged in human rights and democracy projects in Asian countries though the organization is involved in activities that are in common with CCEJ and other policy monitoring organizations, and there are three projects related to Africa.

Since the Arab Spring in 2011, the organization issued statements on democracy ending Libya's Gadhafi dictatorship and Egypt's Mubarak dictatorship where Korean companies have entered these countries' market. They also urged awareness of civil society and the public by holding public lectures about the Jasmine Revolution on the modern history of North Africa in the Middle East, which is as remote and less friendly as African countries. Furthermore, nor were they afraid of the 2012 CNK International government scandal and sharp criticism of the ODA.[19] Since it was revealed that the Prime Minister's Office had chosen Cameroon as the leading strategic partner country for ODA in the process of obtaining mineral rights to develop a diamond in Cameroon, the organization gave a sharp criticism on the issue of the opacity in the selection of crucial cooperative countries and corruption within the government. It became known that the KOICA's aid to Cameroon has jumped sevenfold in two-year periods as diamond development rights were being discussed. Through the CNK scandal, it was revealed that Cameroon's addition as an ODA strategy partner country came through the intervention of former Deputy Minister of Knowledge Economy, Park Young-Joon. Later, the People Power 21 and the CCEJ criticized that the amount of aid that was levied on taxpayer's money was not used to reduce poverty and realize humanitarianism objectives in the recipient country but was applied to pad the pockets of industry.

These policy watchdog groups raised suspicions that the selection of strategic cooperative countries that can receive government ODA was based on ambiguous standards related to resource diplomacy as a means of diplomacy. Therefore, they argued that the establishment of independent aid agency responsible for the overall ODA policy should be considered. As shown in Table 7.5 the list of priority partner countries has changed in every regime, as civic groups have raised. Ironically, the DR Congo and Cameroon, which had doubts what policy watchdogs organizations raised, were selected as strategic partner countries and have a very close relationship with the resource diplomacy of the Myung-bak Lee regime. Most recently, the organization also raised the concerns about an electronic voting system that was implemented by Korean companies as part of an ODA business in DR

Table 7.5 Priority partner countries in Africa continent

Year	No. of countries	Name of priority partner countries	Type of aid
2010	4	Angola, Tanzania, Madagascar, and Mozambique	Priority Partner countries for Concession Loan
2007–2010	5	Nigeria, Senegal, Egypt, Ethiopia, and Tanzania	Priority Partner countries for Grant
October 2010	8	Ghana, DR Congo, Nigeria, Ethiopia, Mozambique, Cameroon, Rwanda, and Uganda	Priority Partner countries for Concession Loan and Grant
In 2015	7	Ghana, Ethiopia, Rwanda, Uganda, Senegal, Mozambique, and Tanzania	Priority Partner countries for Concession Loan and Grant

Source: Rebuilding by the author based on the data of KOICA, the Institute of Audit and Inspection (2011): 20

Congo, formerly a key ODA strategy partner country. Questions were asked about the National Election Commission's 'Korean Election System Overseas Dissemination Project' over concerns regarding the appropriateness of introducing an electronic voting system to local circumstances and instead raised concerns over potential election fraud.

KoFid and KCOC

Korea Civil Society Forum on International Development Cooperation (KoFid) is a network of Korean civil society organizations working to make development cooperation more effective. The network was established on 29 September 2010 through consultations among Korea civil society organizations (KCOC).

There are 26 member organizations registered within KoFid which include research and development NGOs and ODA policy monitoring groups. Through strengthening the capabilities of Korean civil society, KoFid monitors the ODA policy of the Korean government and mainly provides aid and development policy suggestions and advocacy. KoFid, like the aforementioned policy monitoring organizations, criticized the ODA of the Myung-bak Lee and Park Geun-hye governments for making it as a foreign policy and political means.

The previous activities of the CCEJ, the People's Solidarity for Participatory, the PIDA, and the KoFid, which monitor ODA policies and engage citizens, are different from development NGOs, which carries out the development projects directly in African countries. However, they contribute significantly to the process of informing citizens about both the African continent and the government's efforts in the region including the budget by monitoring each administration's ODA policies, selection of key partners, and budget allocation.

Besides, many development NGOs and their significant partners are operating in Africa's poorest countries with the support of KOICA, a crucial government organization. However, there is a significant distinction between policy monitoring NGOs as they have raised issues of aid transparency, as KOICA and other government-related organizations fund many development NGOs.

Since internal reflection within ODA societies has been made by raising the issue of ODA projects in African countries, civil society continues a role that emphasizes the importance of increasing efficiency and transparency in the increasing among of aid. At each time of the establishment of CPS and the readjustment of the strategic partner countries, these aid-monitoring policy groups continued to raise questions about the government's unilateral drive and continue to demand that the opinions of civil society be reflected, and changes were made.

KCOC was established in 1999 and is a consultative body of the Korean Development NGOs, which provide emergency relief and development assistance in many needed areas around the world. The primary activities of the KCOC include enhancing the capabilities of NGOs, policy advocacy and civic education, building a network within domestic and overseas, and dispatching of the volunteer corps. The KCOC has been operating the World Friends NGO Volunteer Group since 2004. Starting with the displacements of 33 volunteers in cooperation with International development NGOs and KOICA in 2004, so far, as many as 3000 volunteers have been dispatched to various fields and jobs around the world. In 2017, 343 volunteers were active in 33 countries through cooperation with 83 NGOs. A total of 33% of the volunteers were sent to African countries, including Ghana and Burkina Faso in the same year.

In terms of capacity enhancement by private organizations, the company is conducting an incubation project for public-private cooperation. The KCOC has organized an integrated capacity improvement program to support the project formation process to find new partners and find outstanding projects in collaboration with the KOICA since 2012 to effectively carry out the international development cooperation projects of development NGOs. A growing number of small and medium-sized civil society organizations are funded by this incubating program to develop new and excellent businesses before embarking on full-scale projects to new locations such as Africa. Regionally, 15 organizations from 8 countries in Asia and 8 organizations from 5 countries in Africa including Ethiopia, Kenya, Rwanda, Tanzania, and Madagascar received support through this program.

Advocacy and Awareness CSOs: Africa Insight

As mentioned earlier, Korean civic groups can be divided into three main categories: Development NGOs/development CSOs that are carrying out community development and education programs, health care, projects in African countries. Second, a policy monitoring civil society organizations that monitor the public-private cooperation project and the use and distribution of

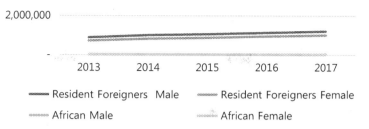

Fig. 7.1 Status for foreign residents in Korea (2013–2017) (Source: Kosis.kr)

the Korean government's aid budget. Lastly, CSOs that conduct an exchange and culture-oriented advocacy campaign with Africans within Korea.

Africa Insight, founded in April 2013, focuses on breaking the widespread prejudice against African countries and increasing the network of Africans in Korea, unlike other NGOs and civic groups that conduct business directly in African countries.

Currently, according to Fig. 7.1, the number of foreigners staying in Korea is increasing every year. As of 2017, about 2.18 million foreigners have visited Korea. Among them, the number of expatriates from Africa was 0.8% of the total foreign population or 18,198 as of 2017.[20]

Despite the growing number of foreigners from African countries entering and staying in Korea, however, most Koreans have a negative perception of Africa created by frequently negative exposure to fundraising campaigns by major CSOs and media focusing on extreme poverty or violence. Although many development NGOs are still engaged in direct and indirect activities to fight poverty in Africa, Africa Insight is the only civil society organization that aims to break the stereotypes that have been hardened by Koreans due to the objectification of poverty eradication. Not many studies have been done by Koreans on the image of Africa as a whole. However, there is a number of reports on Africa's image produced by Korean broadcasters.

Previous studies have confirmed through interviews with views that Africa's image has deteriorated further through a documentary about Africa produced by a significant Korean broadcaster (Park and Lee 2012).

For Koreans, Africa is still geographically remote that carries an image of poverty. The traditional Korean perception of Africa is a reproduction of Western prejudices. By ignorance and bias against Africa, they understand Africa only with its primacy and uncivility or romanticize Africa with vague yearning and curiosity (Han 2006, 2007). The Korean government introduced Africa as the place where Tarzan and Jane shared beautiful love or described Africans as dancing and singing when they were happy or sad. Such perceptions may be repeated or strengthened in the field of education (Kim and Han 2012).

The number of registered non-profit organizations in Korea is also increasing as the amount of interest and assistance to African countries outside of Korea increases. Although private donations are also steadily growing, the importance of individual sponsorship is growing, as non-profit organizations are not provided with sufficient resources (Lee 2018).

Currently, Korea still has too many negative media portrayals of Africa, and it is passing through a transitional period in which the negative public's negative prejudice against Africa is showing up. There is little media research on Africa and Kim Chun-Shik et al. 2015 mainly analyzed content on media coverage, advertising, and fundraising broadcasts, described Africa in a negative frame, along with expressions of poverty, death, despair, as well as devastation. He showed a tendency to a passive structure with an incompetent and lethargic look. In particular, sponsored advertisements, fundraising broadcasts, and media campaigns for African aid by development NGOs that fund child sponsorship often contain dramatic and provocative images and messages, along with negative descriptions of Africa.

The growing interest in African aid in Korean society has increased as aid agencies actively campaigned for media and increased broadcasting content related to African aid. Currently, state aid and charity organizations are conducting active media campaigns such as sponsorship ads and fundraising broadcasts, and in fact, they believe that donations to Africa have increased considerably (Save the Children 2011, 2013).

However, critics are highly critical of the campaign's unilateral and unrealistic image of the region and its people (Park 2013). The images of Africa on the media are familiar primitive and dangerous, a non-social area dominated by death, suffering and disease, and jungle and animals (Park 2013; Park and Ryu 2010; Park and Lee 2012; Ukadike 1990).

If the most major CSOs are operating campaigns and educational programs aimed at encouraging the public to improve and participate in the global issues of global civic education, this organization takes precedence over issues on the subject of Africa. First, the organization's primary campaign is a campaign to improve awareness through the knowledge and respect for Africa, and they are also conducting anti-discrimination campaigns through monitoring of leaders' opinions. One of the most common campaigns about Africa is that Africa is not a country, but a continent. Africa Insight argues that people should know about Africa through reliable facts and data about the continent, which has been biased based on the image of poverty. It also strives to improve the perception that Africa should be respected as a partner, not as a help, to break down the image of a continent that has a keen perception as a beneficiary. Besides, if there are any lawmakers and local celebrities who are influential in opposing disparate, racist comments or acts of aggression against Africa countries, the organization states this through a signature petition movement.[21]

As the ODA's budget increases, the number of African students seeking higher education opportunities in Korea is also increasing. The cumulative number of students are mostly from Priority partner countries since these students came with the Korean government' scholarship as part of ODA programs. As shown in Table 7.6, from 2012 to 2017, the number of students in the top eight countries has been increasing with 8255. In particular, students from Ghana and Kenya, who live in Korea, are organizing an autonomous student association and cooperating with their embassy. The Africa Insight provides a chance to directly participate in improving awareness of Africa in Korea through network and exchanges with student associations from Africa. For example, they run the Seoul Africa festival every May and encouraged African students and African expats group living in Korea to promote their countries and culture to locals. Such efforts are recognized as a CSO specialized only on the African continent, and they are active in various fields, including the operation of Swahili language courses in cooperation with the Tanzania Embassy in Korea. The activities of the African Insight could be an example of a new civil society organization that represents the third and fourth generations defined by Corten, unlike existing development NGOs and FBOs.

Table 7.6 Numbers of African students by nationality in Korea from 2012–2017

Nationality	Cumulative number of students from 2012 to 2017	Proportion
Cameroon	1722	14%
Ethiopia	1343	11%
Nigeria	1177	10%
Ghana	1159	10%
Kenya	890	7%
Uganda	731	6%
Tanzania	620	5%
Rwanda	613	5%

Source: Kosis.kr

Conclusion

It is not easy to establish a link between South Korea's civil society and the African continent. First of all, the author asked the existential question of the existence of Korean civil society. Since the late 1980s when Korea experienced state-led economic growth after the Korean War, modern civil society is thought to have been formed in Korea. In a short history of more than 30 years, the study looked at how Korean civil society has been behaving concerning the African continent with the characteristics of a civil society that characterized by only Korean civil society.

Over the past decade or so, the author has seen an increasing number of people waiting to board a flight to Africa from Incheon International Airport. Most Koreans leave for Africa to carry out international development cooperation projects to fight poverty, for missionary work, or to travel to the unknown continent. Among them, many South Koreans still visiting Africa were mainly involved in the field of development cooperation or traveling on business trips on development cooperation projects by private or public funding. This can be an example of a rebuttal in which aid or NGOs first comes to mind when thinking intuitively about Korean Civil society and Africa.

However, the development cooperation CSOs cannot simply replace the Korean civil society with the development CSOs that focus on eliminating poverty in Africa. Although the amount of aid to African countries has increased, the number of Korea's development CSOs is also increasing, and their scope or field or activity is increasingly comparable to that of any advanced donor country although Africa is geographically more remote than other Asian developing countries, given the scale of projects carried out by the development CSOs.

Besides, many South Korean civil society organization from religious backgrounds are conducting their businesses in developing countries. Among them, a Buddhist-based organization in Korea is mainly focused on Asian countries for development cooperation and community development. This is believed to be because certain religions, like Buddhism, have an advantage in entering a country. Christian-based and Catholic faith-based organizations, like other CSOs, were directly carrying out projects in African countries through regional development projects and emergency relief projects. It is quite encouraging that faith-based organizations are moving away from the primary stage of raising funds and carrying out various direct projects. It was also noted that many NGOs operating overseas projects in Africa or developing countries have far higher numbers or organizations unrelated to their religious base.

As with other donor countries, the support and role of the government agency mainly KOICA were very prominent in strengthening the capacity of civil society in the field of International development cooperation sector. Among them, the KCOC identifies the current status of the organizations that conduct international development cooperation projects every year to determine the size or needs of the organizations. Moreover, it also compiles and publishes a handbook by compiling the overall information of the development CSOs, including the size of their financial resources, and the scope of their activities. And not only does it play a role in coordinating policies with private organizations and government agencies in ODA projects, but it also operates a program to strengthen the capacities of each private organization through the KOICA budget. Most of the existing FBOs belong to the first generation as Corten distinguished. In addition, by considering the areas of activity and focus of Korea's self-reliance development NGOs, these NGOs can be classified to be included in the level of second generation and public service traders as defined by Corten. As the amount of ODA increases, public-private partnership projects where development NGOs also involved increases. It increased the chances of Korean CSOs to enter Africa and implement their projects, but their autonomy to check the government is also limited. As in advanced countries, CSOs such as CCEJ are engaged in ODA policy monitoring to monitor the direction of ODA budgets and policies that affect Africa directly or indirectly. Furthermore, African-related CSOs continue to grow, with young people working or living in African countries since the late 2000s as members of KOICA Volunteer Corps or NGO volunteer groups. The emergence of specialized Korea's CSO such as Africa Insight can be seen as an encouraging achievement in a short period.

Notes

1. In this chapter, rather than using the exact definitions of civil society, NGOs, and CSOs, the three preceding terms are used in a mix. Organizations operating in the field of international development cooperation sector used by Korea civil society organization (KCOC), in particular, are using a mix of development CSOs (as defined by KCOC) and development NGOs (general terms used extensively).

2. Encyclopedia of Korean Culture: http://encykorea.aks.ac.kr/Contents/SearchNavi?keyword=%EC%8B%9C%EB%AF%BC%EC%82%AC%ED%9A%8C&ridx=0&tot=2655.
3. Willets, P. (1982): 15.
4. The Beautiful Foundation 2018, Issue Paper 1, Korea's non-profit organization overview status analysis. https://research.beautifulfund.org/wp-content/uploads/20180620_070638.pdf.
5. How Development Assistance Committee (DAC) members work with civil society organizations (CSOs) in development co-operation: https://www.oecd.org/dac/peer-reviews/48784967.pdf.
6. Cooperation and Participation in Overseas NGOs (http://e.copion.or.kr/).
7. http://heart-heart.org/.
8. According to the KCOC Korea CSOs handbook English version, CSOs established by Koreans and started in Korea engaging with international development cooperation activities were marked as self-reliance organization. Therefore, the author uses the same term.
9. Guide Star Korea (2018), 2018 Public Interest Corporation Analysis Report <Social Welfare Corporation>.
10. http://www.worldvision.or.kr/business/dataCenter/worldReport/wvreport_list.asp?searchType=&searchKeyword=&iPage=3.
11. http://www.worldvision.or.kr/eng/participation/childHealth_campaign/childHealth.asp.
12. Niger, Chad, Cameroon, Uganda, Rwanda, Zambia, South Sudan, Ethiopia, Kenya, Tanzania, Malawi, Mozambique.
13. http://www.caritas.or.kr/business/overseas/cooperation/status/.
14. https://www.cpbc.co.kr/CMS/newspaper/view_body.php?cid=744710&path=201901.
15. http://heart-heart.org/en/.
16. The Saemaul Movement is officially marked as Saemaul Undong by the Saemaul Movement Center, and the term Saemaul Movement or New Community Movement is used in other papers and comments by Korea Institute for International Economic Policy (KIEP).
17. http://pida.or.kr/.
18. http://www.peoplepower21.org/.
19. http://www.peoplepower21.org/International/868092.
20. Korean Statistical Information Services, http://kosis.kr/statisticsList/statisticsListIndex.do?menuId=M_01_01&vwcd=MT_ZTITLE&parmTabId=M_01_01&parentId=A.1;A8.2;#SelectStatsBoxDiv.
21. Korean Statistical Information Services, http://kosis.kr/statisticsList/statisticsListIndex.do?menuId=M_01_01&vwcd=MT_ZTITLE&parmTabId=M_01_01&parentId=A.1;A8.2;#SelectStatsBoxDiv.

REFERENCES

ADB. (2011). ADB Cooperation with Civil Society: Annual Report 2009. https://www.adb.org/sites/default/files/institutional-document/31405/2009-ngo-annual-report.pdf.

An, S. (2010). A Study on Partnership Between Government and Development NGOs. *Future Social Welfare Research, 1*(1), 65–87. Korean Research Society for Social Welfare Practices.

Chang, H. S. (2001). The ODA Policy of OECD/DAC Member Countries and Cooperation with NGO. *Journal of International Area Studies, 5*(1), 49–66.

Clark, J. (1991). *Democratizing Development: The Role of Voluntary Organizations* (No. E51 C593 GTZ-PR). Kumarian.

Clarke, G., Jennings, M., & Shaw, T. (Eds.). (2007). *Development, Civil Society, and Faith-Based Organizations: Bridging the Sacred and the Secular.* Springer.

Ferris, E. (2005, June 5, 6). Faith-based and Secular Humanitarian Organizations. *International Review of the Red Cross, 87*(858).

Green, E. C. (2003, September). US Agency for International Development.

Han, G. S. (2006). Imagination and Consumption of African Culture. In M. Ok-pyo et al. (Eds.), *Foreign Culture in Our Country: Cultural Consumption Through Tourism and Food* (pp. 115–159). Seoul: Sohwa.

Han, G. S. (2007). Korean Imagination and Reproduction of Africa. In *Correcting Errors and Prejudices of World History Textbooks* (pp. 241–299). Seoul: Samin.

Han, G. S. (2013). A Methodological Reflection on African Studies in Korea and a Review for Research Topics. *Asia Review, 3*(1), 159–193.

Im, K. K. (2016). Prospects and Challenges of International Development Cooperation in the Buddhist World: Focused on the Religious-Based Development NGO (FBO). *International Welfare Studies, 6*(2), 27–56.

Institute of Audit and Inspection 2011: The Board of Audit and Inspection. 2011 [Request for Disposal of Audit Results: Status of Implementation of Public Development Assistance (ODA). The Board of the Board of Audit and Inspection. 2012. [Audit Results Report: Audit of the Ministry of Foreign Affairs and Trade's press release).

Jang, J. S. (2012). Measures to Establish a Cooperative Governance System with the Private Sector for the Revitalization of Official Development Assistance (ODA). *Korean Public Management Review, 26*(4), 29–54.

Jung, S. B. (1995). Civil Society and Transnational Citizen Movements. 유럽연구, 3, 383–417.

KCOC. (2017). Korea NGOs for International Development Cooperation.

Kim, C.-S., Chae, Y. I. L., & Jung, N. W. (2015). Exploring Media Portrayals and Public Images About Africa. *Journal of International Area Studies, 18*(5), 219–252. Center for International Area Studies.

Kim, D. W., & Han, G. S. (2012). Viewing Africa based on 'Factual Contents' and 'Representation': Centered on Africa Contents in Elementary and Middle School Social Studies Textbooks. *Journal of the Korean Geographical Society, 47*(3), 440–458. The Korean Geographical Society caritas.or.kr (Caritas Korea).

Kim, E. D. (2010). Alter-Globalization Movement of Korea Civil Society Organization (CSO) – Implications, Limitations, and Tasks. *Social Science Research Review, 26*(4), 371–398.

Kim, T. K., & Park, M. J. (2010). Governance Mechanisms to Mobilize Civil Society Organizations for International Development Cooperation A Comparative Analysis of Japan and Germany and Its Implications for South Korea. *Civil Society & NGO, 8*(2), 193–234.

Korten, D. C. (1990). *Getting to the 21st Century: Voluntary Action and the Global Agenda*. West Hartford, Conne: Kumarian Press.

Lee, T. J. (2004). An Anthropological Study on the International Development, Evaluation and Policy Engagement: An Essay for the Anthropology of International Development. *Comparative Culture Study (비교문화연구), 10*(1), 221–248.

Lee, C. G. (2015). Structural Analysis of the Cooperative Network Between International Development NGOs and Government Agencies – Using the Ecological Approach. *Korean Policy Studies Review, 24*(4), 587–615.

Lee, K. J. (2018). The Fundraising Advertisement's Effect of NGOs. *Journal of Korean Social Welfare Administration, 20*(2), 205–232. Academy of Korean Social Welfare Administration.

Lee, K. S., & Lee, S. J. (2017). The Partnership Between the Government and the Development NGOs International Development Cooperation Study, *9*(4), 83–115.

OECD. (2018). Aid for Civil Society Organizations Statistics Based on DAC Members' Reporting to the Creditor Reporting System Database (CRS), 2015–2016. Retrieved from https://www.oecd.org/dac/financing-sustainable-development/development-finance-topics/Aid-for-Civil-Society-Organisations-2015-2016.pdf.

Park, J. H. (2013). Korean Documentaries' Perspectives on the Third World—Interviews with the Documentary Directors and Writers. *Korean Journal of Broadcasting and Telecommunication Studies, 27*(4), 45–84.

Park, J. H., & Lee, J. (2012). Producers' and Audiences' Perspectives on Korean Documentaries on the Third World: A Case Study of <Tears in Africa> on MBC. *Broadcasting & Communication, 13*(4), 83–122.

Park, J. H., & Ryu, K. H. (2010). The Ideological Implication of the Production Process and Practice of an International Current Affairs Program – The Representation of the West and the Third World on MBC's⟨W⟩. *Media & Society, 18*(2), 2–39.

Save the Children. (2011). Annual Report.

Save the Children. (2013). Annual Report.

Save the Children. (2017). Annual Report.
Sohn. H. S. (2011). International Trade; Human Rights-Based Approach Toward International Development Cooperation and Canada's ODA Accountability Act. *International Area Studies Review, 15*(2), 403–425.
Sohn, H. S., & Han, J. K. (2014). A Study on Government – NGO Partnership in Development Cooperation: The Case of the Netherlands Co-financing Program. *Korean Political Science Review, 48*(1), 221–239.
Sohn, H. S., Han, J. K., & Park, B. G. (2011). A Study of Government-Civil Society Partnership in International Development Cooperation: Focusing on the NGO Assistance Policies of OECD DAC Members. *National Policy, 17*(4), 105–136. The Sejong Institute.
Ukadike, F. N. (1990). Western Film Images of Africa: Geneology of an Ideological Formulation. *The Black Scholar, 21*, 30–48.
UNAIDS. (2009). Partnership with Faith-Based Organizations. UNAIDS Strategic Framework.
Willets, P. (Ed.). (1982). *Pressure Groups in the Global System: The Transnational Relations of Issue-Oriented Non-governmental Organizations.* F. Pinter.

OTHER RELATED WEBSITES

http://www.worldvision.or.kr/index.asp.
https://www.childfund.or.kr/main.do.
https://www.sc.or.kr/.
http://www.ngokcoc.or.kr/.
http://ccej.or.kr/.
http://www.peoplepower21.org/.
http://www.africainsight.or.kr/.
http://www.caritas.or.kr/.
http://obos.or.kr/html/.
http://www.copion.or.kr/ (COPION).
http://www.gcs.or.kr/gcs/index.asp (Global Civic Sharing).
https://www.saemaul.or.kr/eng/ (Samaeul Undong Center).
http://www.goodneighbors.kr (Good Neighbors).

Index[1]

A
Academically neglected areas, 15
Academic sectionalism, 21, 24, 26
Academic sustainability, 21, 23
Addis Ababa, 110, 113–115, 123
Advocacy and Awareness CSOs, 182–185
Advocacy campaign, 164, 171, 183
Advocacy NGOs, 162
Africa Museum of Original Art, 151
African Development Bank (AfDB), 80, 95, 98, 99n5
The African Renaissance statue, 139
African Studies Association of India (ASA-India), 29
Aid Policy Monitoring, 176–180
Anti-Communist Hallstein Doctrine, 141
Apartheid, 52, 53
Asian Africanist Network, 19, 20

B
Better Education for Africa's Rise (BEAR) project, 90
Bibliometric mapping technique, 35
Bilateral aid, 72, 82, 84, 87

C
Cameroon, 47, 49
Center for African Area studies of Kyoto University (CAAS-KU), 19, 30n7
Centre for African Studies, Jawaharlal Nehru University (CAS-JNU), 19
China, 34, 42, 52
Chuncheon, 110, 113, 123
Civil society movement, 176
Civil society organizations (CSO), 160, 162, 163, 170, 176, 182, 183, 185, 187n1, 188n5, 188n8
Cold War, 37, 41, 46, 49, 58, 59

---

[1] Note: Page numbers followed by 'n' refer to notes.

The Committee for International Development and Cooperation (CIDC), 76–78, 82, 99n10
Concessional loans, 72, 75–77, 84, 86, 87, 100n21, 100n23
Corporative social responsibility (CSR), 76, 94, 96, 97
Côte d'Ivoire, 43, 48, 49
Cultural diplomacy, 138–140, 142–146, 152
Cultural ODA, 145, 147–149

D
The Department of African Studies, 13, 29n2
Development Assistance Committee (DAC), 54–56
Development Assistant Committee (DAC), 14, 17, 118
Development CSOs, 160, 161, 167, 169, 170, 182, 186, 187, 187n1
Development NGOs, 160–166, 168, 170–175, 181–185, 187
Development NGOs of self-reliance organizations, 170
Diplomatic rivalry, 43, 50, 59
Doi Moi policy, 85

E
Economic Development Cooperation Fund (EDCF), 72, 75–77, 88, 91, 115
Economic Development Cooperative Fund (EDCF), 51
Effectiveness of ODA, 73
Equatorial Guinea, 49
Ethiopia, 103–128, 129n1, 129n9, 129n10
Ethnic conflict, 53

F
Faith-based organization (FBO), 160, 172–175, 185, 187
Fight poverty, 183, 186
Foreign direct investment (FDI), 81, 85, 97

G
Ghana, 49, 52, 53, 67n7
Good Neighbors, 123

H
Haile Selassie, 105, 106
Hallstein Doctrine, 43, 66–67n4
Hallyu, 144–147, 149, 153, 154n10
Hankuk University of Foreign Studies (HUFS), 10–14, 24
The High-Level Forum 4 (HLF 4), 75
Humanities Korea, 15

I
IAA-HUFS, 12
ICT projects, 93
The Inclusive Business Opportunity Creation Program, 81
International development cooperation, 162, 165, 168, 170, 172–174, 178, 181, 182, 186, 187, 187n1
The internationalization of South Korean African studies, 18
International NGOs, 170, 173

J
The Japanese Association of African Studies (JAAS-Japan), 19, 29, 29n6
Juche, 138

K

Kagnew Battalions, 108–110, 122
Kangnido, 137, 151
Kenya, 45–47, 50–53, 59
Kim Dae-jung, 144
Knowledge-Sharing Program (KSP), 81, 92
Korea-Africa Forum (KOAF), 80
Korea-Africa Foundation, 97
Korea Aid, 145, 152
Korea civil society organizations (KCOC), 167–170, 173, 181, 187, 187n1
Korea International Cooperation Agency (KOICA), 71, 72, 75–77, 81, 87, 91, 92, 113, 115, 120–123, 129n8
The Korean Association of African Studies (KAAS), 12, 14, 27, 29
Korean civic organizations, 159
Korean Cultural Centre, 142, 143
Korean economy, 71, 73, 75, 97, 98n1
Korean NGOs, 164, 166, 173
Korean Veterans Association, 113
Korean War, 103–128, 129n4
Korean War veterans, 110, 113–115, 122–125
Korea's Official Development Assistance, 71–98
Korea Trust Fund, 80

M

Mansudae Overseas Projects, 139
Market entry, 44–47, 56–60
Meles Zenawi (Prime Minister), 114
Mid-term Strategy for Development Cooperation, 76
The Millennium Development Goals (MDGs), 73, 75
Museum of African Art, 151
Myung-bak Lee (President), 114, 122, 124

N

National Museum of Congo, 147–149
National Research Foundation of Korea (NRF), 15, 21, 23, 25, 28
Natural resources, 45, 46, 48, 56, 57, 60
Neutral nation, 41
New Partnership for Africa's Development (NEPAD), 95
Nigeria, 45–48, 50–53, 57, 59
Non-aligned countries, 48–50
Non-Aligned Movement, 137
North Korea, 41–44, 46, 49–52, 58, 59, 66n3, 67n6, 137–141, 144, 152, 153n2, 153n3, 154–155n14

O

ODA Coordination, 78
ODA policies, 179, 181
OECD DAC, 72, 75, 76, 84, 97
Official Development Assistance (ODA), 52–59, 67n7, 103, 110, 115–122, 124, 129n8, 160, 163, 166–169, 176–181, 185, 187
The overseas network of South Korean African studies, 18
Overseas Research Grant, 15

P

Park Geun-hye (President), 115
Partnership for Skill in Applied Science, Engineering and Technology (PASET), 95
The popularization of academic knowledge, 25, 28

President, 104, 110, 111, 114–116, 125
Priority partner countries, 53, 67n7, 172, 180, 185
Public administration, 87, 91, 92
Public diplomacy, 134–136, 138–144, 152, 153n1
Public Diplomacy Act, 140–142
Public-private partnership (PPP), 76, 92, 94, 187

R
Relationship, 103, 107, 110–114, 122, 124, 125
Resources diplomacy, 57, 60, 177
Roh Moo-hyun, 141

S
Saemaul Undong, 81, 93, 99n17, 170, 188n16
Science and Technology Policy Institute (STEPI), 94
Science, Technology and Innovation (STI), 93
Seoul, 112, 114
Seoul Africa Festival, 28, 150
Soft power, 133–136, 144, 145, 152
South Africa, 52

South Korea, 104, 110, 112, 113, 115, 124
Sub-Saharan Africa, 49
Sudan, 43, 49

T
Taekwondo, 142–144, 149
Tanzanian Health Basket Fund, 91
Technical Vocational Education and Training (TVET), 86, 88, 90, 94, 95
Tertiary education, 88, 90
Tiglachin Monument, 139

U
Uganda, 49, 67n7
Unclassified others, 21
United Nations (UN), 37, 42–44, 48, 54, 58, 59, 67n5
UN Village Program, 81

V
Veterans, 109, 110, 113–115, 122–125
The Visualization of Similarities (VOS) Viewer, 35, 36
Volunteers, 108, 114, 115, 121, 122